PACEMAKER®

Basic English Grammar

by Bonnie Walker

PEARSON
AGS Globe

Shoreview, MN

About the Author

Bonnie L. Walker taught for 16 years in secondary schools and college. She holds a Ph.D. in curriculum theory and instructional design from the University of Maryland, an M.Ed. in secondary education, and a B.A. in English. She studied psycholinguistics at the University of Illinois Graduate School and was a curriculum developer at the Model Secondary School for the Deaf at Galludet University. She is the author of Pacemaker® *Basic English,* Pacemaker® *Basic English Composition, Life Skills English,* and numerous curriculum materials in written expression, grammar, and usage. Since 1986, Dr. Walker has been president of a research and development company specializing in the development of training and educational materials for special populations.

Reading Consultant

Timothy Shanahan, Ph.D., Professor of Urban Education, Director of the Center for Literacy, University of Illinois at Chicago; Author, AMP Reading System

Reviewers

The publisher wishes to thank the following educators for their helpful comments during the review process for Pacemaker® *Basic English Grammar.* Their assistance has been invaluable. **Sylvia Berger,** Special Education Resource Teacher, Markham District High School, Markham, ON, Canada; **Raequel Gadsden,** ESE Teacher, Chamberlain High School, Tampa, FL; **William P. LeNoble,** English Teacher, Soledad High School, Soledad, CA; **Wendy Mason,** Special Education Teacher, Magnolia High School, Anaheim, CA; **Karen Oliver,** English Teacher, Florence High School, Florence, AL; **John Petitt,** Resource/Special Education Teacher, Culver Elementary School, Niles, IL; **Monica M. Thorpe,** Language Arts Teacher, El Paso, TX; **Elizabeth Towne,** Special Education/Corrective Reading Teacher, Drew Middle School, Lincoln, AL

Acknowledgments appear on page 403, which constitutes an extension of this copyright page.

ISBN-13: 978-0-7854-6311-5
ISBN-10:   0-78-546311-9

1 2 3 4 5 6 7 8 9 10   11 10 09 08 07

1-800-992-0244
www.agsglobe.com

Table of Contents

How to Use This Book: A Study Guide

Welcome to Pacemaker® *Basic English Grammar.* This book focuses on grammar skills that you can use now and later in life. You may be wondering why you need to study English grammar. When you write, read, or speak, you draw on your knowledge of grammar. Knowing how to write sentences correctly will help you communicate more effectively, both in writing and speaking. Knowing how words fit together in sentences will help you understand what you read. In this book, you will learn about the different parts of speech. You will learn about word placement and punctuation. You will put words together to create sentences and paragraphs. You will also practice your vocabulary and spelling skills.

As you read this book, notice how each lesson is organized. Information is presented and then followed by Examples and Practices. Read the information. Study the Examples. Then do the Practice activities. If you have trouble with a lesson, try reading it again. If you still do not understand something, ask your teacher for help.

It is important that you understand how to use this book before you start to read it. It is also important to know how to be successful in this class. This study guide can help you to achieve these things.

How to Study

These tips can help you study more effectively:

- Plan a regular time to study.
- Choose a quiet place to study that has good lighting.
- Gather all of the books, pencils, paper, and other materials you will need to complete your assignments.
- Decide on a goal. For example: "I will finish reading and taking notes on Lesson 1-1, by 8:00."
- Take a five- to ten-minute break every hour to stay alert.

Before Beginning Each Chapter

■ Read the chapter title and study the photograph.

■ Read the opening paragraphs. How is the photograph related to the chapter?

■ Read the Goals for Learning. These are the main objectives of the chapter. Each goal represents one lesson.

■ Read the Reading Strategy feature on the next page. There are seven different strategies described in this book. They are also summarized in Appendix F. As you read each chapter, try to use the strategy. It will help you become a better reader.

■ Study the Key Vocabulary Words. Say each one aloud. Read its definition. These words will also be defined and explained in the chapter.

Note These Features

▶ **EXAMPLE 1**

Example
Example sentences that show a lesson idea

Practice A

Practice
An activity designed to practice a lesson skill

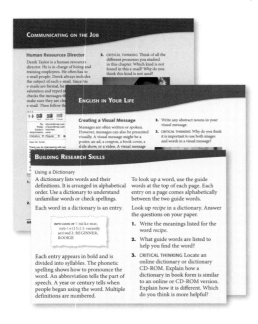

Communicating on the Job
Information about a job that requires writing skills

English in Your Life
A practical application of writing skills

Building Research Skills
Information about a research tool or a research skill

Vocabulary Builder
Vocabulary practice

Spelling Builder
Spelling practice

Putting It All Together
A writing activity designed to practice lesson skills

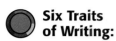
Reading Strategy:
Summarizing

Reading Strategy
A prompt to help you use the chapter's reading strategy (See Appendix F for a description of these strategies.)

**Six Traits
of Writing:**
Ideas message, details, and purpose

Six Traits of Writing
A prompt to remind you about a trait of good writing (See page 362 for a description of the six traits.)

Test Tip

Test Tip
A tip to help you do your best on tests

Writing Tip

Writing Tip
A tip to help you understand lesson ideas and skills

NOTE

Note
Additional information related to the lesson

Technology
Note

Technology Note
Additional information related to using computer technology in writing

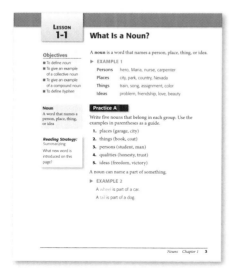

Before Beginning Each Lesson

Read the lesson title and restate it in the form of a question. For example, write: What is a noun?

Look over the entire lesson, noting the following:

- ■ Objectives
- ■ bold words
- ■ text organization
- ■ notes in the margins
- ■ Examples
- ■ Practices
- ■ Lesson Review

As You Read the Lesson

- Read the lesson title.
- Read the subheadings and paragraphs that follow.
- Study the Examples.
- Do the Practices.
- Complete the Lesson Review.
- Make sure you understand the concepts in the lesson. If you do not, reread the lesson. If you are still unsure, ask your teacher for help.

Using the Bold Words

Bold type
words seen for the first time will appear in bold type

Glossary
words listed in this column are also found in the glossary

Knowing the meaning of the red vocabulary words in the left column will help you understand what you read. These words are in **bold type** the first time they appear in the text. They are defined in the lesson text.

> A **noun** is a word that names a person, place, thing, or idea.

All of the boxed vocabulary words are also defined in the **glossary.**

> **Noun** (noun) A word that names a person, place, thing, or idea

Word Study Tips

- Start a vocabulary file with index cards to use for review.
- Write one term on the front of each card. Write the definition, chapter number, and lesson number on the back.
- You can use these cards as flash cards by yourself or with a study partner to test your knowledge.

Noun

A word that names a person, place, thing, or idea

Taking Notes

It is helpful to take notes during class and as you read this book.

■ Use headings to label the main sections of your notes. This organizes your notes.

■ Summarize important information, such as main ideas and supporting details.

■ Do not try to write every word your teacher says or every detail in a chapter.

■ Do not be concerned about writing in complete sentences. Use short phrases.

■ Use your own words to describe, explain, or define things.

■ Sometimes the best way to summarize information is with a graphic organizer or an example. Use simple word webs, charts, and diagrams in your notes. Write your own examples.

■ Try taking notes using a three-column format. Draw two lines to divide your notebook page into three columns. Make the middle column the widest. Use the first column to write headings or vocabulary words. Use the middle column to write definitions and examples. Use the last column to draw diagrams, write shortcuts for remembering something, write questions about something you do not understand, record homework assignments, or for other purposes. An example of three-column note-taking is shown at left.

■ Right after taking notes, review them to fill in possible gaps.

■ Study your notes to prepare for a test. Use a highlighter to mark what you need to know.

Types of Nouns		
Collective	Names a group of people or things	crew, team
Compound	Two words joined to form one new noun	newspaper, flashlight
Common	Name of a general person, place, thing, or idea	state, school
Proper	Name of a certain person place, thing or idea	Illinois, Jan Jones

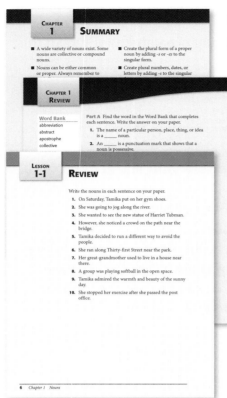

Using the Chapter Summaries

■ Read each Chapter Summary to be sure you understand the chapter's main ideas.

Using the Reviews

■ Complete each Lesson Review. It covers important ideas and skills from the lesson.

■ Complete the Chapter Review. Part A covers the chapter vocabulary words. The rest of the review covers the main ideas and skills taught in the chapter.

■ Read the Test Tip. Try to remember this tip when you take a test.

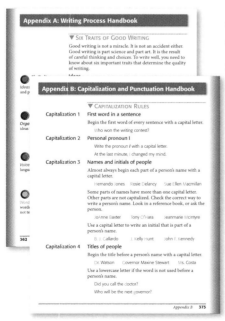

Using the Appendixes

This book contains six appendixes. Become familiar with them before starting your study of English grammar.

■ Appendix A is a Writing Process Handbook. It has seven sections: Six Traits of Good Writing, Steps in the Writing Process, Prewriting, Drafting, Revising, Editing and Proofreading, and Publishing and Presenting.

■ Appendix B is a Capitalization and Punctuation Handbook. If you have a question about writing sentences, look for the answer here.

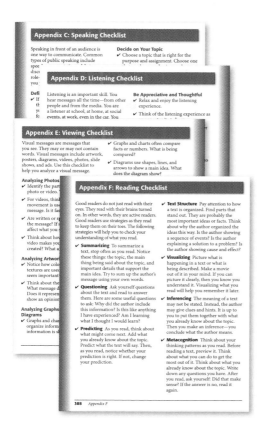

- Appendix C is a Speaking Checklist. Use this list to help you become a better speaker.
- Appendix D is a Listening Checklist. Use this list to help you become a more careful listener.
- Appendix E is a Viewing Checklist. Use this list to help you evaluate a visual message.
- Appendix F is a Reading Checklist. It summarizes the seven reading strategies that are described on the chapter opener pages. Review this list as you read. Using these strategies will help you become a better reader.

Preparing for Tests

- Read the Goals for Learning at the beginning of the chapter. A test may ask questions related to these goals.
- Review the Examples in each lesson. Ask yourself: What main idea does each Example show?
- Complete the Practices in each lesson. Review your work.
- Study the Key Vocabulary Words at the beginning of the chapter. If you made flash cards, use them to study.
- Complete the Lesson Reviews and the Chapter Review.
- Read the Chapter Summary.
- Use a graphic organizer to summarize main concepts.
- Review your notes. Highlight key ideas and examples.
- Review the Writing Process Handbook.
- Make a sample test with a partner. Share your questions.

Nouns

Name the things that you see in the photograph. For example, the picture shows a *coyote*, a *rock*, and *cactuses*. One way to communicate is to name the people, places, and things you experience. You can even name ideas such as *strength* and *speed*. Everything and everyone in the world has a name. Using these names makes it possible to talk about people, places, things, or ideas.

A noun is a word that names a person, place, thing, or idea. In Chapter 1, you will learn about nouns. The lessons will help you use nouns in everyday speech and writing.

GOALS FOR LEARNING

- To identify nouns in sentences
- To identify common and proper nouns
- To identify concrete and abstract nouns
- To write singular and plural nouns
- To write plurals of unusual or proper nouns
- To write possessive nouns

Reading Strategy: Summarizing

Good readers ask questions about what they are reading. This helps them to summarize what they have read. As you read this chapter, ask yourself the following questions:

- What is this chapter about?
- What is the main idea of each lesson?
- What details are important to each main idea?

Key Vocabulary Words

Noun A word that names a person, place, thing, or idea

Collective noun The name of a group of people, places, or things

Compound noun Two words joined together to form one new noun

Hyphen (-) A short dash between parts of a word

Common noun The name of a general type of person, place, thing, or idea

Proper noun The name of a particular person, place, thing, or idea

Abbreviation A short form of a word

Concrete noun A word that names something you can see, touch, hear, smell, or taste

Abstract noun A word that names an idea that you cannot see, touch, hear, smell, or taste

Singular noun The name of one person, place, thing, or idea

Plural noun The name of more than one person, place, thing, or idea

Possessive Showing ownership or a relationship between two things

Apostrophe (') A punctuation mark that shows that a noun is possessive

What Is a Noun?

A **noun** is a word that names a person, place, thing, or idea.

▶ **EXAMPLE 1**

Persons	hero, Maria, nurse, carpenter
Places	city, park, country, Nevada
Things	train, song, assignment, color
Ideas	problem, friendship, love, beauty

Practice A

Write five nouns that belong in each group. Use the examples in parentheses as a guide.

1. places (garage, city)
2. things (book, coat)
3. persons (student, man)
4. qualities (honesty, trust)
5. ideas (freedom, victory)

A noun can name a part of something.

▶ **EXAMPLE 2**

A wheel is part of a car.

A tail is part of a dog.

Practice B

Write four nouns that name a part of each thing.

Example: car
Answer: wheels, engine, gears, seats

1. school

2. forest

3. newspaper

4. library

5. garden

A **collective noun** is the name of a group of people or things.

▶ **EXAMPLE 3**

Groups of People   crew, chorus, team

Groups of Things   litter, bunch, swarm

Practice C

Write the collective noun in each sentence on your paper.

1. The baseball team practiced every day.

2. Alex's club had a meeting every Thursday.

3. The whole neighborhood went to the picnic.

4. Carla decided to join the Peace Corps.

5. The jury found the man innocent.

A **compound noun** is two words joined together to form one new noun.

▶ **EXAMPLE 4**

news + paper = newspaper

flash + light = flashlight

basket + ball = basketball

Practice D

Write a sentence using each compound noun. Be sure to capitalize the first word and use end punctuation. Underline the noun in each sentence.

1. sunflower
2. highway
3. suitcase
4. toothpick
5. classroom

A noun can be a group of related words. Sometimes the noun has a hyphen. A **hyphen** is a short dash between parts of a word. You use a hyphen to join parts of words such as *mid-November* or *father-in-law*.

Other groups of related words without hyphens are also nouns.

▶ **EXAMPLE 5**

swimming pool

Abraham Lincoln

bus stop

Practice E

Write the nouns in each sentence on your paper.

1. Amanda swims on a team with her sister-in-law.
2. Nicole and Ramon formed a committee to clean up Jamison Park.
3. Kaitlin gave the jack-in-the-box to her younger sister.
4. Her favorite author is Stephen King.
5. Mrs. Wong visited the White House in mid-August.

REVIEW

Write the nouns in each sentence on your paper.

1. On Saturday, Tamika put on her gym shoes.

2. She was going to jog along the river.

3. She wanted to see the new statue of Harriet Tubman.

4. However, she noticed a crowd on the path near the bridge.

5. Tamika decided to run a different way to avoid the people.

6. She ran along Thirty-first Street near the park.

7. Her great-grandmother used to live in a house near there.

8. A group was playing softball in the open space.

9. Tamika admired the warmth and beauty of the sunny day.

10. She stopped her exercise after she passed the post office.

Common and Proper Nouns

Objectives

- To identify a common noun
- To identify a proper noun
- To determine when to capitalize a noun
- To capitalize and punctuate titles

Common noun
The name of a general type of person, place, thing, or idea

Proper noun
The name of a particular person, place, thing, or idea

Reading Strategy:
Summarizing

Summarize the difference between common and proper nouns.

A **common noun** is the name of a general type of person, place, thing, or idea. A **proper noun** is the name of a particular person, place, thing, or idea. Capitalize a common noun only if it is the first word of a sentence or part of a title. Always capitalize a proper noun.

▶ **EXAMPLE 1**

Common Nouns	Proper Nouns
school	Springville High School
month	December
writer	Edgar Allan Poe

Practice A

Write each noun on your paper. Write a proper noun next to each common noun. Write a common noun next to each proper noun. Remember to capitalize proper nouns.

Example: university
Answer: university, Harvard University

Example: Alaska
Answer: Alaska, state

1. teacher
2. Super Bowl
3. team
4. France
5. singer

The name of a particular place is a proper noun. The name of a country, state, city, street, or building is a proper noun. Sometimes a proper noun is **abbreviated.** An abbreviation is a short form of a word. Capitalize the abbreviation if the whole word is a proper noun.

▶ **EXAMPLE 2**

Common Nouns	Proper Nouns	Abbreviations
state	New York	NY
street	Lee Street	Lee St.
school	Triton High School	Triton H.S.

Practice B

Write each sentence on your paper. Capitalize the proper nouns. Use abbreviations when you can. Use the U.S. Postal Service abbreviations for states.

1. Roberto mailed a package to houston, texas.
2. His friend lives at 602 river drive, apartment 119.
3. Last year roberto went to a new high school.
4. He liked northview High School very much.
5. I met josie at the corner of elm road and high street.

Names of parts of the country are proper nouns. However, directions are common nouns.

▶ **EXAMPLE 3**

Part of the Country	I visited the West last winter.
Direction	Susan will drive north next summer.

 **Writing Tip**

President can be a common noun or a proper noun. *Tino is president of the class. Today President Juarez will speak.* Are you naming the job or a specific person? If you are naming a specific president, it is a proper noun.

Practice C

Write each sentence on your paper. Capitalize the proper nouns. Not every sentence has a proper noun.

1. When alex graduated from high school, he took a trip to the south.

2. On the first day, he drove 300 miles southwest.

3. He started in baltimore and spent the first night in north carolina.

4. On the second day, alex drove west to visit some friends in tennessee.

5. The next day alex headed southeast to florida.

The name of a language and a particular school course are proper nouns. The name of a school subject is a common noun.

▶ **EXAMPLE 4**

Proper Nouns	Common Nouns
German	language
Introduction to Algebra	algebra

Practice D

Choose the correct word or words in parentheses. Write the sentence on your paper.

1. Karl got an A in (English, english).

2. Alex studies (math and history, Math and History).

3. Jennifer signed up for (math II, Math II).

4. Who teaches your (science, Science) class this year?

5. Miguel decided to take (introduction to music, Introduction to Music) for extra credit.

Books, songs, and movies have titles. A title is a proper noun. Capitalize the first word and all main words in a title. Italicize or underline the title of a movie, book, magazine, opera, or play. Put quotation marks around the title of a song, poem, or short story.

▶ **EXAMPLE 5**

"America the Beautiful" (song)   *Star Wars* (movie)

A Tale of Two Cities (book)   "The Raven" (poem)

Practice E

Write each title on your paper. Capitalize the first word and all main words. Punctuate each title correctly.

1. the red badge of courage (book)
2. the sound of music (movie)
3. the star-spangled banner (song)
4. the world almanac (book)
5. dr. martin luther king, jr. (person)

The Art History class visits the Museum of Modern Art.

REVIEW

Write each noun on your paper. Capitalize the proper nouns.

1. george washington

2. spain

3. alligator

4. labor day

5. river

Read each sentence. If the sentence is correct, write *correct* on your paper. If the sentence has a capitalization or punctuation mistake, write the sentence correctly.

6. Latisha took math 101, not math 201, this year.

7. Armando's favorite holiday is thanksgiving.

8. I am reading a novel called the old man and the sea.

9. Kaitlin's favorite subject is science.

10. Lisa and greg visited wicker park.

Concrete and Abstract Nouns

Concrete noun

A word that names something you can see, touch, hear, smell, or taste

Abstract noun

A word that names an idea that you cannot see, touch, hear, smell, or taste

Reading Strategy: Summarizing

What are some details that help you understand concrete nouns?

A noun may be abstract or concrete. A **concrete noun** is a word that names something you can see, touch, hear, smell, or taste. The name of a person, place, or thing is a concrete noun. An **abstract noun** is a word that names something you can think about or talk about. You cannot see, touch, hear, smell, or taste it. An abstract noun is an idea, quality, or feeling.

▶ **EXAMPLE 1**

Concrete Nouns	Abstract Nouns
money	debt
clock	time
college	education

Practice A

Write the abstract noun in each pair on your paper.

Example: apple, appetite
Answer: appetite

1. teacher, learning

2. bravery, soldier

3. steel, strength

4. value, dollar

5. spirit, cheerleader

Practice B

Write the concrete nouns in each sentence. For each concrete noun, write one of the senses that makes it concrete: *sight, touch, sound, smell,* or *taste.*

Example: Jim heard the laughter in the room.
Answer: Jim—sight; laughter—sound; room—sight

1. Kim earned the respect of her teachers.

2. Maria brought flowers to the birthday party.

3. The boys told jokes around the campfire.

4. Tears of joy ran down her face.

5. Julio stared at his brother with admiration.

Practice C

Write the nouns in each sentence. Decide if each is concrete or abstract. For each noun, write *concrete* or *abstract.*

1. Keiko valued her friendship with Adam.

2. Tonya had too much energy in class.

3. You could see the happiness on his face.

4. Hard work and a little luck got him the contract.

5. The car wash was a success.

Review

Write the nouns in each sentence on your paper. Decide if each one is concrete or abstract. Write *concrete* or *abstract*.

1. Alex Jones wanted a car very much.

2. Every week he saved his paycheck.

3. He put his dollars in a bank to save them.

4. A decision about a vehicle would not be easy.

5. He looked at pictures in the magazines.

6. Alex saw an ad in the newspaper.

7. He called the phone number and planned a meeting.

8. Alex looked at automobiles for a month.

9. He found a seller who was known for his kindness.

10. Alex had a good feeling. He trusted the man.

Vocabulary Builder

Using *Site* and *Sight* Correctly
The words *site* and *sight* are both nouns. They have different meanings. *Site* is a place. *Sight* refers to vision.

We will build our house on that **site.**
The sunset was a beautiful **sight.**

Write the word that completes each sentence.

1. We wanted a (site, sight) with a view of the ocean.
2. Jean was a lovely (site, sight) in her new dress.
3. What is the (site, sight) for the 2008 Olympics?
4. The eye doctor will check your (site, sight).
5. The new park is a perfect (site, sight) for a picnic.

Singular and Plural Nouns

Singular noun

The name of one person, place, thing, or idea

Plural noun

The name of more than one person, place, thing, or idea

Reading Strategy:
Summarizing

Explain how you create a plural noun from a singular noun ending in *-x, -s, -z, -ch,* or *-sh.*

A **singular noun** is the name of one person, place, thing, or idea. A **plural noun** is the name of more than one person, place, thing, or idea.

Nouns Ending in *-x, -s, -z, -ch,* or *-sh*

For many singular nouns, the plural form is created by adding *-s* to the end of the word. However, singular nouns that end with *-x, -s, -z, -ch,* or *-sh* are treated differently. Create the plural form of these nouns by adding *-es* to the end of the word. A plural noun with *-es* has an extra syllable. Say aloud the words below to hear the difference between them.

▶ **EXAMPLE 1**

Singular	Plural
committee	committees
peach	peaches
leash	leashes

Practice A

Decide if each noun is singular or plural. Write *singular* or *plural* on your paper.

1. bosses
2. nations
3. crowd
4. agents
5. circus

Practice B

Write the plural of each singular noun. Add either -s or -es.

1. address

2. car

3. tax

4. patch

5. mountain

Nouns Ending in *-y*

Nouns that end in *-y* and have a consonant before the *y* become plural by changing the *y* to *i* and adding *-es*. Nouns that end in *-y* and have a vowel before the *y* become plural by simply adding *-s*.

▶ **EXAMPLE 2**

Singular	Plural
day	days
pony	ponies

Practice C

Write the plural of each singular noun on your paper.

1. monkey

2. army

3. country

4. body

5. bay

Find the spelling mistakes in each sentence. Write each sentence correctly on your paper.

1. Both pies had berrys and cherrys.
2. He traveled to three different citys on his vacation.
3. The doctors treated the man's injurys at the hospital.
4. The boys attended two partys and two playes.
5. How many butterflyes did you see in the vallies?

Nouns Ending in *-f, -fe,* or *-o*

For most nouns that end in *-f* or *-fe,* you make the plural form by adding *-s.* Some nouns that end in *-f* or *-fe* change the *f* to *v* and add *-s* or *-es.*

▶ **EXAMPLE 3**

Singular	Plural
roof	roofs
chief	chiefs
leaf	leaves
knife	knives

To form the plural of some nouns ending with a consonant and *o,* add *-es.* Some nouns only need *-s.* These words are often musical words.

▶ **EXAMPLE 4**

Singular	Plural
tomato	tomatoes
piano	pianos

NOTE

Pay attention to the pronunciation of a plural noun. It will help you decide whether to change the *f* to *v.* For example, hear the difference between *leaf* and *leaves.* Do you hear the *v* sound in *leaves?* Now say *roof* and *roofs* aloud. Do you hear the *f* sound in *roofs?*

Reading Strategy:
Summarizing

What nouns are described on this page?

To form the plural of a noun ending with a vowel and *o*, add *-s*.

▶ **EXAMPLE 5**

Singular	Plural
radio	radios
rodeo	rodeos

Practice E

Write the plural of each singular noun. Then write a sentence using the plural noun.

Example: belief
Answer: beliefs—He asked me about my beliefs.

1. calf

2. potato

3. safe

4. studio

5. life

We chopped tomatoes, carrots, and avocados with the knives.

REVIEW

Write the plural of each noun on your paper.

1. echo   **2.** lady   **3.** cliff   **4.** month   **5.** wish

Choose the word or words that correctly complete each sentence. Write the letter of your answer.

6. Jamie bought a few new _____ for his baby brother.

A toys   **B** toyes   **C** toies   **D** toy

7. Mel and I looked at the _____ behind the counter.

A prizess   **B** prizzes   **C** prizes   **D** prizies

8. The _____ in our neighborhood have dinner together once a month.

A wifes   **B** wives   **C** wifies   **D** wivies

9. Ricardo had three _____ in the school concert.

A solios   **B** soloes   **C** solos   **D** solo

10. The cafeteria worker writes the _____ for the week on the board.

A lunchies   **B** lunchs   **C** lunches   **D** luncheas

SPELLING BUILDER

Using Suffixes to Form Abstract Nouns

Some suffixes in the English language make abstract nouns. A suffix is a syllable at the end of a root word. You add a suffix to the end of a word to form a new word. Suffixes such as *-dom*, *-hood*, *-ism*, *-ment*, *-ness*, *-ship*, and *-ity* create abstract nouns.

Root Word	free	amaze
Abstract Noun	freedom	amazement

Create five abstract nouns by adding suffixes to root words. Write the root word and the abstract noun on your paper. Check the spelling of each abstract noun by looking it up in a dictionary. Share your abstract nouns with a partner.

More About Plural Nouns

Unusual Plurals

Sometimes the singular and plural forms of a noun are the same.

▶ **EXAMPLE 1**

Singular	Plural
one deer	a herd of deer
one fish	two fish
one series	two series

A few nouns become plural by changing letters within the word.

▶ **EXAMPLE 2**

Singular	Plural
man	men
mouse	mice
tooth	teeth

Practice A

Find the spelling mistakes in each sentence. Write the sentence correctly on your paper.

1. Two deers surprised the mans in the woods.

2. The rancher bought 80 sheeps.

3. We went fishing and caught seven trouts.

4. The Reds won two World Serieses in a row.

5. The womans brushed their tooths after dinner.

Plurals of Proper Nouns

Most proper nouns become plural by adding -*s* to the singular form. If a proper noun ends in -*s*, -*x*, -*sh*, -*ch*, or -*z*, add -*es* to make it plural.

▶ **EXAMPLE 3**

Singular	Plural
the Garcia family	the Garcias
Gina Roberts	the Robertses

Practice B

Write the plural form of each proper noun.

1. the Delp family
2. Wednesday
3. American
4. March
5. the Martinez family

Practice C

Write a sentence using the plural of each proper noun.

1. Friday
2. Canadian
3. Yorkshire Terrier
4. the Jones family
5. the Yamada family

Plurals of Numbers, Dates, and Letters

Make a number, date, or letter plural by adding -s.

▶ **EXAMPLE 4**

My mother had three children during the 1980s.

Many people scored in the 70s on the history test.

Jenelle got three As on her report card.

Practice D

Choose the correct plural to complete each sentence. Write the letter of your answer on your paper.

1. We moved into this home in the _____.

   A 1990's   **B** 1990s   **C** 1990   **D** 1990es

2. Mark needed two _____ to make the honor roll.

   A B   **B** Bes   **C** B's   **D** Bs

3. My young niece sang her _____ in front of the family.

   A ABCs   **B** ABC's   **C** AsBsCs   **D** ABCes

4. Some students scored in the _____ on the Spanish II test.

   A 70es   **B** 70's   **C** 70s   **D** 70

5. In her _____, Janet ran in many races around the country.

   A 20's   **B** 20s   **C** 20es   **D** 20

Practice E

Write a sentence on your paper using the plural of each number, date, or letter.

1. 2000   **2.** 1940   **3.** 60   **4.** C   **5.** 1970

Find the mistakes. Write each sentence correctly.

1. My mother was born in the 1960's.

2. She played with many childs in the park nearby.

3. They liked to dip their foots in the creek.

4. Her family was very close to the Sanchez's.

5. In his 30es, my dad returned to see his old home.

BUILDING RESEARCH SKILLS

Using a Dictionary

A dictionary lists words and their definitions. It is arranged in alphabetical order. Use a dictionary to understand unfamiliar words or check spellings.

Each word in a dictionary is an entry.

> **new-com-er** \\`nü-kə-mər, `nyü-\ *n* (15c) 1: recently arrived 2: BEGINNER, ROOKIE

Each entry appears in bold and is divided into syllables. The phonetic spelling shows how to pronounce the word. An abbreviation tells the part of speech. A year or century tells when people began using the word. Multiple definitions are numbered.

To look up a word, use the guide words at the top of each page. Each entry on a page comes alphabetically between the two guide words.

Look up *recipe* in a dictionary. Answer the questions on your paper.

1. Write the meanings listed for the word *recipe*.

2. What guide words are listed to help you find the word?

3. **CRITICAL THINKING** Locate an online dictionary or dictionary CD-ROM. Explain how a dictionary in book form is similar to an online or CD-ROM version. Explain how it is different. Which do you think is more helpful?

Possessive Nouns

Objectives

- To identify possessive nouns
- To explain the difference between plural and possessive nouns
- To form singular possessive nouns
- To form plural possessive nouns

Possessive

Showing ownership or a relationship between two things

Apostrophe (')

A punctuation mark that shows that a noun is possessive

Reading Strategy:
Summarizing

Explain the difference between plural nouns and possessive nouns.

A **possessive** noun shows ownership or a relationship between two things. It ends in -s and has an **apostrophe** ('). An apostrophe is a punctuation mark that shows that a noun is possessive.

▶ **EXAMPLE 1**

| Ownership | That is Jennifer's jacket. |
| Relationship | Nicole is Devon's sister. |

Remember that most plural nouns end in -s or -es. A noun that is possessive also ends in -s. Plural and possessive nouns sound the same when you say them aloud. Many people mix up plurals and possessives when they write. However, these nouns are written differently. The possessive noun uses an apostrophe. Look at Example 2. Notice the difference in the meaning of the nouns.

▶ **EXAMPLE 2**

Plural	Possessive
I read three books.	The book's cover is torn.
The cars had engine trouble.	This car's engine failed.

Practice A

Write the word in bold in each sentence on your paper. Next to the word, write *plural* or *possessive*.

1. **Alex's** insurance policy came in the mail.
2. The policy had several **pages.**
3. A few of Alex's **friends** stopped by the house.
4. They came to see their **friend's** new car.
5. They went out to inspect the **car's** tires.

NOTE

In Chapter 3, you will learn that a possessive noun acts as an adjective in a sentence.

Reading Strategy:
Summarizing

Explain the rules of singular nouns and possessive nouns in one sentence.

Singular and Plural Possessive Nouns

A possessive noun can be singular or plural.

Rule 1 Make a singular noun possessive by adding an apostrophe and -s ('s).

▶ **EXAMPLE 3**

Wes	Wes's laptop
principal	principal's office

Rule 2 Make a plural noun possessive by adding only an apostrophe (').

▶ **EXAMPLE 4**

ladies	ladies' purses
magazines	magazines' covers

Rule 3 When a plural noun does not end in -s, make it possessive by adding an apostrophe and -s ('s).

▶ **EXAMPLE 5**

women	women's shoes
geese	geese's feathers

Practice B

Each sentence has a possessive noun. Write the possessive noun on your paper. Write *singular* or *plural*.

1. The principal canceled the teachers' meeting.
2. The cat slept on the sofa's cushion.
3. Gabriel had to replace the camera's batteries.
4. The mice's tracks led under the baseboard.
5. Last week we painted the children's room.

Practice C

Write the singular possessive and plural possessive of each noun on your paper.

Example: book
Answer: book's, books'

1. chapter
2. church
3. person
4. crowd
5. fox

Possessives in Phrases

Use apostrophes in phrases such as "one cent's worth." If the noun is plural and ends in -s, add only an apostrophe.

▶ **EXAMPLE 6**

Singular	one dollar's worth	a week's vacation
Plural	twenty dollars' worth	two weeks' vacation

Practice D

Write the possessive noun that correctly completes each sentence.

1. Mark likes to put in his two (cents', cent's) worth.
2. Michelle gets two (weeks', week's) vacation every year.
3. You will have only a (minutes', minute's) wait.
4. I would like four (dollar's, dollars') worth of stamps.
5. We hoped for a rest at the (week's, weeks') end.

REVIEW

Each sentence has the wrong possessive noun. Write the correct possessive noun. Add an apostrophe if it is needed.

1. Billys job is very important to him.

2. He has worked in the Wilsons store for one year.

3. Mr. Wilson sells mens sports clothes.

4. Every week at the salespersons meeting, they talk about their work.

5. Mr. Wilsons plan is to make Billy a manager.

Decide if each noun in bold is plural or a possessive. Write the word in bold on your paper. Add an apostrophe if it is needed. Next to the word, write *plural* or *possessive*.

6. Jennifer and Jay went to New York with their **parents.**

7. **Jennifers** favorite place was the Statue of Liberty.

8. One of the **familys** favorite places was Lincoln Center.

9. On their way to lunch, they saw a **womens** street band.

10. The **crowds** of people and the subways were exciting.

PUTTING IT ALL TOGETHER

Ask five friends or family members to name their favorite book or movie. Write one sentence about each person and the book or movie he or she chose. Include a possessive noun in each sentence. Circle the proper nouns. Remember to underline movie and book titles. Then make a list of all of the nouns in the sentences. Identify each noun as singular or plural. Write *singular* or *plural* after each noun in the list.

Six Traits of Writing:
Conventions correct grammar, spelling, and mechanics

Creating a Visual Message

Messages are often written or spoken. However, messages can also be presented visually. A visual message might be a poster, an ad, a coupon, a book cover, a slide show, or a video. A visual message might contain photos, drawings, or art. It might come with sound effects, music, or a voice track. Most visual messages contain words. Some of the words are abstract nouns. For example, a car ad might include abstract nouns such as *freedom* or *power*.

Create a visual message for an event at your school. Begin by brainstorming about the event—write down all the ideas that pop into your mind. Think about the pictures or images (concrete nouns) that could represent the event. Also think of abstract nouns related to the event. Ask yourself, "What message do I want to send to my audience about the event?" Create your visual message in the form of a poster, flyer, or slide show. Use both pictures and words to show your message.

1. Write each concrete noun in your visual message. For each one, write whether it is singular or plural. In addition, identify any proper nouns or possessive nouns.

2. Write any abstract nouns in your visual message.

3. **CRITICAL THINKING** Why do you think it is important to use both images and words in a visual message?

VIEWING

Have other students view your visual message. Ask them to summarize the main idea. Then explain your message by giving the meaning of several details. To be a critical viewer, take notes while viewing a visual message. This will help you remember details. Pay attention to the effect of images and words together.

- A wide variety of nouns exist. Some nouns are collective or compound nouns.

- Nouns can be either common or proper. Always remember to capitalize proper nouns.

- Nouns can be either concrete or abstract. You can experience a concrete noun with one or more of the five senses.

- Nouns can be either singular or plural. Often you create a plural noun by adding *-s* or *-es* to a singular noun.

- For some nouns, the singular and plural forms are the same. Other singular nouns are made plural by changing a few letters within the word.

- Create the plural form of a proper noun by adding *-s* or *-es* to the singular form.

- Create plural numbers, dates, or letters by adding *-s* to the singular form.

- A possessive noun shows ownership or relationship. Create a possessive noun by adding an apostrophe and *-s* to a singular noun. Only add an apostrophe after a plural noun ending in *-s*. If a plural noun does not end in *-s*, add an apostrophe and *-s*.

Word Bank

abbreviation

abstract

apostrophe

collective

common

compound

concrete

hyphen

noun

possessive

plural

proper

singular

Part A Find the word in the Word Bank that completes each sentence. Write the answer on your paper.

1. The name of a particular person, place, thing, or idea is a _____ noun.

2. An _____ is a punctuation mark that shows that a noun is possessive.

3. A short form of a word is an _____.

4. A word that names one person, place, thing, or idea is a _____ noun.

5. A _____ noun names a group of people, places, or things.

6. A _____ noun shows ownership or a relationship.

7. Two words can join together to form one _____ noun.

8. A word that names something you can see, touch, hear, smell, or feel is a _____ noun.

9. The name of two or more people, places, things, or ideas is a _____ noun.

10. A _____ noun is the name of a general type of person, place, thing, or idea.

11. A _____ is a word that names a person, place, thing, or idea.

12. A short dash between parts of a word is a _____.

13. An _____ noun names an idea, quality, or feeling.

Part B Write the nouns in each sentence. Write *concrete* or *abstract* after each noun. Underline any nouns that are compound nouns.

14. It had been a big surprise for their teacher.

15. A group of students gathered in the classroom.

16. Raf played Jennifer's guitar at the high school.

17. Tammy and Jennifer cleaned up their friends' mess.

Part C Write the letter of the answer that correctly completes each sentence.

18. Miguel went to _____.
  A Wade high school   **C** wade high school
  B Wade High school   **D** Wade High School

19. "Did you get your _____ worth?" she asked.
  A moneys   **C** monies
  B money's   **D** moneys'

20. We baked four _____ of bread.
  A loafs   **B** loaves   **C** loaves'   **D** loaf's

21. I like to read _____ stories.
  A Charles Dickens'   **C** Charles Dickens's
  B Charles Dickens   **D** Charles Dickenses

Part D Find the mistakes in each sentence. Write the sentence correctly.

22. Next year jennifer will be a senior at jackson h.s.

23. His favorite book great expectations was written in the 1800es.

24. This year tonya is taking Math and Science.

25. Carly and sam headed west after finishing their lunchs.

Pronouns

Imagine that someone asks you, "What are the two eagles in the photograph doing?" You might answer, "*They* are watching something." You might add, "*They* are sitting together. *One* is looking to the left. The *other* is looking to the right." Each word in italic type refers to the word *eagles*. What if there was just one eagle in the picture? You would say, "*It* is watching something." *It* refers to a single *eagle*. These words are pronouns, or words you use in place of nouns.

In Chapter 2, you will learn how to recognize and use pronouns. Each lesson focuses on the correct use of pronouns in writing and speaking.

GOALS FOR LEARNING

- To identify pronouns in sentences, and to identify the antecedent of a pronoun
- To identify and use personal pronouns in sentences
- To identify and use relative pronouns in sentences
- To identify and use interrogative pronouns in sentences
- To identify and use demonstrative pronouns in sentences
- To identify and use indefinite pronouns in sentences
- To write contractions with pronouns

Reading Strategy: Questioning

Asking questions as you read will help you understand and remember the information. Questioning what you read will also help you to be a more active reader. As you read, ask yourself:

- What is my reason for reading this?
- What decisions can I make about the facts and details that I am reading?
- What connections can I make between what I am reading and my own life?

Key Vocabulary Words

Pronoun A word that replaces a noun in a sentence

Antecedent The noun that a pronoun replaces

Personal pronoun A pronoun that refers to a person or a thing

First-person pronoun A pronoun that refers to the person who is speaking

Second-person pronoun A pronoun that refers to the person who is being spoken to

Third-person pronoun A pronoun that refers to the person or thing that is being talked about

Compound personal pronoun A pronoun formed by combining a singular personal pronoun with *-self* or a plural personal pronoun with *-selves*

Relative pronoun A pronoun that relates or connects words to an antecedent; *who, whom, whose, which, that,* or *what*

Compound relative pronoun A pronoun formed by combining a relative pronoun with *-ever; whoever, whomever, whatever,* or *whichever*

Interrogative pronoun A pronoun that asks a question; *who, whom, which, what,* or *whose*

Demonstrative pronoun A pronoun that points out a particular person or thing; *this, these, that,* or *those*

Indefinite pronoun A pronoun that does not refer to a specific person or thing

Contraction A word made from two words by replacing one or more letters with an apostrophe

What Is a Pronoun?

A **pronoun** is a word that replaces a noun in a sentence. Without pronouns, you would have to repeat the same nouns over and over again.

▶ **EXAMPLE 1**

Chang said that Chang was going to call Chang's brother.

Chang said that he was going to call his brother.

Identifying Pronouns and Antecedents

Every pronoun has an **antecedent.** The antecedent is the noun that a pronoun replaces. The antecedent is not always in the same sentence as the pronoun.

▶ **EXAMPLE 2**

Maria is a junior. She is on the student council. (*Maria* is the antecedent for the pronoun *she.*)

Pronoun
A word that replaces a noun in a sentence

Antecedent
The noun that a pronoun replaces

| **Practice A** |

Write the pronoun in bold on your paper. After it, write the antecedent that the pronoun replaced.

Example: Erica is a writer. **She** lives in Chicago.
Answer: she—Erica

1. David and Amy joined the gym last week. **They** received a student discount.
2. The gym is easy to find. **It** is on the corner of Elm Street and Park Avenue.
3. Mr. Cruz teaches a class in weight lifting. **He** won a medal in last year's state contest.
4. Amy plans to go to the gym before school. **She** has a job after school.
5. David says that **he** wants to go to Mr. Cruz's afternoon class.

Pronoun-Antecedent Agreement

A pronoun must agree with its antecedent. The antecedent and pronoun must be the same in number. If the antecedent is singular, the pronoun must be singular. If the antecedent is plural, the pronoun must be plural.

Singular Pronouns: I, me, you, he, him, she, her, it
Plural Pronouns: we, us, you, they, them

▶ **EXAMPLE 3**

Jerry brought the apple for lunch and ate it. (singular)

Andrea spoke to Li and Juan when they arrived. (plural)

The antecedent and pronoun must also be the same in gender. If the antecedent is masculine, the pronoun must be masculine. If the antecedent is feminine, the pronoun must be feminine. *Masculine* pronouns refer to males, and *feminine* pronouns refer to females.

Masculine Pronouns: he, him, his
Feminine Pronouns: she, her, hers

▶ **EXAMPLE 4**

Ed was here, but he had to leave. (masculine)

Diane invited Cal to visit her next week. (feminine)

Some pronouns, like *it* and *them*, are neither masculine nor feminine.

Practice B

Complete each sentence with a pronoun that agrees with the antecedent.

1. Jake asked Lauren if _____ wanted to go to the mall.
2. Open the door for Nancy and Jose when _____ arrive.
3. Tyrone and I got lost as _____ explored the woods.
4. After you read the magazine, where did you put _____?
5. Andy said hello when we saw _____ yesterday.

REVIEW

Write each bold word or phrase on your paper. After it, write a pronoun that could replace it.

1. Brittany searched the halls of **Brittany's** school.
2. **Brittany** could not find the art classroom.
3. Brittany saw Alex and waved at **Alex.**
4. **Alex** pointed out the room.
5. **Brittany and Alex** agreed to meet after class.

Write each bold pronoun. After it, write the antecedent.

6. Jack and I went to the game, and then **we** ate dinner.
7. Pete drove **his** father's van.
8. Alicia's history book is in **her** locker.
9. Mr. and Mrs. Martinez drove **their** daughter to school.
10. Jane bumped the vase, and **it** fell off of the table.

SPELLING BUILDER

Contractions vs. Possessive Pronouns
Some possessive pronouns and contractions sound alike. The relative possessive pronoun *whose* sometimes is confused with the contraction *who's*. *Who's* means who is. It is not possessive. Confusing possessive pronouns and contractions:

| **Pronouns** | your | its | their | theirs |
| **Contractions** | you're | it's | they're | there's |

Write the correct pronoun or contraction for each sentence.

1. Look at (it's, its) cover to find the author's name.
2. Are (your, you're) gloves in the bag?
3. (They're, Their) going sledding.
4. This one is mine, but that one is (theirs, there's).
5. (Who's, Whose) coming with us?

Personal Pronouns

Objectives

- To define *personal pronoun*
- To identify first-person, second-person, and third-person pronouns
- To use a personal pronoun in a sentence
- To identify compound personal pronouns

Personal pronoun
A pronoun that refers to a person or a thing

First-person pronoun
A pronoun that refers to the person who is speaking

Second-person pronoun
A pronoun that refers to the person who is being spoken to

Third-person pronoun
A pronoun that refers to the person or thing that is being talked about

Personal Pronouns

Personal pronouns refer to people or things. They refer to one of these: the speaker, the person being spoken to, or the person or thing being talked about.

A **first-person pronoun** refers to the speaker. A **second-person pronoun** refers to the person being spoken to. A **third-person pronoun** refers to the person or thing being talked about.

▶ **EXAMPLE 1**

First Person	I am late.
Second Person	You are late.
Third Person	He is late.

Pronoun-Antecedent Agreement

Personal pronouns express number. They can be singular or plural. A singular pronoun refers to one person or thing. A plural pronoun refers to more than one person or thing. A pronoun must agree with its antecedent in number.

▶ **EXAMPLE 2**

Singular	I am late.	She is leaving.
Plural	We are late.	They are leaving.

Some personal pronouns are masculine or feminine. You must replace a feminine noun with a feminine pronoun. You must replace a masculine noun with a masculine pronoun.

▶ **EXAMPLE 3**

Masculine	John is tall. He is taller than his uncle.
Feminine	Mary is my friend. She lives on the next block.
Neither	The notebook is lost. It has a red cover.

Uses and Forms of Personal Pronouns

You use personal pronouns in different ways:

- as the subject of a sentence
- as an object
- as a possessive pronoun that shows ownership

Personal pronouns change in form depending on how you use them. The chart below shows the personal pronouns.

Reading Strategy:
Questioning

Ask yourself: Do I understand this chart?

 NOTE
You will learn more about objects in Chapter 7 and Chapter 10.

Personal Pronouns

	Subject	Object	Possessive Pronoun
Singular			
First Person	I	me	my, mine
Second Person	you	you	your, yours
Third Person	he, she, it	him, her, it	his, hers, its
Plural			
First Person	we	us	our, ours
Second Person	you	you	your, yours
Third Person	they	them	their, theirs

Practice A

Read the description. Write each pronoun on your paper.

1. third person, plural, subject
2. third person, singular, object, neither masculine nor feminine
3. first person, singular, object
4. second person, plural, subject
5. third person, singular, masculine, possessive

**Compound
personal pronoun**

A pronoun formed by
combining a singular
personal pronoun
with -*self* or a plural
personal pronoun
with -*selves*

Compound Personal Pronouns

Form a **compound personal pronoun** by adding -*self* to a
singular personal pronoun or -*selves* to a plural personal
pronoun. These pronouns are the "-*self* pronouns."

▶ **EXAMPLE 4**

I hurt myself.
(*Myself* refers to the pronoun *I*.)

The baby played by herself.
(*Herself* refers to the noun *baby*.)

Vince ate the whole salad himself.
(*Himself* refers to *Vince* and is used for emphasis.)

-*Self* Pronouns

	Singular	Plural
First Person	myself	ourselves
Second Person	yourself	yourselves
Third Person	himself, herself, itself	themselves

Practice B

Write the compound personal pronoun in each sentence.
After the pronoun, write *singular* or *plural*.

1. The glass fell off the shelf by itself.
2. Samantha and Janet cleaned the kitchen themselves.
3. We cooked dinner by ourselves.
4. The baby sat up by himself.
5. Can you do your homework by yourself?

REVIEW

List the pronouns in each set of sentences. After each pronoun, write its antecedent. One set has three pronouns.

1. Laura and Jami are both seniors. They are old friends.

2. Ms. Bell is the math teacher. She also teaches science.

3. James is in the class. Jennifer knows him well.

4. "Can I borrow your book?" James asked Jennifer. "Here it is," Jennifer said.

Write the personal pronouns in each sentence. After each personal pronoun, write one of these: *first person, second person,* or *third person.* Then write either *singular* or *plural.* One sentence has two personal pronouns.

5. It had been a very pleasant day at the beach.

6. The students enjoyed seeing their old teachers.

7. Yolanda and I are going to the mall to see our friends.

Write the *-self* pronoun in each sentence. After each *-self* pronoun, write *first person, second person,* or *third person.*

8. Did you paint the picture by yourself?

9. Rosa walked home by herself after school.

10. I finished my homework by myself.

Relative Pronouns

Objectives

- To identify a relative pronoun in a sentence
- To identify the antecedent of a relative pronoun
- To identify a compound relative pronoun
- To use relative pronouns correctly in sentences

The **relative pronouns** are *who, whom, whose, which, that,* and *what*. Relative pronouns are often used to relate or connect words to an antecedent. Like personal pronouns, relative pronouns must agree with their antecedents. *Who, whom,* and *whose* refer to people.

▶ **EXAMPLE 1**

He is the man who is fixing lunch. (*Who* refers to *the man.*)

The person whom I met for lunch was late. (*Whom* refers to *the person.*)

Mia has a friend whose mother is a poet. (*Whose* refers to *a friend.*)

Practice A

Write the relative pronoun in each sentence on your paper.

1. Anita is the girl whose brother works at a radio station.
2. Jamal wants a car that has four doors.
3. Tina has a friend who is a mechanic.
4. The mechanic works at Sal's, which is on Elm Street.
5. Mary also had a friend whom I knew from school.

Practice B

Write the bold relative pronoun. Then write its antecedent.

1. The man **who** owns the garage sold Tina new tires.
2. He is the man **whom** I met last week.
3. Andy likes cars **that** have four-wheel drive.
4. The mechanic has an old car, **which** he stores there.
5. Did you see the screwdriver **that** I was using?

Relative pronoun

A pronoun that relates or connects words to an antecedent; *who, whom, whose, which, that,* or *what*

Reading Strategy:
Questioning

Think of a recent conversation you had with someone. Did you use relative pronouns?

Compound Relative Pronouns

Compound relative pronouns are formed by adding -*ever* to relative pronouns. The four compound relative pronouns are *whoever, whomever, whichever,* and *whatever.* The antecedent of a compound relative pronoun may not be stated, but it is understood by the listener or reader.

▶ **EXAMPLE 2**

Jackets and coats are on sale. I'll buy whichever is warmest. (The antecedents of *whichever* are *jackets* and *coats*.)

Whoever wants to go hiking should come now. (The antecedent of *whoever* is not stated but is understood.)

Practice C

Write the compound relative pronoun in each sentence.

1. Do whatever you think should be done.

2. You may choose whichever of these soups you like.

3. Whoever wants to go first should come upstairs now.

4. You can find whatever you need at the store.

5. You can invite whomever you want.

Practice D

Write the pronouns in each set on your paper.

1. himself, he, car

2. whoever, Ms. Woo, you

3. Katie, I, bus

4. which, what, its

5. that, whom, friend

Practice E

Write the relative pronouns in each set on your paper.

1. we, whose, you
2. that, whichever, which
3. mine, what, ours
4. I, themselves, whom
5. who, whoever, us

Practice F

Complete each sentence with the correct pronoun.

1. There are the shoes (who, that) I want.
2. The puppy (who, that) I found is so lovable.
3. There is the girl (whom, what) I met at the library.
4. I like a house (who, that) has a big yard.
5. Did you see the man (which, who) was singing?

Reading Strategy:
Questioning

Look at the photo and read the caption. How does the caption relate to what you are reading?

Diego is the student who studies the most.

REVIEW

Each sentence has a relative pronoun or a compound relative pronoun. Write this pronoun and its antecedent.

1. The mechanic who checked Roy's car did a good job.

2. Carol said, "Whoever wants a ride should come now."

3. When you rent a video, choose whatever you want.

Write the pronoun that completes each sentence.

4. She is the one (what, who) joined the rugby team.

5. The skateboard (who, that) Tara bought was expensive.

VOCABULARY BUILDER

Denotation and Connotation

Denotation is the dictionary definition of a word. *Connotation* is a feeling suggested by a word. A word can have a positive (good) or negative (bad) connotation. For example, *cheap* and *inexpensive* both mean something does not cost very much. However, *cheap* has a negative connotation. *Inexpensive* has a positive connotation. Some words are neutral—they do not have a positive or negative connotation.

Think about the connotation of each bold word. Write *positive, negative,* or *neutral.*

1. The boy in the blue sweater is **bony.**
2. The boy in the blue sweater is **slender.**
3. Why are you **chuckling?**
4. Why are you **sniggering?**
5. Why are you **laughing?**

Pronouns That Ask Questions

The **interrogative pronouns** are *who, whom, which, what,*
and *whose.* They are called interrogative pronouns because
they ask questions.

▶ **EXAMPLE 1**

Who is planning the party?

Whom did you ask to join us?

Which purse did Jennifer buy?

What books are we to read for homework?

Whose backpack is on the floor?

Interrogative vs. Relative Pronouns

Who, whom, which, what, and *whose* are interrogative
pronouns only when they ask a question. Otherwise, they
are relative pronouns.

▶ **EXAMPLE 2**

Interrogative	Who is going to the party?
Relative	Ramon asked a girl who lives on his street.

**Interrogative
pronoun**

A pronoun that asks a
question; *who, whom,
which, what,* or *whose*

Reading Strategy:
Questioning

As you read, think
beyond the lesson.
Consider the ways you
use pronouns when
you write and speak.

Practice A

Write each bold pronoun on your paper. After it, write
interrogative or *relative.*

1. **Which** season of the year do you like best?

2. **What** is the name of your book?

3. Tell me about the people **who** are going to the dance.

4. **Whom** do you like the most?

5. He is the man **whose** wallet I found.

Direct and Indirect Questions

You can use an interrogative pronoun to ask a direct question or an indirect question.

▶ **EXAMPLE 3**

Direct Question	What are you doing?
Indirect Question	She asked what you are doing.
Indirect Question	Tell me what you are doing.

Practice B

Decide whether each sentence is a direct question or an indirect question. Write *direct* or *indirect* on your paper.

1. Who is going?
2. Ben asked Alex where he went.
3. Which kind of sandwich would you like?
4. Show me what book you are reading.
5. How do you feel today?

Interrogative Antecedents

An interrogative pronoun must agree with its antecedent. Unlike personal and relative pronouns, an interrogative pronoun does not have a stated antecedent. The antecedent is the answer to the question that the interrogative pronoun asks.

Use *who, whom,* or *whose* when the answer to the question is a person or people.

▶ **EXAMPLE 4**

Subject	Who is your neighbor?
Object	Whom did you see at the mall?
Possessive	Whose decision was that?

Reading Strategy:
Questioning

What do the details in this lesson tell you about pronouns that ask questions?

Use *what* when the answer to the question is a thing, place, or idea.

▶ **EXAMPLE 5**

What are your assignments for the next week?

Use *which* when the answer to the question is a choice between two or more definite people or things.

▶ **EXAMPLE 6**

Which magazines do you read?

Practice C

Write the pronoun that completes each question.

1. (Which, What) of these fish is larger?
2. (Whom, Whose) did Kevin ask to the dance?
3. (Who, What) will win the World Series?
4. (Who, Whose) mother teaches at our school?
5. (Which, What) do you want for dinner?

Practice D

Write each interrogative or relative pronoun on your paper. After it, write *interrogative* or *relative*.

1. Beth has a friend whose uncle lives in Canada.
2. Which tree is taller?
3. Name all of the cities that you have visited.
4. Tell me which book you like best.
5. Who is the coach of your baseball team?

REVIEW

Write the interrogative pronoun in each question. Then identify the question as *direct* or *indirect*.

1. Which ocean is bigger: the Atlantic or the Pacific?

2. He asked who wrote that book.

3. What country did Queen Elizabeth rule?

4. Tell me whose jacket is on the chair.

5. Whom did you see at the mall?

Write the pronouns in each sentence on your paper. Next to each pronoun, write *personal*, *relative*, or *interrogative*.

6. Li and Patty talked about what they would like to do.

7. "What is playing at the movies?" Patty asked.

8. "Which theater should we go to?" Li asked.

9. "Who else might like to go with us?" Patty asked.

10. "I think that I will ask Susan," Li answered.

Demonstrative Pronouns

Objectives

■ To identify a demonstrative pronoun in a sentence

■ To use demonstrative pronouns correctly

Demonstrative pronoun

A pronoun that points out a particular person or thing; *this, these, that,* or *those*

Reading Strategy:
Questioning

How might you use the content in this lesson in your own writing or speaking?

Demonstrative pronouns point out particular persons or things. The four demonstrative pronouns are *this, these, that,* and *those.* Use *this* and *that* with singular nouns. Use *these* and *those* with plural nouns.

▶ **EXAMPLE 1**

Singular	Plural
This is my pen.	These are my pens.
That is an old car.	Those are old cars.

This and *these* point out persons and things that are near.

▶ **EXAMPLE 2**

Singular	This is my house.
Plural	These are the tickets to tonight's concert.

That and *those* point out persons and things that are far.

▶ **EXAMPLE 3**

Singular	That is my house on the corner.
Plural	Those are my boots near the front door.

Practice A

Write the demonstrative pronoun in each sentence.

1. Is that the movie you saw?

2. Those are new socks.

3. Are these your favorite colors?

4. Is this the book you wanted?

5. That color is so bright.

Practice B

Write the pronoun that completes each sentence.

1. (This, These) is my house.

2. Are (that, those) the people who just moved in?

3. "(This, Those) just came for you," Mrs. Thomas said as she handed Jennifer the package.

4. Tom bought two new CDs. "(These, That) are really great!" he said to Jamal.

5. A fire truck went speeding down the street. "Did you see (this, that)?" asked Amanda.

Practice C

Write the demonstrative pronoun in each sentence. Then write *singular* or *plural* after each pronoun.

1. That is my backpack on the bench.

2. "Who sent that?" asked Jennifer.

3. Which of these do you want to try?

4. This is my e-mail address.

5. Those were the only choices.

Practice D

Write four sentences. Use a different demonstrative pronoun in each: *this*, *that*, *these*, and *those*. Make some of the sentences statements and some questions.

REVIEW

Write the demonstrative pronoun in each sentence. After each pronoun, write *singular* or *plural*.

1. Do you think Nicole would like these?

2. Those are exactly alike.

3. Pick that up, please.

4. Is this yours?

5. Does that belong to Anna?

Write the pronouns in each sentence. Next to each pronoun, write *personal, relative, interrogative,* or *demonstrative.*

6. He works at a store that sells men's clothes.

7. "What department am I in tonight?" Daniel asked.

8. "Go to the stockroom and help them with the inventory," Daniel's boss replied.

9. Daniel asked the people who were in the stockroom what he should do first.

10. "You can start by counting those," said the woman who was in charge.

Indefinite Pronouns

Indefinite pronouns do not refer to specific people or things. They replace nouns that are understood by the listener or reader.

Singular and Plural Indefinite Pronouns

Some indefinite pronouns are singular. Some indefinite pronouns are plural.

Singular Indefinite Pronouns

another	each other	much	one
anybody	either	neither	something
anyone	everybody	nobody	somebody
anything	everyone	no one	someone
each	everything	nothing	your, yours

Use the singular form of the verb with a singular indefinite pronoun. Do not get confused by words that come between the pronoun and the verb.

▶ **EXAMPLE 1**

Singular	Everyone has a sweatshirt.
Singular	Neither of us wants to miss the play.

Plural Indefinite Pronouns

both	few	many	others	several

Use the plural form of the verb with a plural indefinite pronoun.

▶ **EXAMPLE 2**

Plural	Several of the athletes have arrived.
Plural	The others are on their way.

Write the indefinite pronoun in each sentence.

1. Everyone brought food to the picnic.

2. Jack did not know anyone at the party.

3. Several of the boys were late.

4. Try to be nice to one another.

5. Everything is ready for the party.

Some indefinite pronouns may be singular or plural, depending on their use.

Indefinite Pronouns That Can Be Singular or Plural

all	any	half	most	none	some

When an indefinite pronoun refers to a singular noun, the indefinite pronoun is singular. When an indefinite pronoun refers to a plural noun, the indefinite pronoun is plural.

Reading Strategy:
Questioning

Think about the purpose of this lesson. Ask yourself: Am I finding the information I expected to when I began reading?

▶ **EXAMPLE 3**

All of the garden looks beautiful.
(*All* refers to *garden,* a singular noun.)

All of the roses look beautiful.
(*All* refers to *roses,* a plural noun.)

When an indefinite pronoun is the antecedent of another pronoun, be sure that both pronouns agree in number.

▶ **EXAMPLE 4**

All of the girls took their jackets.
(*All* is plural and is the antecedent of *their.*)

Each of the boys has his wallet.
(*Each* is singular and is the antecedent of *his.*)

Find the mistakes. Write each sentence correctly.

1. Each girl brought their own supplies.

2. None of the coats are missing its buttons.

3. Neither of the girls are wearing a coat.

4. Nobody are as smart as Jordan.

5. Half of the boys are wearing his or her watches.

Singular Indefinite Pronouns with *His* or *Her*

Sometimes a singular indefinite pronoun clearly refers to a masculine or feminine noun. Choose either *his* or *her*.

▶ **EXAMPLE 5**

Everyone on the boys' team has his duffle bag.

Somebody in the audience lost her purse.

Sometimes it is not clear whether a singular indefinite pronoun is masculine or feminine. Use the phrase *his or her*, or rewrite the sentence using plural pronouns.

▶ **EXAMPLE 6**

Everyone brought his or her ticket.

All of the students brought their tickets.

Practice C

Write the word or words that completes each sentence.

1. Everyone carried (his or her, their) lunch on the bus.

2. Many parents went with (his or her, their) children.

3. Few could drive (his or her, their) cars to the museum.

4. Each student (has, have) the key to his or her locker.

5. Everyone put (his or her, their) bags by the curb.

REVIEW

Write a sentence using each indefinite pronoun.

1. someone
2. everyone
3. no one
4. anybody
5. nothing

Write the word or phrase that completes each sentence.

6. Everyone in Al's store (prepare, prepares) for the sale.

7. All of the salespeople (arrives, arrive) at work early.

8. Everybody is quiet as (they, he or she) works.

9. "Why (is, are) everyone so quiet?" one man asks.

10. "Some of us (remembers, remember) last year."

BUILDING RESEARCH SKILLS

Finding a Topic

To find a topic to write about, first list topics that you find interesting. For example, you may be interested in the Internet. Choose a general topic to develop. Then think of topics that are narrower, or more specific. A graphic organizer helps you narrow a general topic. If you are interested in the Internet, you might create this diagram:

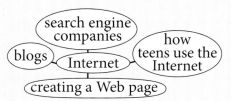

Next, choose one of your narrower topics, such as blogs. Learn more about this topic by doing an Internet search

or by talking to an expert. Finally, develop a thoughtful question about the topic. One question about blogs might be "How have blogs changed the way we communicate?"

1. Choose a topic. Use an organizer or diagram to narrow your topic.

2. Use an encyclopedia or an Internet search to find more information. Write three questions you have after learning more about your topic.

3. **CRITICAL THINKING** Evaluate your questions. Are they interesting and challenging? Do they require more than just a single fact for an answer? Choose the question you think would be best to write about. Explain your choice.

Pronouns in Contractions

Objectives

■ To identify a contraction that contains a pronoun
■ To form a contraction from two words

Contraction
A word made from two words by replacing one or more letters with an apostrophe

Reading Strategy:
Questioning

Which of these common contractions do you use every day?

In Chapter 1, you learned how to use an apostrophe (') to show the possessive form of a noun.

▶ **EXAMPLE 1**

Annie's cat   the fans' cheers

You also use an apostrophe in a **contraction.** A contraction is a word made from two words by leaving out one or more letters. An apostrophe takes the place of the missing letters. Some contractions are made from a pronoun and a verb.

Common Contractions

I'd = I would, I had	who's = who is
I'll = I will	we'll = we will
I'm = I am	we're = we are
I've = I have	we'd = we would, we had
you'll = you will	we've = we have
you're = you are	they'd = they would, they had
you've = you have	they're = they are
he's = he is, he has	they've = they have
she's = she is, she has	that's = that is
it's = it is, it has	what's = what is

🔖 **NOTE**
To contract means "to make shorter or smaller." You form contractions by taking out letters and combining two words.

Practice A

Write the contraction for each set of words.

1. who is

2. let us

3. they are

4. you have

5. they would

Reading Strategy:
Questioning

What rules or details about possessive nouns do you remember from Chapter 1?

 Writing Tip

You can use contractions in informal writing, such as in a letter or note to a friend. You can also use contractions in everyday speech. Avoid using contractions in formal writing.

Practice B

Write the contraction in each sentence as two words.

1. We're studying the solar system in our science class.
2. We've already studied the sun.
3. I'd like to know more about Mars.
4. It's the fourth closest planet to the sun.
5. We'll study other galaxies next semester.

Practice C

Write a sentence using each contraction.

1. we'd
2. that's
3. let's
4. she's
5. I'll

We're riding to the park. It's fun!

REVIEW

Find the contractions in each sentence, and write them on your paper. Then rewrite each contraction as two words. Some sentences have two contractions.

1. I'd like to meet Maya Angelou.

2. We're studying her writing in English class.

3. I'm surprised to learn that she knew Martin Luther King Jr.

4. She's been a dancer and a singer.

5. However, that's not what has made her famous.

6. Let's read about her in the textbook.

7. If you've read her books, you know why she's so well liked.

8. She's written two books about her life.

9. I'm sure that you'd like her poetry, too.

10. We'll be studying Robert Frost's poetry next.

PUTTING IT ALL TOGETHER

Write five questions to ask another student about his or her activities during the past week. Be sure to use interrogative pronouns. Then find a partner and take turns asking and answering questions. Write three or four sentences about what your partner did during the past week. Use at least three of these pronoun types: personal, relative, demonstrative, indefinite, or contractions. Now list each pronoun in the questions and answers you wrote. Next to each pronoun, write what type of pronoun it is.

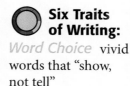

Six Traits of Writing:

Word Choice vivid words that "show, not tell"

Human Resources Director

Derek Taylor is a human resources director. He is in charge of hiring and training employees. He often has to e-mail people. Derek always includes the subject of each e-mail. Since his e-mails are formal, he also includes a salutation and typed signature. Derek checks the messages that he sends to make sure they are clear. Read his e-mail. Then follow the directions.

Send | Send Later | Forward | Save | Delete | Address

To: ASmith@mail.com
From: DTaylor@mail.com
Subject: Interview
▶ **Attachments:** *none*

Helvetica ▼ | Regular ▼ | **B** *I* U | ≡ ≡ ≡

Dear Mr. Smith,

Thank you for interviewing with our company last week. Vice President Sanders requested that you come in for a second interview. Each of the board members will speak to you during this visit. Which day next week would work best for you? Also tell me what time works well for you.

Sincerely,

Derek Taylor
Human Resources Director

1. Make a list of the personal pronouns in Derek's e-mail. Next to each pronoun, write first person, second person, or third person.

2. List the interrogative pronouns in the e-mail.

3. **CRITICAL THINKING** Think of all the different pronouns you studied in this chapter. Which kind is not found in this e-mail? Why do you think this kind is not used?

🖊 SPEAKING

In office settings, people may communicate by e-mail, fax, or phone. When leaving a phone message, speak clearly and slowly. Give your name, phone number, time that you called, and a brief reason for your call. Keep your message short. Imagine a phone call that Derek may need to make after Mr. Smith gives Derek a day and time. Practice "leaving a message" with a partner.

■ A pronoun must agree with its antecedent. Choose a plural pronoun to go with a plural antecedent. Choose a singular pronoun to go with a singular antecedent. If an antecedent is masculine or feminine, choose a pronoun that matches.

■ Personal pronouns can be first-person, second-person, or third-person pronouns. Personal pronouns can be the subject of a sentence, an object, or a possessive pronoun.

■ Compound personal pronouns are formed by adding -*self* or -*selves* to personal pronouns.

■ The relative pronouns *who*, *whom*, and *whose* refer to people. *Which* and *what* refer to things. *That* can refer to people or things.

■ Compound relative pronouns are formed by adding -*ever* to relative pronouns.

■ Interrogative pronouns are different from relative pronouns. Relative pronouns show relationship, while interrogative pronouns ask questions.

■ Interrogative pronouns can ask direct or indirect questions.

■ The demonstrative pronouns are *this*, *that*, *these*, and *those*. They point out particular people or things.

■ Indefinite pronouns can be either singular or plural. Some indefinite pronouns can be both. Sometimes it is unclear whether an indefinite pronoun refers to a masculine or feminine noun.

■ A contraction is created by combining two words into one word. An apostrophe shows where one or more letters are missing.

Word Bank

antecedent

compound personal

compound relative

contraction

demonstrative

first-person

indefinite

interrogative

personal

pronoun

relative

second-person

third-person

Part A Find the word or words from the Word Bank that complete each sentence. Write the answer on your paper.

1. A word that replaces a noun is a _____.

2. An _____ pronoun is used to ask a direct or indirect question.

3. The _____ is the noun that a pronoun replaces.

4. A _____ pronoun refers to the person who is speaking.

5. A _____ is a word made from two words and an apostrophe.

6. A _____ pronoun refers to the person being spoken to.

7. A _____ pronoun refers to the person or thing being talked about.

8. The _____ pronouns are *who*, *whom*, *whose*, *which*, *that*, and *what*.

9. *Whoever* is an example of a _____ pronoun.

10. A _____ pronoun, such as *I* or *it*, refers to a person or a thing.

11. A _____ pronoun, such as *that*, points out a particular person or thing.

12. An _____ pronoun, such as *someone*, does not refer to a specific person or thing.

13. A _____ pronoun is also called a *-self* pronoun.

Part B Write the letter of the pronoun that correctly completes each sentence.

14. Chris is a person _____ likes to be active.

    A whom   **B** which   **C** who   **D** whose

15. Biking is an exercise _____ he enjoys.

    A that   **B** whom   **C** who   **D** whatever

16. He wears a helmet to protect _____.

    A herself   **B** ourselves   **C** oneself   **D** himself

Part C Write the pronoun in each sentence. Then write the antecedent next to each pronoun.

17. It was Jennifer's first day at the new high school.

18. Jennifer looked for her new homeroom.

19. "Lucky us!" laughed Laura and Jennifer.

Part D Write the pronouns in each sentence. After each pronoun, write the type of pronoun it is: *personal, relative, interrogative, demonstrative,* or *indefinite.*

20. Everyone was watering his or her yard.

21. "What should we do?" one of the neighbors asked.

22. "I suggest that each of us waters only once a week," Mrs. Mendez said.

Part E Find the contractions in each sentence. Write each contraction as two words.

23. Alex decided that he'd take the puppy for a walk.

24. Jennifer said she'd go to the mall, and we'd meet her there.

25. I'll let you know when I'm ready to leave.

Test Tip

When you have vocabulary to learn, make flash cards. Write a word on the front of each card. Write its definition on the back.

Adjectives

How would you describe this photograph to a friend? You might describe the *bright pink* and *green* flowers. You also might say that the *small, spotted* butterfly sits on a *delicate* plant. Using these descriptive words, readers can imagine what the flowers and butterfly look like. These descriptive words are adjectives.

An adjective is a word that describes or tells about a noun or pronoun. You can make your writing clearer and more interesting by using adjectives.

In Chapter 3, you will learn about adjectives. Each lesson focuses on a type of adjective and its use in writing and speaking.

GOALS FOR LEARNING

- To identify adjectives in sentences and identify the nouns or pronouns they describe
- To identify definite and indefinite articles as adjectives
- To identify common nouns and proper nouns used as adjectives
- To identify possessive nouns and pronouns used as adjectives
- To identify numbers and indefinite pronouns used as adjectives
- To identify demonstrative pronouns used as adjectives
- To use adjectives to make comparisons

Reading Strategy: Predicting

Previewing a text helps readers think about what they already know about a subject. It also prepares readers to look for new information—to predict what will come next. Keep these things in mind as you make predictions:

- Make your best guess about what might happen next.
- Add details about why you think certain things will happen.
- Check your predictions. You may have to change your predictions as you learn more information.

Key Vocabulary Words

Adjective A word that describes a noun or pronoun

Definite article The word *the*, which is used to talk about a particular person or thing

Indefinite article The words *a* or *an*, which are used to talk about a general group of people or things

Proper adjective A proper noun used as an adjective, or the adjective form of a proper noun

Demonstrative adjective The word *this*, *that*, *these*, or *those* used as an adjective

Positive form The form of an adjective used to describe one person or thing

Comparative form The form of an adjective used to compare two people or things

Superlative form The form of an adjective used to compare more than two people or things

What Is an Adjective?

Objectives

- To define *adjective*
- To identify the noun or pronoun that an adjective describes

An **adjective** is a word that describes a noun or pronoun. An adjective may tell what kind, which one, how many, or how much. You can use more than one adjective to describe a noun or pronoun.

▶ **EXAMPLE 1**

What Kind?	We stayed in a small mountain cabin.
Which One?	I live in the blue house.
How Many?	We have lived in five cities.
How Much?	They had some time.

Adjective
A word that describes a noun or pronoun

Reading Strategy:
Predicting

Preview the lesson title. Predict what you will learn in this lesson.

Practice A

Write each adjective in bold on your paper. Next to each adjective, write the noun that the adjective describes.

Example: Carlos bought an **expensive new** reel.
Answer: expensive new—reel

1. What a **fun summer** vacation they had at the lake!
2. We did not have **enough** time to do everything.
3. On the **first** day we were there, Jill caught a **huge** fish.
4. The **next** day, Carlos hooked **three** trout.
5. At night, a **large black** bear came into **our** camp.

Writing Tip

Practice B

Add adjectives to describe each noun in bold.

1. Students brought **books** to class.
2. **People** brought food.
3. **School** started early.
4. I saw **mountains** and **rivers.**
5. Janaya planted **tomatoes** and **cucumbers.**

Most adjectives come before the noun that they describe. However, adjectives may follow the noun for emphasis. When an adjective follows the noun, the adjective is set off with commas.

▶ **EXAMPLE 2**

The sleepy boy was crying.

The boy, sleepy and hungry, was crying.

Sometimes an adjective comes after the verb.

▶ **EXAMPLE 3**

He was sleepy and hungry.

They seem happy.

Practice C

Write the adjectives in each sentence. Next to each adjective, write the noun or pronoun that it describes.

1. The lake was beautiful on that morning.
2. The water was clear and cool.
3. Rajeev saw a large fish jump out of the sparkling water.
4. Vince used a trusty old rod.
5. By late afternoon, they had caught many fish.

REVIEW

Write the adjectives in bold in each sentence on your paper. Next to each adjective, write the noun or pronoun that the adjective describes.

1. The boys fished for **eight** hours.

2. For a **long** time, nothing happened.

3. They remained **hopeful.**

4. They were **tired** and **cold.**

5. Perhaps their **next** trip will bring **better** luck.

Rewrite each sentence. Add at least one adjective to each sentence. Then underline the adjectives that you added.

6. Diana has a dog.

7. David bought a coat.

8. The store had a sale.

9. Ramon plays piano.

10. My sister bought shoes.

The Articles—*a, an, the*

Objectives

- To identify *definite* and *indefinite articles*
- To decide when the definite article is used
- To decide when the indefinite articles are used

When to Use Definite and Indefinite Articles

The articles *a, an,* and *the* are always adjectives. They come before nouns in sentences.

The **definite article** is *the.* Use *the* when you are talking about a particular person or thing.

▶ **EXAMPLE 1**

Eric saw the musical yesterday.
(Eric saw a particular play.)

The **indefinite articles** are *a* and *an.* Use *a* or *an* when you are talking about a general group of people or things.

▶ **EXAMPLE 2**

Rhea wanted to go to a play.
(Rhea does not have a particular play in mind.)

Tony would like to see an adventure movie.
(Tony wants to see any adventure movie.)

Definite article

The word *the,* which is used to talk about a particular person or thing

Indefinite article

The words *a* or *an,* which are used to talk about a general group of people or things

Reading Strategy:
Predicting

Based on what you have read in this lesson, predict what the next page will be about.

Practice A

Write each sentence on your paper. Underline the articles.

1. The math class was the first class of the day.
2. The students had a homework assignment.
3. The first part of the class was easy.
4. The class discussed the answers to the problems.
5. "I got a different answer to the problem," Jamal said.

NOTE

A word beginning with a *y* sound uses *a*: *a* unit. A word beginning with an unpronounced *h* uses *an*: *an* hour.

Technology Note

Use your computer's grammar checker to see whether you have used *a* or *an* incorrectly. Some grammar programs also explain exceptions when using *a* and *an*.

Reading Strategy: Predicting

Think about your prediction. What details can you now add to make your prediction more specific?

When to Use *A* or *An*

Use the article *a* before a word that begins with a consonant sound. Use the article *an* before a word that begins with a vowel sound.

▶ **EXAMPLE 3**

a large orange   an orange

a mistake   an honest mistake

Practice B

Write the correct article for each sentence on your paper.

1. Suki packed (a, an) apple for her lunch.
2. They waited for (a, an) hour.
3. The teacher spoke in (a, an) soft voice.
4. They had (a, an) English lesson.
5. I read (a, an) book about elephants.

Singular and Plural Articles

Use the articles *a* and *an* with singular nouns. You can use the article *the* with both singular and plural nouns.

▶ **EXAMPLE 4**

I bought a magazine.   (*Magazine* is singular.)

David bought the magazine.   (*Magazine* is singular.)

He bought the magazines.   (*Magazines* is plural.)

Practice C

Write the correct article for each sentence on your paper.

1. She had (a, an) message for her boss.
2. Look up the topic in (a, the) index.
3. They saw (the, an) horror movies.
4. Susan likes (a, the) blue coats in the window.
5. Jack is (an, a) honest man.

REVIEW

Write the correct article for each sentence on your paper.

1. Look at all (a, the) traffic.

2. Did you enjoy eating (a, the) peaches?

3. Mrs. Jones put (a, the) groceries on the table.

4. We went to Toronto to see (a, an) play.

5. Chicago is (a, an) American city.

6. They did (a, the) activity in class.

7. A hammer is (a, an) useful tool.

8. Did you see (a, the) pencils I left here?

9. Being invited was (a, an) honor.

10. I was in (a, an) earthquake in California.

SPELLING BUILDER

Words That Are Almost Alike
In the English language, many words look and sound almost alike. Examples include *loose, lose; quite, quiet;* and *than, then.* Say the words *loose* and *lose* aloud. Note the different meanings and uses.

Loose (adjective) Free; not tight   **Lose** (verb) To misplace; to fail to win

Write the word that correctly completes each sentence.

1. The team will (loose, lose) without its best player.
2. Be careful not to (loose, lose) your homework.
3. Ned's pants are too (loose, lose) without a belt.
4. The gate keeps the dog from getting (loose, lose).
5. Josie hates to (loose, lose) at checkers.

Nouns as Adjectives

Proper adjective

A proper noun used as an adjective, or the adjective form of a proper noun

Reading Strategy:
Predicting

After reading this page, predict what other type of nouns might be used as adjectives.

Common Nouns as Adjectives

People often use common nouns as adjectives. Look at how the writer uses the word in the sentence. If the word is a person, place, thing, or idea, it is a noun. If the word describes a noun, it is an adjective.

▶ **EXAMPLE 1**

Noun	Luke plays the piano.
Adjective	Luke enjoys his piano lessons. (*Piano* describes the noun *lessons.*)

Practice A

Write each word in bold. Write whether it is a noun or an adjective. If it is an adjective, write the noun it describes.

1. I am looking for a **summer** job.

2. My sister found a great job for the **summer.**

3. Vera will be working as a **park** leader.

4. She will probably work at the **park** near our house.

5. She gets to be outdoors and play **basketball** with kids.

Proper Adjectives

Proper adjectives are proper nouns used as adjectives. Proper adjectives can also be adjective forms of proper nouns. A proper adjective always begins with a capital letter.

▶ **EXAMPLE 2**

Proper Noun	He is a Canadian.	I visited Italy.
Proper Adjective	He is a Canadian citizen.	I love Italian food.

NOTE

Some people use the proper adjective *American Indian* instead of *Native American*. Both describe people whose ancestors lived in the Americas before settlers arrived from Europe.

Practice B

Write each proper adjective. Then write the noun or pronoun the proper adjective describes. Not all capitalized words are proper adjectives.

1. Bess had Spanish class during first period.

2. Then she almost forgot her French book.

3. Bess studies Shakespearean literature in English class.

4. In the library, we studied American Indian culture.

5. Bess had never tasted Chinese food.

Practice C

Complete each sentence with a proper adjective.

1. We ordered _____ dressing for our salad.

2. Mr. Cruz likes _____ cheese.

3. Latasha studied the _____ language last year.

4. They live in Germany, but they are _____ citizens.

5. We saw examples of _____ art.

Bess loves Chinese food!

Reading Strategy:
Predicting

Think about your last prediction. How well did you predict other nouns that could be used as adjectives?

Proper Noun or Proper Adjective?

A proper noun is the name of a particular person, place, thing, or idea. Remember that a proper adjective is a proper noun that you use as an adjective.

▶ **EXAMPLE 3**

Tomorrow is Labor Day.
(*Labor Day* is a proper noun.)

We are going on a trip for Labor Day weekend.
(*Labor Day* describes *weekend*. It is a proper adjective.)

Practice D

Write the words in bold. Next to each word, write whether it is used as a proper noun or a proper adjective.

1. I like **French** onion soup.
2. Chang lives in **Philadelphia.**
3. He is a **Philadelphia** boy.
4. Kareem watched the **Russian** jugglers.
5. The band will march in the **Thanksgiving** parade.

Practice E

Use each proper noun as a proper adjective in a sentence. You may need to change the form of the word. Underline the noun or pronoun each proper adjective describes.

1. Asia
2. Fourth of July
3. India
4. United States
5. China

REVIEW

Write the common noun used as an adjective in each sentence. Next to the adjective, write the noun it describes.

1. Jovan grabbed his lunch bag and ran out the door.

2. He was going to be late for the newspaper meeting.

3. Jovan enjoyed working on the school paper.

4. As the sports reporter, he went to all the games.

5. Talking to team members before and after the games was fun.

Write the proper noun or proper adjective in each sentence. Next to each one, write whether it is a proper noun or a proper adjective.

6. The girl speaks Russian.

7. She is a Danish citizen.

8. Did you go to the New Year's Eve party?

9. The young man has a Boston accent.

10. The instructions are in Japanese.

Possessive Nouns and Pronouns as Adjectives

Objectives

- To identify possessive nouns as adjectives in a sentence
- To identify possessive pronouns as adjectives in a sentence
- To identify the nouns that possessive nouns and pronouns describe in a sentence

Possessive nouns shows ownership or a relationship. They end in *-s* and have an apostrophe. Because they describe nouns, possessive nouns can also be possessive adjectives.

▶ **EXAMPLE 1**
Rosa's aunt lives in Texas.
(*Rosa's* is an adjective that describes *aunt.* It shows a relationship by telling whose aunt lives in Texas.)

We made the puppy's bed out of blankets.
(*Puppy's* is an adjective that describes *bed.* It shows ownership of the bed.)

Some possessive nouns work with other adjectives to describe a noun.

▶ **EXAMPLE 2**
Have you bought the man's birthday present?
(*Man's* is an adjective that describes *present. Birthday* is an adjective that describes *present.* Both describe the present.)

Reading Strategy:
Predicting

Based on what you have read, do you think possessive pronouns could also be adjectives? Explain.

Practice A

Write each possessive adjective and the word it describes.

1. The children's names all began with an *s*.
2. I took my brother's small stereo to the beach.
3. Do you want to stop by Rachel's house?
4. James needs to fill the dogs' water bowls.
5. We all need to follow the game's rules.

Possessive Pronouns

Possessive pronouns can also be possessive adjectives. They describe nouns.

▶ **EXAMPLE 3**

His house is next door. (Which house is next door?)

Is that their yard? (Whose yard is that?)

Practice B

The possessive adjectives are in bold. Write them on your paper. Next to each one, write the noun it describes.

1. I always like to get **my** money's worth.
2. **Our** family has always shopped in their store.
3. **Your** dog has a guilty look on its face.
4. We are having **her** birthday party next Saturday.
5. **His** picture was in the newspaper yesterday.

A possessive adjective can describe a possessive noun.

▶ **EXAMPLE 4**

That is my sister's bike.
(The possessive adjective *my* describes *sister.* The possessive noun *sister's* shows ownership.)

Practice C

Write each possessive adjective and the noun it describes.

1. His bike is missing.
2. Your coat was in the living room.
3. I helped my mother's friend look for her ring.
4. A rabbit was in his garden.
5. Their dog likes to hide its bones under our porch.

REVIEW

Find the possessive adjectives in these sentences. Write them on your paper. Next to each one, write the word it describes.

1. Dave and Vince did their math homework together.

2. The teacher's instructions were listed on the board.

3. Vince's older brother checked their answers.

4. "Your second answer is wrong," Dave said.

5. They compared their answers to the book's examples.

BUILDING RESEARCH SKILLS

Using an Encyclopedia

Suppose you wanted to find some information about your state. One place to find information is in an encyclopedia. An encyclopedia gives general information on many topics. The articles are in alphabetical order by topic. You can find a variety of print encyclopedias in the library. You can also find them on CD-ROM or the Internet.

Start your search by choosing a specific topic. Use the guide words or letters on a print encyclopedia to find your topic. For a computer encyclopedia, type your topic in the search window. Select "enter."

1. Use a print or computer encyclopedia to find an article about your state.

2. Write the name of your state on your paper and list five facts from the article.

3. CRITICAL THINKING Decide which of the following would be information found in an encyclopedia. Explain why some information would not appear in an encyclopedia.

   • reasons to expand Interstate 465

   • the sun's distance from the moon

   • the number of bones in the human body

   • the plans for a new airport

Numbers and Indefinite Pronouns as Adjectives

Numbers as Adjectives

A number can be an adjective. You use numbers as adjectives to describe nouns. Numbers describe by telling how many.

▶ **EXAMPLE 1**

Ten people came to the party. (How many people came?)

He bought sixty-one pears. (He bought how many pears?)

Practice A

Write the number word used as an adjective in each sentence. Next to the adjective, write the noun it describes.

1. Twenty-five people signed up for the class.
2. One student dropped out.
3. After two weeks, the teacher gave a test.
4. Seven members of the class got a perfect grade.
5. We measured out two and one-half cups of water.

Indefinite Pronouns as Adjectives

An indefinite pronoun can be an adjective. Indefinite pronouns used as adjectives describe by telling how many. However, the amounts they describe are not exact.

▶ **EXAMPLE 2**

Few students got roles in the play.

The cafeteria workers serve lunch to all students.

Reading Strategy:
Predicting

Think about the title of this lesson. How might indefinite pronouns be used as adjectives?

Practice B

Use each word as an adjective in a sentence. Write the sentence on your paper. Underline the noun or pronoun that each adjective describes.

1. few

2. several

3. each

4. some

5. most

Indefinite Pronoun or Adjective?

Remember, an indefinite pronoun refers to a noun that is not named. A word is an adjective if it describes a noun or pronoun. A word is a pronoun if it replaces a noun in a sentence.

▶ **EXAMPLE 3**

| Pronoun | Several of the athletes arrived late. |
| Adjective | Several months went by before I saw her again. (How many months? *several*) |

Practice C

Write each bold word. After it, write *pronoun* or *adjective*.

1. The hurricane winds scared **some** of the people.

2. The storm lasted for **several** hours.

3. **Everyone** on the block watched the storm.

4. **Many** trees blew down in the neighborhood.

5. **No one** could cook dinner or watch TV.

REVIEW

Write the number words and indefinite pronouns used as adjectives in each sentence. Write the noun each describes.

1. One Sunday, several friends visited the San Diego Zoo.
2. Each animal was in a natural setting.
3. We watched three chimpanzees swing from trees.
4. Eight lions and six tigers climbed over a rocky ledge.
5. Many birds flew around the park.

Complete each sentence by adding a number word or an indefinite pronoun used as an adjective.

6. Winds blew at _____ miles an hour.
7. _____ friends on our block are going on a picnic.
8. Nathan is taking _____ classes this year.
9. The movie lasted for _____ minutes.
10. _____ people were unhappy about the decision.

VOCABULARY BUILDER

Less or *Fewer*

Use *less* when comparing things that have volume (like water). Also use *less* when comparing abstract nouns (like love). Use *fewer* when comparing things you can count (like pencils).

> Jackie drank **less** milk than Jorge.
> Tomas finished **fewer** of the math problems than Tara.

Complete each sentence with either *less* or *fewer*.

1. This pan holds _____ water than that one.
2. This book has _____ pages than that one.
3. Chin spent _____ hours studying than Pam.
4. Tino's face has _____ freckles than mine.
5. Kevin's party was _____ fun than Madri's.

Demonstrative Adjectives

Objectives

- To define *demonstrative adjective*
- To identify demonstrative adjectives in a sentence
- To explain the difference between demonstrative pronouns and demonstrative adjectives

Demonstrative adjective

The word *this, that, these,* or *those* used as an adjective

Reading Strategy:
Predicting

Think about what you know about demonstrative pronouns. What might be the purpose of demonstrative adjectives?

Remember that a demonstrative pronoun points out a particular person or thing. When a demonstrative pronoun appears before a noun, it can act as an adjective. The **demonstrative adjectives** are *this, that, these,* and *those.* They act as adjectives because they answer the question *which one* or *ones?*

▶ **EXAMPLE 1**

Pronoun	That is an error.
	(*That* is the subject. It does not describe anything. It points out a particular thing.)
Adjective	That error was Todd's.
	(*That* describes *error.* It describes which error was Todd's.)

Practice A

Write each demonstrative adjective in bold. Next to each adjective, write the word it describes.

1. "**This** Sunday, let's go to the football game together," Maurice said.

2. "My sister gave me **these** tickets," said Justine.

3. "Do you think **that** team will win a game **this** year?" Andy asked.

4. "Some of **those** new players are great," Maurice answered.

5. "**This** season should be a good one," Andy said.

Reading Strategy:
Predicting

After reading about demonstrative adjectives, what details can you add to your prediction?

Practice B

Write each sentence on your paper. Underline each demonstrative adjective. Then draw two lines under the noun that each demonstrative adjective describes.

1. The football game that day was exciting.

2. Where are those snacks you promised?

3. Look in this cabinet next to the stove.

4. My mother keeps those things in the closet.

5. These sandwiches look good enough to eat.

Practice C

Write the demonstrative pronouns and demonstrative adjectives in each sentence. Write *pronoun* or *adjective*.

1. "We need to repair this watch," Karen said.

2. "How are we going to fix that?" Tyra asked.

3. "This mall has that repair shop," Karen replied.

4. "Can I bring these earrings for the owners to repair?"

5. "They could probably also fix those."

These purses are on sale. Oh, look at this one!

REVIEW

Write the demonstrative adjectives in each sentence on your paper. Next to each one, write the noun it describes.

1. On that day, we went to a baseball game.

2. Those people behind us yelled through the whole game.

3. I would have liked to see that last play again.

4. We could have watched this game on TV at home.

5. That would have been less fun than this game has been.

6. I felt bad for those umpires when the fans booed them.

7. Would you like to keep these ticket stubs?

8. Do you think that friend of yours could get us tickets again?

9. I want to keep these plastic cups from our sodas.

10. My sister has a set of those cups.

Adjectives That Are Used To Compare

Adjective Forms

Adjectives describe people or things. You also use adjectives to compare two or more people or things. Adjectives have three forms—the **positive form,** the **comparative form**, and the **superlative form.**

Use these rules to form comparisons.

Rule 1 Use the positive form to describe one person or thing.
That bike is fast.

Rule 2 Use the comparative form to compare two people or things.
That bike is faster *than this bike.*

Rule 3 Use the superlative form to compare more than two people or things.
Of all the bikes, this one is the fastest.

Objectives

- To explain the difference between positive, comparative, and superlative forms of adjectives
- To identify the positive, comparative, and superlative forms of adjectives in a sentence
- To make comparisons using the comparative and superlative forms in sentences

Positive form
The form of an adjective used to describe one person or thing

Comparative form
The form of an adjective used to compare two people or things

Superlative form
The form of an adjective used to compare more than two people or things

▶ **EXAMPLE 1**

Positive	Alice wears large shoes.
Comparative	Alice's shoes are larger than mine.
Superlative	Alice has the largest shoes of all.

Practice A

Complete each sentence with the correct adjective.

1. Who is (taller, tallest)—Jennie or Olivia?

2. Mrs. Kim knits the (softer, softest) blankets.

3. Miko is the (funnier, funniest) of all my friends.

4. Orange juice is (tasty, tastiest).

5. I think apples are (sweeter, sweetest) than oranges.

Reading Strategy:
Predicting

Preview the section title. What might you learn about in this section?

Adding *-er* and *-est* to Adjectives

Make most one-syllable words their comparative form by adding *-er*. Form their superlatives by adding *-est*.

▶ **EXAMPLE 2**

Positive	Comparative	Superlative
small	smaller	smallest

Practice B

Write each adjective on your paper. Then write the comparative and superlative forms for each one.

1. young   **4.** short

2. old   **5.** green

3. kind

Using *More/Most* and *Less/Least*

Make other longer adjectives their comparative and superlative forms by using *more* and *most*. Use *more* and *most* with some adjectives of two syllables. Use *more* and *most* with adjectives of three or more syllables.

▶ **EXAMPLE 3**

Positive	Comparative	Superlative
easy	easier	easiest
boring	more boring	most boring
popular	more popular	most popular

Also make longer adjectives their comparative and superlative forms by using *less* or *least*.

▶ **EXAMPLE 4**

Positive	Comparative	Superlative
powerful	less powerful	least powerful
relaxed	less relaxed	least relaxed

Reading Strategy:
Predicting

Based on what you have read, predict when you might use the superlative form.

Practice C

Write the adjectives in bold. Next to each one, write whether it is positive, comparative, or superlative.

1. That is the **least comfortable** chair.

2. Taylor thought the movie was **terrible.**

3. The girl was the **most talented** actress in the play.

4. I have never seen a **sadder** face.

5. This coat is **less expensive** than the other one.

A few adjectives make their comparative and superlative forms in an irregular way.

▶ **EXAMPLE 5**

Positive	Comparative	Superlative
good	better	best
bad	worse	worst

Practice D

Write each adjective in a sentence on your paper.

1. better   **4.** lighter

2. worst   **5** less careful

3. heaviest

Practice E

Complete each sentence with the correct adjective.

1. That is the (redder, reddest) sunset I have ever seen.

2. Which of those two buildings is (taller, tallest)?

3. St. Augustine is the (oldest, older) city in Florida.

4. That movie was the (goodest, best) I have ever seen.

5. Sita is (gracefuller, more graceful) than I could ever be.

REVIEW

Write the adjectives in bold on your paper. Next to each one, write *positive, comparative,* or *superlative.*

1. This fabric feels **nice,** but that one feels **nicer.**

2. Of the two athletes, Brandon is the **faster** runner.

3. That story was **funny.**

4. Hector plays tennis **better** than his twin brother Paco.

5. Of all the photographs, this one is the **best.**

Write these adjectives on your paper. Next to each one, write the comparative and superlative forms.

6. bad

7. useful

8. angry

9. famous

10. stern

PUTTING IT ALL TOGETHER

Write a short note to a friend. Describe a trip to a place you have been. Use at least one example of each kind of adjective.

- proper adjective
- number used as an adjective
- comparison using the comparative or superlative form
- definite or indefinite article
- possessive noun as an adjective
- demonstrative pronoun

Share your note with a classmate. Point out the different kinds of adjectives in your note.

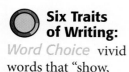

Six Traits of Writing:

Word Choice vivid words that "show, not tell"

Writing an Autobiography

An autobiography is a true story that a person writes about his or her life. Many people such as Benjamin Franklin and Martin Luther King Jr. have written autobiographies.

Think of the events in your life. Choose one moment that you can describe in a paragraph. For example, you could write about a time that you learned something or took an exciting trip. You could also write about a time when you were proud, happy, or sad.

Use details in your autobiography. Use dialogue if possible. Focus on *showing* the reader a moment in your life, not just *telling* it. Use adjectives to help the reader experience the moment you describe. Recall the types of adjectives from this chapter. You can also use more than one adjective to describe a noun.

1. List an example of a definite or indefinite article from your autobiography. Also list a pronoun and a noun used as adjectives.

2. Write an example of an adjective used as a comparison from your autobiography. Identify the adjective as comparative or superlative. If you do not have an example, write one and add it to your story.

3. **CRITICAL THINKING** Why is it important to use adjectives in an autobiography? Explain.

VIEWING AND LISTENING

You can use music, sound effects, and images to set a mood, reinforce an idea, or help tell a story. Suppose you gave your story as a speech. What sounds, music, images, or visual aids would improve your story? Be sure to explain the specific moments when you would include certain sounds or images.

- An adjective may tell what kind, which one, how many, or how much.

- An adjective may come before or after the noun that it describes.

- Definite and indefinite articles are two types of adjectives. They always come before the noun.

- Common nouns can be used as adjectives in a sentence.

- Proper adjectives always begin with a capital letter. They can be proper nouns or a form of a proper noun.

- Numbers can be adjectives when they describe how many. Add a hyphen to numbers between twenty-one and ninety-nine.

- Add a hyphen to a fraction that describes another word.

- An indefinite pronoun can be an adjective when it describes a noun in a sentence.

- The demonstrative adjectives are *this*, *that*, *these*, and *those*. They appear before the nouns that they describe.

- Adjectives can be in the positive, comparative, or superlative form.

- Create the comparative or superlative form of a shorter adjective by adding -*er* or -*est*. For longer adjectives, use *more* and *most* or *less* and *least*.

Word Bank

adjective

comparative form

definite article

demonstrative
  adjective

indefinite article

positive form

proper adjective

superlative form

Part A Find the word or words in the Word Bank to complete each sentence. Write the answer on your paper.

1. The _____ is used to talk about a general group of people or things.

2. A _____ can be a proper noun used as an adjective.

3. A word that describes or tells about a noun or pronoun is an _____.

4. The _____ describes one person or thing.

5. Use the _____ *the* to talk about a particular person or thing.

6. The _____ compares more than two people or things.

7. The _____ compares two people or things.

8. A _____ is the word *this, that, these,* or *those* used as an adjective.

Part B Write the adjectives on your paper. Be sure to include articles.

9. Jane's mom bought fifty-three red apples and ten gallons of cider.

10. The weather is cooler and drier than two weeks earlier.

11. Everyone is happy about these beautiful spring days.

12. After their Spanish class, Akio and Maria went for a long walk.

13. Several young children, noisy but cheerful, got on the bus.

Part C Choose the answer that completes each sentence.

14. Elena was _____ to help than Russ.
   A eagerest   **C** eagerer
   B eager   **D** more eager

15. The day was clear and _____.
   A bright   **C** most bright
   B brightly   **D** brightest

16. She felt bad before the movie and _____ after.
   A badder   **C** worse
   B worst   **D** more worse

Part D Write the adjectives in bold on your paper. Next to each one, write the noun or pronoun it describes.

17. **The** students in **her** homeroom had a meeting.

18. They elected **three** officers for the **school** year.

19. "Li is **smart, loyal,** and **fun,**" said Sue Ann.

20. **That** election was **close,** but Li won.

Part E Write the words in bold on your paper. Next to each, write whether it is a noun, pronoun, or adjective.

21. They all went to the **meeting** room.

22. The **meeting** began at three o'clock.

23. The **south** wind was warm.

24. The wind came from the **south.**

25. **All** wanted a piece of **that** pie.

Test Tip

If you do not understand test directions, read them again. If you still cannot figure it out, ask the person giving the test to help you.

Action Verbs

Y ou could describe the wolf in this photograph as *running, darting, dashing, chasing,* or *racing.* These strong action words help bring the wolf's movement to life. You can also use action words to describe quieter actions like *eating, planning,* or *thinking.* Think of other words that could describe a wolf's actions. All of these action words are called verbs.

Verbs express action or state of being. An action verb tells what someone or something does, did, or will do.

In Chapter 4, you will learn about action verbs. Each lesson focuses on the form and correct use of action verbs in sentences.

GOALS FOR LEARNING

- To identify action verbs and verb phrases in sentences
- To identify simple and perfect verb tenses and use them in sentences
- To recognize regular and irregular verbs
- To identify progressive tenses and use them in sentences
- To use verbs that agree with their subjects
- To use the correct form of verbs such as *have, be,* and *do* in sentences
- To identify and use conditional verbs
- To recognize active and passive verbs

Reading Strategy: Text Structure

Before you begin this chapter, look at how it is organized. Look at the title, headings, boldfaced words, and art. Ask yourself: Is the text a problem and solution, description, or sequence? Does it compare and contrast or give cause and effect? Summarize the text by thinking about its structure.

Key Vocabulary Words

Verb A word that expresses action or state of being

Action verb A word that tells what someone or something (subject) does, did, or will do

Subject The part of a sentence that tells who or what the sentence is about

Verb phrase A main verb and one or more helping verbs

Main verb The last verb in a verb phrase

Helping verb A verb that combines with a main verb to form a verb phrase

Tense The time when an action takes place

Infinitive *To* plus the present tense of a verb

Simple tenses Present, past, and future

Present perfect Shows an action started in the past and continuing to the present

Past perfect Shows one action completed before another action began

Future perfect Shows an action that will be completed before a certain time in the future

Past participle The verb form used to form the perfect tenses

Regular verb A verb that forms its past tense and past participle by adding *-ed* or *-d*

Irregular verb A verb that does not form its past tense and past participle by adding *-ed* or *-d*

Progressive form The form of a verb that ends in *-ing* and shows continuing action

Present participle A verb form that shows continuing action

Verb agreement When a verb agrees in number (singular or plural) with its subject

Conditional verb A helping verb that puts a condition or requirement on an action

Active verb A verb form used when the subject is doing the action

Passive verb A verb form used when the action happens to the subject

What Is an Action Verb?

Action Verbs

A **verb** is a word that expresses action or state of being. An **action verb** is a word that expresses the action in a sentence. The verb tells what the **subject** does, did, or will do. The subject tells who or what the sentence is about. Find the subject and verb in a sentence by asking yourself two questions:

1. Who or what is doing something? (subject)

2. What are they doing? (verb)

▶ **EXAMPLE 1**

Every evening Jiro reads the mail.

Who is doing something? Jiro (subject)

What does he do? reads (verb)

A sentence can have more than one verb.

▶ **EXAMPLE 2**

Antonia washed and dried the glasses after dinner.

She opened her notebook and began her assignment.

Some verbs express mental action.

▶ **EXAMPLE 3**

Pedro likes his car.

Tanesha thinks about her test.

Practice A

Write the verbs in each sentence on your paper.

1. Mr. Okada parked his car.
2. Several of his friends shouted and waved to him.
3. He likes all the people at the office.
4. Yoshimi called her boss.
5. Yoshimi reminded her about the meeting.

Practice B

Write the subject and verb in each sentence. Write *S* next to the subject and *V* next to the verb.

1. In the office everyone works hard.
2. Some people sort mail.
3. Mrs. Davis prepares the payroll.
4. Her assistant enters the information into a computer.
5. The computer prints the checks.

Practice C

Write the verb or verbs in each sentence on your paper.

1. Mr. Ochoa rode his bike to work on Tuesday.
2. He drank some juice and ate a bagel.
3. Mr. Ochoa called the new client, Ms. Peters.
4. He sat in the meeting room and prepared a report.
5. Ms. Peters and her assistant arrived on time.

Verb Phrases

A **verb phrase** contains a main verb and one or more helping verbs. A **main verb** is the last verb in a verb phrase. A **helping verb** combines with a main verb to form a verb phrase.

▶ **EXAMPLE 4**

Mr. Lopez has poured his water.
poured—main verb   *has*—helping verb

Pat will come with us.
come—main verb   *will*—helping verb

Practice D

Write the verb phrase in each sentence. Underline the main verb in each verb phrase once. Underline the helping verb in each verb phrase twice.

1. Mrs. Stamos had spoken to Mr. Franklin.

2. Later, he had remembered their talk.

3. He did recognize the problem immediately.

4. They will help each other.

5. Mr. Franklin has announced a new policy.

Practice E

Write a sentence for each verb or verb phrase. Underline each subject once and each verb or verb phrase twice.

1. accept

2. write

3. will comfort

4. contain

5. had lifted

REVIEW

Write the subject and verb in each sentence. Write *S* next to the subject and *V* next to the verb.

1. Ms. Ando enjoys her work.

2. She writes for a magazine.

3. Mr. Sweeney helps her.

4. A photographer takes pictures for the articles.

5. Many people read the magazine.

Write the verb or verb phrase in each sentence. Some sentences have more than one verb or verb phrase. Underline the main verb in each verb phrase once. Underline the helping verb in each verb phrase twice.

6. Mr. Turner scrambled the eggs and put bread into the toaster.

7. He smiled at his wife.

8. She had set the table and had poured their juice.

9. They sat and read the paper.

10. Mr. and Mrs. Turner will start every day the same way.

Simple and Perfect Tenses

Objectives

- To define *tense* and *infinitive*
- To use the verb *have* correctly in a sentence
- To identify and use verbs in the simple tense
- To identify and use verbs in the perfect tense

Tense

The time when an action takes place

Infinitive

To plus the present tense of a verb

Simple tenses

Present, past, and future

Reading Strategy:
Text Structure

Note the material in boxes like this one on the side of the pages in this lesson. What is often included in them?

The verb in a sentence expresses **tense.** A verb tense tells the time when an action takes place. Verbs use endings, helping verbs, or both to express tense.

Every verb has an **infinitive** form. The infinitive form is *to* plus the present tense of the verb. Verbs can express three **simple tenses**—present, past, and future. Use the present tense when the action is happening now or if it usually happens. Use the past tense when the action has already happened. Use the future tense when the action will happen in the future.

▶ **EXAMPLE 1**

Infinitive	to fish
Present Tense	I fish in that river all summer.
Past Tense	I fished in that river last summer.
Future Tense	I will fish in that river next summer.

Practice A

Write each verb or verb phrase in bold. Next to each verb, write its tense—*present, past,* or *future.*

1. The team **will play** their first game on Saturday.
2. The team **practices** every day.
3. Team members **wondered** about the other team.
4. The coach **called** the team together.
5. He **talked** to them about the game plan.

Present perfect

Shows an action started in the past and continuing to the present

Past perfect

Shows one action completed before another action began

Future perfect

Shows an action that will be completed before a certain time in the future

Perfect Tense

The three perfect tenses are **present perfect, past perfect,** and **future perfect.** The perfect tenses use the helping verb *have* with the past tense of a verb. Present perfect shows an action that started in the past and continues to the present. Use past perfect for an action that was completed before another action began. Future perfect shows an action that will be completed before a certain time in the future.

▶ **EXAMPLE 2**

Present Perfect
Denbe has tackled the player many times.
(shows an action started in the past and continuing to the present)

Past Perfect
Denbe had tackled him before the whistle.
(shows one action completed before another action began)

Future Perfect
In two seconds, Denbe will have tackled him.
(shows action that will be completed before a certain time in the future)

Practice B

Write a sentence for each verb. Use the tense listed to write your sentence. Underline the verb phrase in each sentence.

1. act   past perfect
2. pass   future perfect
3. yell   present perfect
4. lock   future perfect
5. move   past perfect

Reading Strategy:
Text Structure

Why do you think this text is in a box?

The Verb *Have* in the Simple and Perfect Tense

The chart below shows the simple and perfect tenses of the verb *have*. Notice the different ways *have* is used. You will learn more about how to form these tenses in lesson 4-3.

Forms of the Verb *Have*

Present	(singular)	Denbe **has** the ball now
	(plural)	They **have** six points.
Past		The team **had** the lead.
Future		The team **will have** the ball.
Present Perfect	(singular)	He **has had** the ball four times.
		(has + past tense of verb)
	(plural)	They **have had** the ball once.
		(have + past tense of verb)
Past Perfect		By halftime, they **had had** enough.
		(had + past tense of verb)
Future Perfect		In a week, they **will have had** 10 wins.
		(will have + past tense of verb)

Practice C

We use the different forms of *have* to form the perfect tenses. Write the verb phrase in each sentence on your paper.

1. The Wilson Wildcats have had a great season.
2. The team has scored many touchdowns.
3. Coach Shaw has planned a team party.
4. The Wildcats have earned the celebration.
5. The coach has ordered trophies for the players.

The verb *have* can be a main verb or a helping verb. When it is a helping verb, it is part of a verb phrase.

▶ **EXAMPLE 3**

I have good friends. (main verb)
(*have* used alone)

I have made good friends. (helping verb)
(*have* forms the present perfect tense of the verb *made*)

Practice D

Decide whether *have* is the main verb or the helping verb in each sentence. Write *main verb* or *helping verb*.

1. The quarterback has worked hard today.

2. He has thrown several good passes.

3. The team has a good record so far.

4. They have one win and no losses.

5. The coach has expressed high hopes for the season.

Practice E

Write a sentence using each verb. Use a different tense in each sentence. Then underline the verb or verb phrase in each sentence.

1. walk

2. work

3. fish

4. listen

5. clean

Practice A

Complete each sentence with the correct form of the verb in parentheses.

1. Mrs. Kim (be) the coach two years ago.
2. The children have already (eat) their lunch.
3. Amir has (have) his job for nearly a year.
4. They (do) their chores every night.
5. Carlos has (go) to band practice.

You use the past participle with *have*, *has*, or *had* to form the perfect tenses of irregular verbs. For some irregular verbs, the past tense and past participle are the same.

Irregular Verbs with Same Past Tense and Past Participle

Present	Past	Past Participle
bend(s)	bent	(has) bent
cut(s)	cut	(has) cut
cost(s)	cost	(has) cost

Other irregular verbs with the same past tense and past participle are: feed, find, hear, keep, lose, make, and send.

Practice B

Complete each sentence with the past tense or past participle form of the verb in parentheses.

1. Ms. Lee has (find) the answer.
2. Carol (keep) her old clothes.
3. Leon has (cut) his finger on the glass.
4. They have (hear) that joke before.
5. Phillip had (feed) the dogs already.

Reading Strategy:
Text Structure

Study the chart on this page. How does it help you understand this lesson?

For some irregular verbs, the past tense and past participle are different.

Irregular Verbs with Different Past Tense and Past Participle

Present	Past	Past Participle
begin(s)	began	(has) begun
break(s)	broke	(has) broken
choose(s)	chose	(has) chosen
drive(s)	drove	(has) driven
fall(s)	fell	(has) fallen
fly (flies)	flew	(has) flown
forget(s)	forgot	(has) forgotten
give(s)	gave	(has) given
grow(s)	grew	(has) grown
hide(s)	hid	(has) hidden
know(s)	knew	(has) known
ride(s)	rode	(has) ridden
see(s)	saw	(has) seen
swim(s)	swam	(has) swum
take(s)	took	(has) taken
write(s)	wrote	(has) written

Practice C

Complete each sentence with the correct form of the verb in parentheses.

1. Mitsu has (know) Brad for many years.

2. Kiara (ride) in the holiday parade last year.

3. Hasan has (write) his cousin in Africa.

4. The vase (break) when it fell off the counter.

5. Calvin has (saw) that musical twice.

The words in a verb phrase are usually written together. However, they may be separated by another word or words in the sentence. The words in the verb phrases in Example 2 are underlined.

▶ **EXAMPLE 2**

She <u>has</u> finally <u>written</u> the report.

<u>Has</u> Rica really <u>gone</u> to the store?

John <u>will</u> not <u>finish</u> his assignment.

Practice D

Write the verb phrase in each sentence. Ignore any words that come between the helping verb and the main verb.

1. James has always given his best.
2. Have you ever heard that song before?
3. Victor has often seen him at the field.
4. I had not known the answer until today.
5. Have you ever ridden a scooter?

Practice E

Write the tense of each verb or verb phrase in bold.

1. She **will drive** me to the store tomorrow.
2. Yesterday Beth **lost** her gloves.
3. Ms. Potter **feeds** the rabbits.
4. Melissa **had known** most of the players for years.
5. A reporter **has written** about many of the games.

REVIEW

Write the correct form of the verb in parentheses to complete each sentence. Then write the tense next to each verb or verb phrase.

1. We have (eat) dinner at that cafe before.

2. Jeff had (be) at practice all afternoon.

3. I will (keep) my thoughts to myself.

4. The members will have (swim) every week.

5. Have the girls (go) to the movies?

Write the verb phrase in each sentence on your paper.

6. Helen has written a poem for English class.

7. Did you ever do your report?

8. Ramon has often fed the ducks.

9. He had not broken his promise.

10. Have you chosen your topic?

Progressive Forms

The **progressive form** of a verb ends in *-ing* and shows continuing action. Compare these two sentences.

▶ **EXAMPLE 1**

Present	Kim practices the guitar twice a week. (shows an action that is done frequently)
Present Progressive	Kim is practicing the guitar. (shows an action that is being done now)

The **present participle** shows continuing action.

▶ **EXAMPLE 2**

Present	see	seeing
Present Participle	work	working

Practice A

Write the verb phrase in each sentence on your paper.

1. Hai Sin practices her flute on Saturdays.
2. Tom is practicing the drums.
3. Sam plays the clarinet in the band.
4. Cathy works at the store after school.
5. Cathy is working tonight.

You have learned six tenses: present, past, future, present perfect, past perfect, and future perfect. Each of these tenses has a progressive form. It is made from a form of the verb *be* plus the present participle.

▶ **EXAMPLE 3**

Present Progressive	He is working.
Past Progressive	He was working.
Future Progressive	He will be working.
Present Perfect Progressive	He has been working.
Past Perfect Progressive	He had been working.
Future Perfect Progressive	He will have been working.

Practice B

Write the tense of each verb phrase in bold on your paper.

1. Mario **has been going** to Texas every year.
2. He **is flying** there for a vacation.
3. He **will be leaving** at noon.
4. Mario **had been packing** all morning.
5. He **will have been flying** for three hours.

Practice C

Write a sentence for each verb. Use the tense given in parentheses. Underline each verb or verb phrase.

1. drive   (future progressive)
2. have   (past progressive)
3. see   (future perfect progressive)
4. pour   (past perfect progressive)
5. jump   (present perfect)

The Verb *Be*

Be is an irregular verb. Study the different forms of *be*.

Simple Tenses of *Be*

Present	Past	Future
I am	I was	I shall be
you are	you were	you will be
he is	he was	he will be
we are	we were	we shall be
you are	you were	you will be
they are	they were	they will be

Perfect Tenses of *Be*

Present	Past	Future
I have been	I had been	I shall have been
you have been	you had been	you will have been
he has been	he had been	he will have been
we have been	we had been	we shall have been
you have been	you had been	you will have been
they have been	they had been	they will have been

Practice D

Complete each sentence with the correct form of the verb *be*.

1. I have _____ on an airplane six times.

2. Jack will _____ going to Seattle next week.

3. Doris has _____ in my class every year.

4. By noon, Mac will have _____ painting for four hours.

5. Sara _____ leaving for Florida on Friday.

Complete each sentence with the correct verb form.

1. Rosa has been (playing, played) the oboe for a year.

2. She has (playing, played) in the band for two months.

3. This year the band is (going, gone) to Florida for a national contest.

4. The band members have been (raising, raised) money all year.

5. So far they have (raising, raised) more than one thousand dollars.

Reading Strategy:
Text Structure

How do the photograph and caption relate to the progressive tense?

Our team is scoring many points. The players are working hard!

REVIEW

Write each sentence using the verb *sharpen*. Use the tense listed. *Sharpen* is a regular verb.

1. future
2. present perfect
3. past perfect
4. future perfect
5. present progressive

6. past progressive
7. future progressive
8. present perfect progressive
9. past perfect progressive
10. future perfect progressive

BUILDING RESEARCH SKILLS

Evaluating the Credibility and Reliability of Sources

Bias is a leaning toward a certain way of thinking. When writers are biased they present only the facts that support their opinion. Companies wanting to sell a product present product information in a biased way.

Think about whether a source may be biased when you begin your research. Some Internet sources are not reliable. Keep these things in mind when you look at Internet sites:

• Is the site sponsored by an expert?
• Does the site give facts, not opinions? Does it offer references?
• Does the site present a variety of expert opinions?
• Has the site been updated recently?

Choose a topic to research on the Internet. Visit at least three Web sites. Then answer these questions.

1. Which ones have the best information? Explain.

2. Which ones are not useful for research? Explain.

3. **CRITICAL THINKING** Why is it important to look for possible bias in a source or media message? Explain.

Subject-Verb Agreement

Objectives

- To use verbs that agree with the subject of the sentence
- To use correct verb agreement with indefinite pronouns
- To use correct verb agreement with collective nouns

Verb agreement

When a verb agrees in number (singular or plural) with its subject

A verb must agree in number (singular or plural) with its subject. This is called **verb agreement.** The present tense of a regular verb has two forms. You use one form with a singular subject. You use another form with a plural subject.

Add *-s* or *-es* to the present tense of the verb when the subject is a singular noun.

▶ **EXAMPLE 1**

| **Singular Subject** | Mel's puppy always cries for treats. |
| **Plural Subject** | Both puppies cry for treats. |

When the subject is a singular pronoun (*he*, *she*, *it*), add *-s* or *-es* to the verb.

▶ **EXAMPLE 2**

| **Singular Subject** | She likes to write. |
| **Plural Subject** | They like to write. |

When the subject is *I* or *you*, use the plural form of the verb.

▶ **EXAMPLE 3**

I enjoy holidays with my cousins.

Do you enjoy holidays?

NOTE

Hearing the correct verb forms can help you write them correctly. Read aloud sentences that are correct. Listen to the sound of correct usage.

Practice A

Write each sentence with the correct verb on your paper.

1. Jack (hope, hopes) to win the tournament.
2. They (love, loves) history class.
3. I (want, wants) a new box of colored pencils.
4. He (watch, watches) his neighbor's cat.
5. The robin (fly, flies) to the feeder.

Verb Agreement with Indefinite Pronouns

Most indefinite pronouns are singular even though their meanings are plural. They take a singular form of the verb.

Reading Strategy:
Text Structure

What does Example 4 show you about indefinite pronouns?

▶ **EXAMPLE 4**

| Incorrect | Everyone go to the mountains in the fall. |
| Correct | Everyone goes to the mountains in the fall. |

Some indefinite pronouns may be singular or plural depending on the way we use them. These are *all, any, most,* and *none.*

▶ **EXAMPLE 5**

| Singular | All of the picnic food is in the cooler. |
| Plural | All of the girls are going to the mall. |

Practice B

Write the correct verb to complete each sentence.

1. All of the noise (has, have) stopped.
2. Anyone (is, are) welcome at the play.
3. Most of the members (go, goes) to Angie's for snacks.
4. None of us (are, is) going.
5. Everyone that I know (travel, travels) to Toronto.

Some indefinite pronouns are always plural: *both*, *many*, *few*, and *several*. These indefinite pronouns take a plural form of the verb.

▶ **EXAMPLE 6**

Several of the students want to take the test.

Practice C

Write the correct verb to complete each sentence.

1. Everyone (is, are) coming to the football game.
2. Both of the teachers (announces, announce) an exam.
3. Few of them (was, were) prepared for the exam.
4. Nothing (sound, sounds) as noisy as a hockey game.
5. Several of the club members (plan, plans) the party.

Collective Nouns

Remember that a collective noun names a group of people, places, or things. Examples include *army*, *audience*, *jury*, *committee*, *troop*, and *crowd*. A collective noun usually takes the singular form of a verb.

▶ **EXAMPLE 7**

The crowd is ready for the performance.

The committee makes a decision.

Practice D

Write the correct verb to complete each sentence.

1. The group (was, were) planning a party.
2. I hope the team (score, scores)!
3. The flock of birds (flies, fly) south.
4. Your club (meet, meets) on Friday.
5. The herd of cows (eat, eats) meadow grass.

Reading Strategy:
Text Structure

Describe the structure of this lesson.

REVIEW

Find the mistake in each sentence. Write each sentence correctly on your paper.

1. Jay teach people to play tennis.

2. Several of his students wants to play professionally.

3. Many hopes to play in college.

4. The tennis team always win.

5. Each of Jay's students learn a lot.

6. Everyone enjoy winning.

7. They practices forehands during their lessons.

8. Nothing are better than hitting a smash.

9. He participate in the tournament.

10. Both of the umpires calls the ball out.

VOCABULARY BUILDER

Synonyms

Synonyms are words with the same or nearly the same meaning as another word. For example, *snicker* and *cackle* are synonyms for *laugh*. Improve your writing by using verbs with specific meanings. A thesaurus will help you find words to use.

Rewrite each sentence on your paper. Replace the bold verb with a more specific or unusual verb.

1. The wind **blew** during the storm.
2. Mr. and Mrs. Perez **walk** every evening.
3. He **washed** the stain out of his shirt.
4. Stefan **moved** down the basketball court.
5. Ming **looks** through the telescope.

The Verb *Do*

Do as a Main Verb

The verb *do* can be a main verb. When *do* is a main verb, it means "to perform an action."

Objectives

- To use the verb *do* as a main verb
- To use the verb *do* as a helping verb
- To use the verb *do* for emphasis

▶ **EXAMPLE 1**

Keiko does her chores on the weekend. (main verb)

You can use the verb *do* in all tenses.

▶ **EXAMPLE 2**

	Progressive
Present	Yola does her exercises early.
Past	Rishi did his report well.
Future	Everyone will do his or her best.
Present Perfect	The team has done its work well.
Past Perfect	We had done the chores by noon.
Future Perfect	Soon he will have done his chores.

Reading Strategy:
Text Structure

How does the structure of this lesson compare with the rest of the chapter?

Practice A

Write a sentence using the verb *do* as a main verb. Use the tense listed.

1. present progressive
2. past
3. present
4. future perfect
5. past perfect progressive

Do as a Helping Verb

The verb *do* can also be a helping verb. You use the helping verbs *do* and *did* only with the present form of the main verb.

▶ **EXAMPLE 3**

He did dust the cabinets.

Did you go home? (The verb *go* is present.)

▶ **EXAMPLE 4**

Alonzo did enjoy the match. (emphasis)

Many stores do not close on holidays. (with the word *not*)

Do you like pears? (question)

Practice B

Write the verb or verb phrase in each sentence.

1. Did you see Anita at lunch?
2. Jack never did find his gloves.
3. The family is doing the dishes.
4. Do you read the newspaper?
5. They did not trim the fruit trees this year.

Practice C

Write the verb phrase in bold. Decide whether *do* is a main verb or a helping verb. Write *main verb* or *helping verb*.

1. Finally they **had done** all their chores.
2. "**Did** you **see** my math book?" Eric asked.
3. "What **did** you **do** with it this time?" she asked.
4. **Did** Eric ever **find** his book?
5. Soon he **was doing** his math.

Reading Strategy:
Text Structure

How well do you feel this lesson is organized? Would you organize it differently?

REVIEW

Write the verb or verb phrase in each sentence on your paper. Next to each verb or verb phrase, write its tense.

1. Yesterday, Monica did her yard work.

2. She was doing yard work all afternoon.

3. Soon she will have done the entire yard.

4. She had done all of the weeding too.

5. Who does the yard work at your house?

Write the verb or verb phrase in bold. Then write *helping verb* or *main verb* next to each verb or verb phrase.

6. In the fall, people **do** extra yard work.

7. **Did** you **rake** your leaves yet?

8. They **have** already **done** the raking.

9. **Does** your family **plant** grass seed in the fall?

10. Soon they **will have done** the whole yard.

Conditional Verbs

Objectives

- To define *conditional verb*
- To identify verb phrases that express the conditional form
- To use conditional verbs in sentences

Conditional verb

A helping verb that puts a condition or requirement on an action

Reading Strategy:
Text Structure

How does the list in Example 1 help you better understand the conditional form?

Some helping verbs put a condition on an action. You use a **conditional verb** to express possibility or requirement. The conditional verbs are *may, might, can, could, shall, should, will, would,* and *must.* Look carefully at the main verbs in the verb phrases in Example 1. They are all present-tense verbs.

▶ **EXAMPLE 1**

may—might	She may succeed.
	She might succeed.
can—could	He can sing.
	He could sing.
shall—should	You shall leave.
	You should leave.
will—would	He will like that show.
	He would like that show.
must	I must go now.
	You must find your report.
	They must leave quickly.

Practice A

Write the verb phrase in each sentence on your paper.

1. You may stay at the party until ten o'clock.

2. David can play the trombone.

3. The basket will hold a dozen tomatoes.

4. She should do her homework.

5. She must finish her report tonight.

Reading Strategy:
Text Structure

Use a graphic organizer to show the organization of topics in this lesson.

 Writing Tip

Use *can* when referring to ability. Use *may* when referring to permission. For example: *Phil* can *play the piano.* (ability); May *I play the piano?* (permission)

Practice B

Write a conditional helping verb to complete each sentence.

1. Lily said that Latasha _____ use the school computer.

2. With a computer, Latasha _____ write a better paper.

3. That computer program _____ catch grammar and spelling errors.

4. Saul _____ like that program.

5. The movie _____ start soon.

All of the conditional verbs are followed by a plural verb form.

▶ **EXAMPLE 2**

Incorrect   He must does his homework before he goes.

Correct   He must do his homework before he goes.

Practice C

Write the correct verb to complete each sentence.

1. Every day Deshawn will (exercise, exercises) at the gym.

2. They could (exercise, exercises) on a regular basis.

3. Julian (might, mights) exercise today.

4. He would (goes, go) every day if he had the time.

5. Carmen (must, musts) leave early.

Change each verb to the conditional tense. Remember to make the main verb plural.

1. George wants a sandwich for lunch.
2. Paco and I make a card for our sick friend.
3. Tommy drops off his friend at the mall.
4. Andrea hopes to win the soccer game.
5. Juanita carries the bags in the store.

Jorge must walk Fido every morning.
Fido could run all day long.

REVIEW

Write the verb phrase in each sentence on your paper.

1. Next week, I might be going to Indiana.
2. I could have gone last year.
3. This year I must go.
4. I would leave on Monday if possible.
5. Should I take an umbrella?

Write a conditional helping verb to complete each sentence.

6. Julia _____ go to the movies with Guy.
7. Guy _____ ask her to go.
8. Al _____ finish his work by noon.
9. He _____ finish sooner if he hurries.
10. Robert _____ be late.

SPELLING BUILDER

Words with _ie_ or _ei_

Several action verbs include the letters _ie_ or _ei_. Say these words aloud: _achieve, believe, receive, shriek, weigh, neigh,_ and _reign._ This verse will help you spell words with _ie_ or _ei:_

- Put _i_ before _e_
- Except after _c_
- Or when sounded like _a_
- As in _neighbor_ and _weigh._

Exceptions to this rule are _science, either, seize,_ and _height._ Write the correct spelling of each word on your paper.

1. friend, freind
2. relieve, releive
3. neighbor, nieghbor
4. piece, peice
5. reciept, receipt

Active and Passive Verbs

Objectives

■ To decide if a verb is active or passive in a sentence

■ To use active and passive verbs in sentences

Active verb
A verb form used when the subject is doing the action

Passive verb
A verb form used when the action happens to the subject

Reading Strategy:
Text Structure

As you read the lesson, use a graphic organizer to compare and contrast active and passive verbs.

Action verbs can be **active** or **passive.** A verb is active when the subject is doing the action. A verb is passive when the action happens to the subject.

▶ **EXAMPLE 1**

| Active | Alvaro wrote a play. |
| Passive | The play was written by Alvaro. |

Practice A

Write the verb or verb phrase in each sentence. Next to each one, write whether it is active or passive.

1. Lois Lowry writes many stories.

2. *The Giver* was written by Lois Lowry.

3. Lois Lowry won a Newberry Award for *The Giver*.

4. That cake was baked by my aunt.

5. My aunt baked that cake.

Passive verbs use the helping verb *be* with the past participle. Sentences with passive verbs often have *by* and a noun following the passive verb.

▶ **EXAMPLE 2**

The song was sung by Amy.

Reading Strategy:
Text Structure

Review this lesson and others in this chapter. What kinds of boxes like this one are found throughout the chapter? Why are these included?

Technology Note

Many grammar checks in software programs will catch passive verbs. However, do not depend solely on the software.

Practice B

Write two sentences for each verb. In the first sentence, make the verb active. In the second, make the verb passive.

1. cover
2. hit
3. cook
4. answer
5. teach

In some passive sentences, the writer does not name the person doing the action. The person is "understood."

▶ **EXAMPLE 3**

Today the safe was robbed. (by someone)

The pass was thrown well. (by someone)

Practice C

Write the verb phrase in each sentence on your paper.

1. The home run was scored by Tuvel.
2. The decorations were brought by the dance committee.
3. The annual fund-raiser was held by the chess club.
4. The picnic was prepared by Mrs. Choy.
5. The students were tested by the teacher.

REVIEW

Write the verb or verb phrase in each sentence. Next to each one, write *active* or *passive*.

1. Eli Whitney invented the cotton gin.

2. Cotton seeds are removed from the cotton.

3. *Gone With the Wind* was written by Margaret Mitchell.

4. Her book was made into a successful movie.

5. Tecumseh, a Shawnee leader, lived in Ohio.

Rewrite each sentence on your paper. Change the verb in bold from passive to active.

6. The batter **was hit** by the wild pitch.

7. John's bag **was packed** by his mother.

8. The telephone **was answered** by the secretary.

9. The neighbors **were disturbed** by the barking dog.

10. The oil **was changed** last month by the mechanic.

PUTTING IT ALL TOGETHER

Write care instructions for a pet. Explain how the pet has behaved the last few days. Include instructions that the caretaker will have to follow on the day that you leave. Also include instructions that the caretaker will have to follow in a few days. In your instructions, be sure you use the past, present, and future tenses. In addition, use active verbs and one or more conditional verbs.

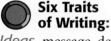

Six Traits of Writing:

Ideas message, details, and purpose

Restaurant Shift Supervisor

Kristen Schultz is a restaurant shift supervisor. She makes sure that things run smoothly during a restaurant shift. She checks food quality, addresses customer concerns, and completes paperwork. In addition, she trains employees and assigns them tasks.

Ms. Schultz uses clear instructions when working with employees. She often writes down directions for employees to learn. She writes how to run the cash register or take an order using clear steps.

Read the steps for closing down the restaurant at night, and then answer the questions that follow.

1. *Existing checks are closed out by waiters.*
2. *Store food and clean the grill.*
3. *Clean all tables and fill salt, pepper, and ketchup bottles.*
4. *Sweep and mop the floors.*
5. *Each of the waiters musts record tips and hours worked.*
6. *The supervisor will count the cash with another employee.*

1. Are the directions clear and direct? Rewrite step number 1 so that it uses an active verb, not a passive verb. Correct the subject-verb agreement in step number 5.

2. Who or what is the subject of the verb in steps 2, 3, and 4?

3. **CRITICAL THINKING** Write the verb tenses and forms used in this list. Which is used most often? Why?

SPEAKING AND LISTENING

Make sure verbal instructions are clear. Use precise words. Do not skip any steps or speak too fast. Choose a topic and explain how to do something while demonstrating it. For example, show a student how to draw something. Ask for feedback. Then repeat your instructions using more precise words.

- Find the subject in a sentence by asking who or what is doing something. Find the action verb in a sentence by asking what they are doing.

- A verb phrase has a main verb and one or more helping verbs.

- Verbs express tense. *Simple* and *perfect* are two types of tenses.

- Verbs have three main forms—infinitive (present), past, and past participle. Most verbs form the past and past participle by adding *-d* or *-ed,* but others are irregular.

- *Have* is an irregular verb. It helps to form the perfect tense.

- Use the simple and perfect tenses in the progressive form to show continuing action.

- *Be* is one example of an irregular verb. It forms the progressive tense.

- A verb must agree in number (singular or plural) with its subject. Indefinite pronouns can be singular, plural, or both.

- *Do* is an irregular verb that can be a helping verb or main verb. Use *do* to add emphasis in a sentence.

- Conditional verbs put a condition or requirement on an action.

- Action verbs can be either active or passive.

Word Bank

action verb

active verb

conditional verb

future perfect

helping verb

irregular verb

main verb

passive verb

past perfect

progressive form

simple tenses

subject

tense

verb

verb phrase

Part A Find the word or words in the Word Bank to complete each sentence. Write the answer on your paper.

1. The time when an action takes place is called _____.

2. An _____ tells what someone or something does, did, or will do.

3. A _____ is the last verb in a verb phrase.

4. A word that expresses action or state of being is a _____.

5. A _____ is a main verb plus one or more helping verbs.

6. The present, past, and future forms of verbs are all _____.

7. The _____ tells who or what the sentence is about.

8. A _____ combines with a main verb to form a verb phrase.

9. A _____ puts a condition or a requirement on an action.

10. An _____ shows that the subject is doing the action.

11. The _____ shows an action that will be completed before a certain time in the future.

12. A _____ shows that the action happens to the subject.

13. The _____ is a verb that ends in *-ing* and shows continuing action.

14. The _____ shows one action completed before another action began.

15. A verb that does not form its past tense and past participle by adding *-ed* or *-d* is an _____.

Part B Choose the verb that completes each sentence. Write the letter of your answer on your paper.

16. Did Kim _____ home yet?
    A go   **C** goes
    B went   **D** going

17. The herd _____ over the hill.
    A runned   **C** run
    B running   **D** runs

18. There _____ jugglers and clowns at the party.
    A is   **C** were
    B was   **D** be

Part C Write the verb or verb phrase in bold on your paper. Write the tense of each verb. Then write whether the verb is active or passive.

19. Everyone **will cheer** them on.

20. We **have been running** for an hour.

21. Your portrait **can be drawn** by Flora.

22. Damon **should leave** the room.

Part D Complete each sentence with the correct form of the verb in parentheses.

23. He _____ many times. (present perfect tense of *drive*)

24. He _____ to school every day. (present tense of *drive* with the helping verb *do*)

25. Devon _____ too sick to drive today. (present tense of *be*)

Test Tip

Look over a test before you begin. See how many parts there are. Think about what you are being asked to do in each part.

State-of-Being Verbs

Look at the photograph. Imagine seeing such a sight! How might you describe this moment to a friend? You could say "It *seems* quiet. The trees *look* dark and bare. The wind *feels* crisp and cold. The air *smells* clean and fresh. The sky *appears* soft and warm. The moon *grows* brighter and brighter." The verb in each of these sentences is a state-of-being verb. Other words like *remain, stay,* and *become* are also state-of-being verbs. How might you use them to describe this photograph?

A state-of-being verb tells something about the condition of the subject of a sentence.

In Chapter 5, you will learn about state-of-being verbs. Each lesson focuses on the correct use and form of state-of-being verbs in sentences.

GOALS FOR LEARNING

- To identify state-of-being verbs and verb phrases in sentences
- To identify the tenses of state-of-being verbs
- To decide if a verb is a state-of-being or action verb in a sentence

Reading Strategy: Visualizing

Visualizing is another strategy that helps readers understand what they are reading. It is like creating a movie in your mind. Use the following methods to visualize a text:

- Look at the photographs, illustrations, and descriptive words.
- Think about experiences in your own life that may add to the images.
- Notice the order in which things are happening and what you think might happen next.

Key Vocabulary Word

State-of-being verb A verb that tells something about the condition of the subject of a sentence

What Is a State-of-Being Verb?

An action verb tells what someone or something does, did, or will do. A **state-of-being verb** tells something about the condition or state of the subject of a sentence. A state-of-being verb does not tell what the subject is doing.

▶ **EXAMPLE 1**

State-of-Being Verb   Dan is a tackle on the football team.
(The verb *is* helps to make a statement about Dan.)

Action Verb   Dan plays on the football team.
(The verb *plays* tells an action that Dan does.)

The Word *Be*

The most common state-of-being verb is *be*. Other forms of the verb *be* include *am, are, is, was, were, being,* and *been. To be* means "to exist, to live, or to happen."

The Verb *Be*

Present	(singular)	(I) am, (he, she, it) is
	(plural)	are
Past	(singular)	was
	(plural)	were
Future		will be
Present Perfect	(singular)	has been
	(plural)	have been
Past Perfect		had been
Future Perfect		will have been
Present Progressive	(singular)	(I) am being, (he, she, it) is being
	(plural)	are being
Past Progressive	(singular)	was being
	(plural)	were being
Future Progressive		will be being

Write each verb or verb phrase. Then, write the verb tense.

1. Alex and Jennifer have been at the museum.

2. Mike was at the mall.

3. Mike and Alex are good friends.

4. They had been friends since second grade.

5. Mike and Alex will be at practice this evening.

Other State-of-Being Verbs

appear	grow	seem
become	keep	smell
feel	look	stay
get	remain	taste

Practice B

Read the example. Write five more sentences about Keiko. Use state-of-being verbs. Underline each verb.

Example: Keiko <u>seems</u> nice.

Reading Strategy:
Visualizing

What things come to mind when you think about some of these verbs?

Be as a Helping Verb

The verb *be* can also be a helping verb. Use *be* with a main verb to form progressive tenses. Use the present participle form (*-ing*) of the verb to form the progressive tenses.

▶ **EXAMPLE 2**

Pedro is feeling sick.

Yumi was looking tired.

Practice C

Write the present participle for each of these state-of-being verbs. Then write a sentence using each present participle.

1. be

2. seem

3. look

4. feel

5. appear

NOTE

You also use *be* to form passive verb phrases. *Be* is a helping verb in these verb phrases. For example: *The mural was painted by Pablo Picasso.*

Practice D

Write the verb or verb phrase in each sentence. Then write whether the verb *be* is a main verb or a helping verb.

1. Carlita was feeling fine yesterday.

2. Today she is sick.

3. She is looking pale.

4. Carlita will be absent from school.

5. She probably will be better tomorrow.

State-of-Being Verbs with Conditional Verbs

You can use the conditional helping verbs with state-of-being verbs. The conditional helping verbs are *may, can, should, might, could, will, must, shall,* and *would.*

▶ **EXAMPLE 3**

Martha should be happy after seeing her favorite movie.

The soccer player must be upset after losing the game.

Write each state-of-being verb or verb phrase on your paper.

1. The team must be early.

2. The pitcher may appear nervous.

3. He could become tired.

4. Will our team be a winner?

5. Emily must feel happy today.

State-of-Being Verbs and Tenses

State-of-being verbs have the same tenses as action verbs. Each of the tenses below can make the progressive form.

▶ **EXAMPLE 4**

Present	The blanket feels warm.
Past	He looked good yesterday.
Future	Maria will be 15 next week.
Present Perfect	I have been hungry all morning.
Past Perfect	Jack had seemed tired by evening.
Future Perfect	Mel will have been sick twice tomorrow.

Practice F

Write the verb or verb phrase in each sentence. Next to each verb or verb phrase, write its tense.

1. Sam will not be happy about that.

2. Mrs. Franco has been our neighbor for two years.

3. She was a Spanish teacher.

4. We had been the winners twice.

5. We will have become tired by then.

REVIEW

Write each state-of-being verb or verb phrase. Then write whether the verb *be* is a main verb or a helping verb.

1. My aunt is 80 years old.
2. She is looking well.
3. She always has been healthy.
4. Aunt Marie is a good cook.
5. She has been keeping very active.

Write the state-of-being verb or verb phrase in each sentence. Then write the verb tense next to it.

6. Dinner should smell very inviting.
7. The food was wonderful.
8. That turkey looks delicious.
9. The drumstick can be my favorite part.
10. Nothing will taste better than the stuffing.

BUILDING RESEARCH SKILLS

Using the Table of Contents

The table of contents appears at the beginning of a book. It lists the book's main sections and the topics of each section. The table of contents lists the page number where each part begins.

Use the table of contents to decide if a book will be useful to you. Also use it to find general information about a topic in a book. To find a specific topic, use the index in the back of a book. A menu is a form of an online table of contents.

Look at the table of contents for this textbook and follow these directions.

1. Where could you find information about recognizing adverbs?
2. Can you use this textbook to find information about writing a letter? Explain your answer.
3. CRITICAL THINKING Search different Web sites and look at their menus. How are the table of contents of books and online menus similar? How are they different?

Using State-of-Being Verbs

Objectives

- To form the tenses of state-of being verbs correctly
- To use a state-of-being verb that agrees with the subject of a sentence
- To identify the forms of the irregular verb *be*
- To use the correct form of the verb *be* in sentences

Reading Strategy:
Visualizing

What words on this page help you visualize the steps to form a singular or plural state-of-being verb?

Subject-Verb Agreement and Tenses

In a sentence, the verb must agree in number (singular or plural) with its subject. The rules for subject-verb agreement for state-of-being verbs and action verbs are the same. Add *-s* or *-es* to the present tense when the subject is singular. *Be* is the only state-of-being verb that does not follow this rule.

▶ **EXAMPLE 1**

| Singular Subject | Jerome looks happy. |
| Plural Subject | They look happy. |

The past tense of the verb stays the same for singular and plural subjects.

▶ **EXAMPLE 2**

| Singular Subject | Laura looked nice. |
| Plural Subject | Both girls looked nice. |

Practice A

Complete each sentence with the present tense of the verb in parentheses. Be sure the subject and the verb agree.

1. Joey (feel) sure that his answer is correct.
2. Jennifer (appear) pleased with the results of the test.
3. Gabe and Mike (look) sad.
4. The bread that is cooling on the counter (smell) delicious.
5. The hot apple cider (taste) good.

Put state-of-being verbs in the correct tense. When writing about past events, make all your verbs past tense. When writing about present events, use present-tense verbs.

Reading Strategy:
Visualizing

How could the first paragraph on this page be written differently to create a stronger picture in your mind?

The Verb *Be*

The verb *be* is an irregular verb. Its form depends on whether it is used with a singular or plural subject. Its form also depends on whether the subject is first, second, or third person.

Present and Past Forms of *Be*

Singular	Present	Past
First Person	I am	I was
Second Person	you are	you were
Third Person	he is	he was
	she is	she was
	it is	it was

Plural	Present	Past
First Person	we are	we were
Second Person	you are	you were
Third Person	they are	they were

Fresh homemade bread tastes great.

Writing Tip

When using *be*, do not leave out the verb. "He tall" is incorrect. "He is tall" is correct. Do not use *be* instead of the correct present form. "He be tall" is incorrect. "He is tall" is correct.

Practice B

Write the verb in each sentence on your paper.

1. I am busy today.

2. They were happy to get the award.

3. They are friends of mine.

4. She is a careful driver.

5. The crowd was anxious for the game to be over.

The past participle of *be* is *been*. Use *been* with *have*, *has*, and *had* to form the perfect tenses.

▶ **EXAMPLE 3**

Mrs. Fong has been sick. (present perfect—singular)

They have been busy all week. (present perfect—plural)

Seth had been their coach. (past perfect—singular)

Remember that a present participle shows continuing action. The present participle of *be* is *being*. Use *being* with the helping verb *be* to show the progressive form.

▶ **EXAMPLE 4**

Kim is being nice. (present progressive)

Shanice was being friendly. (past progressive)

Complete each sentence with the correct form of the verb *be*.

1. Megan's report _____ due yesterday.
2. She was _____ stubborn about the decision.
3. Has he ever _____ a teacher?
4. Yellowstone Park _____ a national park.
5. The children were _____ silly.

Use the verb *be* to show future tense.

▶ **EXAMPLE 5**

Future	He will be home soon.
Conditional	Jamie must be late.

Complete each sentence with the correct form of the verb *be*.

1. Will you _____ my project partner?
2. I should _____ more careful.
3. Must I always _____ the first one?
4. Can I _____ the last one?
5. Howard will _____ disappointed about the game.

REVIEW

Complete each sentence with the correct form of the verb *be*. The tense of each sentence is in parentheses.

1. In May there _____ a contest at Rove School. (future)
2. Mitu _____ entering the contest. (present)
3. Her talent _____ playing the tuba. (past progressive)
4. After the contest, Mitu's parents _____ excited. (past)
5. Before the contest, Mitu _____ nervous. (past perfect)

Complete each sentence with the correct form of the verb in parentheses. Be sure the subject and the verb agree.

6. Tanya should (keep) warm in that jacket.
7. We will (feel) tired after the hike.
8. The teacher (seem) happy with the students.
9. Her perfume (smell) wonderful yesterday!
10. The hearty stew had (appear) delicious.

VOCABULARY BUILDER

Replacing the *Be* Verb
The verb *be* means "to exist, to live, or to happen." Make your writing more interesting by replacing *be* verbs with more specific verbs.

> The apple *is* delicious.
> The apple *tastes* delicious.

Rewrite each sentence. Replace each verb in bold with a more specific word. You may need to change other words.
1. Will Frances and Brandon **be** here very long?
2. That ham **is** too salty.
3. Tanya **is** my best friend.
4. Zach **was** responsible for the goal.
5. Hiro **is** in need of a backpack.

Action or State of Being?

- To locate verbs and verb phrases in sentences
- To determine whether a verb is an action or state-of-being verb in a sentence

Reading Strategy:
Visualizing

Draw a picture to help you visualize what this page is about. How does this image help you remember?

The verb *be* expresses state of being when it is the main verb in a sentence.

▶ **EXAMPLE 1**

The chicken is golden brown.

The chicken was delicious.

Many state-of-being verbs can also be action verbs. To decide whether a verb expresses action or a state of being, think about the meaning of the sentence.

If the subject is doing something, the verb is an action verb.

▶ **EXAMPLE 2**

Action Verb	Gabi tasted the mashed potatoes. (*Tasted* expresses action.)
State-of-Being Verb	The mashed potatoes tasted salty. (*Tasted* expresses a state of being.)

Practice A

Write the verb in each sentence. Next to each one, write *action* or *state of being*.

1. The sky looks very stormy.
2. My jacket keeps me warm.
3. Corey appeared calm.
4. Jamal and Kim became ill after the trip.
5. Everyone smelled the burning rubber.

Verbs often have more than one meaning. Some meanings express action and some express state of being.

Verbs That Express Action and State of Being

Appear	Action	The firefighters **appeared** quickly.
	State of Being	The firefighters **appeared** strong.
Feel	Action	Ling **felt** the heat of the sun on her face.
	State of Being	Ling **felt** relaxed.
Grow	Action	The vegetables **grew** in the garden.
	State of Being	The sky **grew** darker.
Smell	Action	Brenda **smelled** the baking bread.
	State of Being	The bread **smells** delicious.
Look	Action	Ling **looked** at the ocean.
	State of Being	Ling **looks** worried.
Taste	Action	Colin **tasted** the juice.
	State of Being	The juice **tasted** sour.
Get	Action	I **got** my skis.
	State of Being	It **gets** windy during a storm.
Become	Action	This color **becomes** you.
	State of Being	Devon **became** angry.

Practice B

Write *action* or *state of being* for each bold word.

1. She could **smell** the smoke in the air.
2. The warm rolls **smelled** inviting.
3. The oven **felt** too hot.
4. Mary **felt** a hole in her pocket.
5. Joe **grows** orange trees in Arizona.

Substituting Words

If you are not sure whether a verb is a state-of-being verb, try this test. Substitute a form of the verb *be* for the verb. If the meaning of the sentence is almost the same, the verb is a state-of-being verb. You cannot substitute a form of *be* for an action verb.

▶ **EXAMPLE 3**

State-of-Being Verb	They remained members. (You can say: They *were* members.)
Action Verb	He got a new hat. (You cannot say: He *was* a new hat.)

Practice C

Write two sentences for each verb. In the first sentence, use the verb as an action verb. In the second sentence, use the verb as a state-of-being verb.

1. feel
2. taste
3. get
4. look
5. appear

NOTE

The words *seem* and *seam* sound alike. *Seem* is a state-of-being verb. A *seam* is a line formed when two or more items are joined together.

The Verb *Seem*

The verb *seem* is always a state-of-being verb.

▶ **EXAMPLE 4**

Seem   to be; to appear

Alex seems afraid.

Practice D

Write each verb or verb phrase. Write *action* or *state of being* next to each one.

1. Smell these beautiful flowers.
2. The grass seems greener this time of year.
3. That cute little puppy in the window is looking at us.
4. The plants in our yard appeared yellow and shriveled.
5. Did you taste the vegetable pizza?

Reading Strategy:
Visualizing

Study this photograph. How does the picture represent an idea in this lesson?

The puppies in the window look so cute.

REVIEW

Write whether the verb in bold expresses *action* or *state of being.*

1. Howard finally **appeared**.

2. He **seems** strong and healthy.

3. The cloth **felt** soft to me.

4. I **felt** the soft cloth.

5. The taco sauce **tasted** bland.

Write the verb or verb phrase in each sentence. Next to each verb or verb phrase, write *action* or *state of being.*

6. Mr. Klein was looking for the newspaper.

7. Suddenly the newspaper appeared!

8. The newspaper appeared wrinkled.

9. Mr. Klein grew thoughtful for a moment.

10. He smelled the eggs and bacon downstairs.

PUTTING IT ALL TOGETHER

Draw a picture of yourself. Then write a caption using five sentences. Use state-of-being verbs in your sentences to tell about yourself. Use at least three different tenses in your caption. Underline all of the state-of-being verbs and verb phrases. Put the verb tense in parentheses after each sentence.

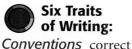

Six Traits of Writing:

Conventions correct grammar, spelling, and mechanics

Completing a Job Application

When you apply for a job, you often have to fill out a job application. A job application asks for basic information such as your phone number, address, and e-mail address. It also asks about your work history and experiences.

On a job application, you will often use state-of-being verbs. For example, the application might ask about your strengths. You might say that you are reliable or hard-working.

When filling out a job application, keep in mind the following:

- Fill out the application completely. Do not leave blank spaces.
- Provide specific details that show your strengths. Use action verbs if possible.
- Be honest. Every detail on an application must be true.
- Double-check your spelling and grammar. This includes verb tenses and subject-verb agreement.

Fill out a job application from a local business. Then follow the directions.

1. Give examples of state-of-being verbs that you used on the application.

2. Give examples of a form of *be* used as a helping verb on your application. If you do not have one, add a sentence using *be* to your application.

3. **CRITICAL THINKING** Why should you use more action verbs than state-of-being verbs on your application?

LISTENING AND SPEAKING

At a job interview, provide appropriate details from your experiences. Show that you are qualified for the job. Answer the questions clearly and directly. Write five job interview questions. Practice asking and answering these questions with a partner. Evaluate your partner's nonverbal communication, such as eye contact, tone, posture, and gestures.

SUMMARY

- State-of-being verbs are different from action verbs. They show the condition or state of the subject of the sentence.

- *Be* is the most common state-of-being verb. However, you can use many other state-of-being verbs such as *taste*, *look*, or *appear*.

- You can use the conditional helping verbs with state-of-being verbs.

- State-of-being verbs have the same verb tenses as action verbs.

- Rules for subject-verb agreement for state-of-being verbs and action verbs are the same.

- *Be* is the only state-of-being verb that is irregular.

- Forms of *be* can act as helping verbs to form the progressive tense. The past participle *been* forms the perfect tense when used with *has*, *have*, or *had*.

- Many state-of-being verbs can also be action verbs. Sentence and verb meaning determine if a word is a state-of-being or action verb.

SPELLING BUILDER

Homonyms: Words That Sound Alike
Homonyms sound alike but have different meanings and spellings. Examples are: *break, brake; past, passed; through, threw; plain, plane;* and *their, they're, there.* Complete each sentence with the correct word. Use a dictionary for help.

1. Have you given the workers a (break, brake) yet?

2. He forgives her for her (past, passed) mistakes.

3. We drove (through, threw) a long tunnel.

4. The passengers boarded the (plain, plane).

5. Teachers should help (their, they're, there) students.

Part A Choose the verb form that correctly completes each sentence. Write the letter of the correct form.

1. Will Carol _____ at the meeting tomorrow?

    A be   **B** been   **C** being   **D** is

2. She _____ almost always on time.

    A be   **B** been   **C** is   **D** being

3. They _____ old friends of Antonio's.

    A is   **B** be   **C** was   **D** are

4. Everyone _____ happy about the news.

    A were   **B** be   **C** was   **D** been

5. Janaya _____ glad about the new car.

    A seem   **B** seems   **C** seeming   **D** do seem

6. The orange juice _____ cool and refreshing yesterday.

    A tastes   **B** must taste   **C** tasted   **D** tasting

7. Natasha _____ tired after the long test yesterday.

    A look   **B** looked   **C** looking   **D** is look

Part B Write the verb or verb phrase in each sentence. Then write the verb tense next to it.

8. The last days of November grow cold.

9. Winter winds are feeling chilly.

10. The days will have been growing shorter.

11. The sky had become dark early in the evening.

12. Soon the first snowfall could be here.

13. We will go sledding tomorrow.

Part C Decide whether each verb in bold expresses action or a state of being. Write *action* or *state of being* on your paper.

14. The weather in December **stayed** cold.

15. People **got** out their winter coats.

16. "The air **feels** frosty," Dave complained.

17. One day the sky **looked** gray.

18. "I can **smell** snow in the air," said Eli.

19. The snow **fell** gently down.

Part D Write the verb or verb phrase in each sentence on your paper. Then write whether the word *be* is a main verb or a helping verb.

20. Angela has been studying all week.

21. The test is tomorrow.

22. Angela is feeling confident.

23. She always has been a good student.

24. Angela is appearing good at math.

25. She had been captain of the math team.

Test Tip

Review tests or quizzes that you took earlier over the same information. Make sure to get the correct answers for any items that you missed.

6

Adverbs

Look at the photograph. What would you think if you saw this scene out your window? You might think, "The owl is approaching *quickly*. It soars *quietly* and *smoothly*." You might also think, "The owl is flying *low* to the ground. It is turning *left*." These words allow you to describe the owl's actions. They are adverbs. Adverbs can answer questions about verbs. They can also answer questions about adjectives or other adverbs. Try adding *very* or *too* to each of the sentences above. How does it change the meaning of each sentence? These words are often used to describe adjectives or other adverbs.

In Chapter 6, you will learn about adverbs. Each lesson in the chapter focuses on recognizing and using adverbs correctly in sentences.

GOALS FOR LEARNING

- To identify adverbs and explain the questions that they answer
- To identify and use adverbs of degree
- To identify and use adverbs of negation
- To use adverbs correctly to make comparisons
- To explain the difference between adjectives and adverbs

Reading Strategy: Inferencing

Sometimes the meaning of a text is not directly stated. You have to make an inference to figure out what the text means.

- What You Know + What You Read = Inference

To make inferences, you have to think "beyond the text." Predicting what will happen next and explaining cause and effect are helpful strategies for making inferences.

Key Vocabulary Words

Adverb A word that answers questions about a verb, an adjective, or another adverb

Adverb of degree An adverb that answers questions about adjectives and other adverbs

Adverb of negation The adverbs *never* and *not*, which tell that an action will not happen or that a state of being is not present

What Is an Adverb?

An **adverb** is a word that answers questions about a verb, an adjective, or another adverb.

Some Common Adverbs

again	lately	previously	today
already	next	quickly	tomorrow
badly	now	shortly	upstairs
easily	once	slowly	usually
forever	often	soon	well
here	presently	there	yesterday

Adverbs That Tell *How*

Use adverbs to answer the question *how* with action verbs. These adverbs describe the way the action happened.

▶ **EXAMPLE 1**

The bird chirped loudly.

Marty guessed right.

Deion works quickly.

Practice A

Write the adverb that answers the question *how did the action happen*.

1. The ballerina danced gracefully.
2. The acrobat climbed the ladder quickly.
3. Kiera helped us gladly.
4. Slowly Tiffany found the answers.
5. Jorge played the game hard.

Complete each sentence with an adverb that answers the question *how* about each verb in bold.

   1. The children **ate** their dinner _____.

   2. Willis **drives** his car _____.

   3. Amanda **sews** _____.

   4. Mrs. Barrett **sang** _____.

   5. We **cleaned** the house _____.

Adverbs That Tell *When, How Often, How Long, How Many Times*

Adverbs also answer the questions *when*, *how often*, *how long*, or *how many times*. They tell something about the time of the action or state of being.

▶ **EXAMPLE 2**

   Dora will be home soon.

   Ramon is usually happy.

Practice C

Write the adverb in each sentence on your paper.

   1. Please begin immediately!

   2. I will go first.

   3. They jumped up instantly.

   4. The newspaper is delivered daily.

   5. Sometimes I enjoy baseball.

The tense of the verb in a sentence and the adverb must agree. *Ago* indicates past time. *Later* indicates future time.

▶ **EXAMPLE 3**

Lila sang long ago.

Reggie will sing later.

Practice D

Write each sentence using the correct form of the verb. The adverb is in bold. Add a helping verb if needed.

1. We (go) there a year **ago.**
2. **Yesterday** we (be) late to class.
3. Felice (arrive) **soon.**
4. The dog (eat) his dinner **now.**
5. We (paint) the house **before.**

Adverbs That Tell *Where* and *In What Direction*

Adverbs also answer the questions *where* or *in what direction*. They tell about the place of the action or state of being.

▶ **EXAMPLE 4**

Leave your coat downstairs.

You should turn left.

Practice E

Reading Strategy:
Inferencing

How does what you just read fit with what you know about adverbs?

Write the adverb in each sentence on your paper.

1. The team advanced the ball forward.
2. The storm was near.
3. Turn right at the corner.
4. Hang your coat here.
5. The bedrooms are upstairs.

REVIEW

Write the adverbs in each sentence. There may be more than one. Write the question each adverb answers.

1. Yesterday, the dog happily buried his toys.

2. Today, he looked for them.

3. He barked loudly at Carla.

4. "I bet you lost your toys again," Carla scolded gently.

5. The dog jumped up and down constantly.

Complete each sentence by adding an adverb. The adverb should answer the question in parentheses.

6. The students **rushed** to their desks (how?).

7. (How often?) their teacher **gave** them a surprise quiz.

8. Otis **came** in late (how often?).

9. Mr. Wong **walked** (where?).

10. The silence seemed to **last** (how long?).

VOCABULARY BUILDER

Biannually and Biennially
Biannually and *biennially* answer the question *when*.
Biannual (adjective) means "twice in one year."
    We do a *biannual* feeding of the lawn.
Biennial (adjective) means "every two years."
    Next fall is the *biennial* election for mayor.
Complete each sentence with *biannual, biennial, biannually,* or *biennially.*
1. We hold meetings _____ or every other year.
2. The store has a _____ sale in spring and fall.
3. We get our report cards _____ in January and June.
4. I sell tickets every other year, during the _____ raffle.

Adverbs of Degree

Adverb of degree
An adverb that answers questions about adjectives and other adverbs

Reading Strategy:
Inferencing

After reading this page, what can you infer about where adverbs of degree appear in a sentence?

Adverbs that answer questions about adjectives and other adverbs are **adverbs of degree**. They answer these questions: *how much, how little, how often,* and *to what degree.*

Some Adverbs of Degree

almost	entirely	nearly	so
altogether	extremely	partly	too
awfully	just	quite	unusually
completely	little	rather	very

The adverb of degree comes before the adjective or adverb.

▶ **EXAMPLE 1**

How Cold?	It is very cold here.
	(The adverb *very* tells about the adjective *cold.*)
How Fast?	I work extremely fast.
	(The adverb *extremely* tells about the adverb *fast.*)

Practice A

Write each sentence. Underline the adverbs of degree.

1. His old truck is so noisy.
2. Your puppy is quite friendly.
3. That is an unusually large pumpkin.
4. He has an extremely bad headache.
5. Mark has a rather interesting idea for the project.

Reading Strategy:
Inferencing

How well did you predict where an adverb of degree appears in a sentence?

 Writing Tip

Using adverbs like *very* too often can become a bad habit. Use words that add to your meaning. Overusing *very* makes your writing wordy.

Practice B

Find the adverb of degree in each sentence. Write whether the adverb is describing an adjective or another adverb.

1. I am almost ready to go.

2. That coat is too small for you.

3. That was a very odd thing for him to do.

4. I am not entirely sure of my plans.

5. Your kitten is so energetic!

Practice C

Add an adverb of degree before each adjective or adverb in bold. Use a different adverb in each sentence.

1. The **strong** man lifted 500 pounds.

2. Pedro is **ready.**

3. Your new sweater is **pretty.**

4. Mel plays basketball **often.**

5. Lin works **quickly.**

Mel plays basketball almost every day after school.

REVIEW

Write the adverb of degree in each sentence on your paper. Then use each adverb of degree in a sentence of your own.

Example: Pamela said the turkey looks almost done.
Answer: almost—He was almost satisfied with his work.

1. Rashid enjoyed his job at the bookstore very much.

2. Saturday was an unusually busy day.

3. Rashid worked quite hard.

4. Tess was completely satisfied with Rashid's work.

5. "You are an exceptionally good worker," she told him.

Add an adverb of degree to tell about each adjective or adverb in bold. Use a new adverb in each sentence.

6. I will be ready to go shopping **tomorrow.**

7. The wind was **noisy** all night.

8. Reggie was **proud** of his accomplishment.

9. Everyone was **happy** about the holiday.

10. Jia Li arrived **later.**

SPELLING BUILDER

A lot and All right

The words *a lot* and *all right* are often misspelled. Both of these are two words. Complete each sentence with *a lot* or *all right.*

1. We got _____ of rain this summer.
2. Yesterday I was tired but today I feel _____.
3. The washing machine works _____ since my dad fixed it.
4. Jan has _____ of books about horses.
5. You ask _____ of questions.

Adverbs of Negation

Adverb of negation

The adverbs *never* and *not*, which tell that an action will not happen or that a state of being is not present

Reading Strategy:
Inferencing

What do you know about contractions?

 NOTE

Most contractions of verbs with *not* use the verb and the shortened version of *not*. The contraction for *will not* is irregular–it is *won't*.

Never and *Not*

Never and *not* are **adverbs of negation.** A negative adverb tells that the action will not happen. It can also tell that the state of being is not present.

▶ **EXAMPLE 1**

She is never lazy.

Anita is not at practice today.

They did not find the key.

Practice A

Write the adverb of negation in each sentence.

1. There is not enough snow to ski.
2. Susan would never quit her job.
3. She never answers the phone during dinner.
4. It was not his fault.
5. I have never met him.

Adverbs of Negation in Contractions

You have learned that in a contraction, you make two words into one. To make a contraction, replace one or more letters with an apostrophe. Examples of contractions are *you'll* (*you will*) and *what's* (*what is*). A verb and the adverb *not* make up some contractions. In these contractions, the *o* in the adverb *not* is replaced by an apostrophe.

▶ **EXAMPLE 2**

Ty and Sam aren't coming to the party. (are + not = aren't)

We couldn't find the park. (could + not = couldn't)

Write the contraction with an adverb of negation in each sentence. Then, write the contraction as two words.

1. Fernando couldn't find his pencil.
2. They haven't been there before.
3. Isn't that a beautiful painting?
4. The play didn't start on time.
5. The store won't be busy today.

Reading Strategy:
Inferencing

What can you infer about what happens when two negative words are used in a sentence?

Writing Tip

When writing or speaking, do not use *can't* and *won't* with the adverb *hardly*. When used together, these words create a double negative.

Double Negatives

When you use a contraction with the word *not*, do not use another negative word in the sentence. This is called a double negative. Some examples of negative words are *nobody*, *none*, *nothing*, *no one*, and *nowhere*.

▶ **EXAMPLE 3**

Incorrect	John isn't doing nothing.
Correct	John isn't doing anything.
Correct	John is doing nothing.

Practice C

Rewrite each sentence to remove the double negative.

1. Lynn hasn't never been on an airplane.
2. Aren't none of you going to the movie?
3. Tammy couldn't drive nowhere without car keys.
4. Christopher didn't have time to see nobody.
5. They don't do nothing on the weekends.

Write the adverb of negation in each sentence on your paper.

1. Ahmed won't be at play practice tonight.

2. He does not think that he is good enough.

3. The director never praised Ahmed.

Rewrite each sentence using a contraction with an adverb of negation.

4. Ahmed should not quit acting.

5. We must not let him quit.

6. Yoko did not find her book.

Rewrite each sentence to correct the double negative. Write *correct* if the sentence does not have any mistakes.

7. Greg couldn't never swim across the pool.

8. Valerie shouldn't go nowhere alone.

9. I haven't time for lunch.

10. Our neighbors didn't bring nothing to the park.

Comparing with Adverbs

Positive, Comparative, and Superlative Forms

You can use adverbs to make comparisons. The three forms of comparison are positive, comparative, and superlative.

Use these rules to form comparisons:

Rule 1 Use the positive form to describe one action.

Rule 2 Use the comparative form to compare two actions.

Rule 3 Use the superlative form to compare more than two actions.

More/Most and *Less/Least*

Some adverbs are more than one syllable. Use *more* and *most* to form the comparative and superlative forms for most adverbs. You can also use *less* and *least*.

▶ **EXAMPLE 1**

Positive	Comparative	Superlative
fast	faster	fastest
slowly	more slowly	most slowly
happily	less happily	least happily

Practice A

Write each adverb on your paper. Next to each adverb, write its comparative and superlative forms.

1. cheerfully   **4.** angrily

2. skillfully   **5.** clearly

3. hard

Write the adverbs in each of these sentences on your paper.

1. This shoe fits less comfortably than that one.

2. Of the three, that shoe fits most comfortably.

3. Victor is speaking calmly.

4. He speaks more calmly when he has practiced.

5. Mr. Hong changes the oil in his car regularly.

Irregular Adverbs

A few adverbs, such as *well*, are irregular. The comparative and superlative of *well* are *better* and *best*.

▶ **EXAMPLE 2**

Kevin paints well.

Wanda paints better than Kevin.

Of the whole class, Cleo paints the best.

Practice C

Complete each sentence with the correct form of the adverb in parentheses. Next to each sentence, write *positive*, *comparative*, or *superlative*.

Example: He writes (well) this year than last year.
Answer: He write better this year than last year.—
             comparative

1. The lights shone (brightly) tonight than any other night.

2. Elsa sings (well) of all the soloists.

3. Dan works (hard) when he is interested.

4. Of all the students, Kim worked (quickly).

5. Zeke played the trumpet (loudly) than his brother.

Reading Strategy:
Inferencing

After reading this page, what can you infer about using *better* and *best* in sentences?

REVIEW

Write the adverb in each sentence on your paper. Next to each adverb, write the form of comparison.

1. Gordon runs the mile faster than Rafael.

2. I work best when I am rested.

3. Hans reads less quickly than Mike.

4. The choir sang the chorus more loudly than the verses.

5. Everyone worked least happily at the end of the day.

Write a sentence for each adverb. Use the form in parentheses.

6. bravely   (superlative)

7. sweetly   (comparative)

8. well   (superlative)

9. sadly   (positive)

10. politely   (comparative)

Adverb or Adjective?

Objectives

- To identify differences between adjectives and adverbs
- To determine whether a word in a sentence is an adjective or an adverb

Sometimes it is difficult to tell if a word is an adjective or an adverb. Review the definitions of these parts of speech.

An adjective describes a noun or pronoun.

▶ **EXAMPLE 1**

Nina is tall.
(*Tall* describes the noun *Nina.*)

An adverb answers a question about a verb, an adjective, or another adverb.

▶ **EXAMPLE 2**

Nina walked outside.
(*Outside* tells where Nina walked.)

Practice A

Write each word in bold on your paper. Next to each word, write whether it is an adjective or an adverb.

1. Baiko is **late.**
2. He is **here.**
3. Do **daily** exercises.
4. We practice **daily.**
5. She is a **hard** worker.

Adding -ly

You can change many adjectives into adverbs by adding the ending -*ly*.

▶ **EXAMPLE 3**

Adjectives	Adverbs
The blanket is soft.	He sang softly.
The fruit is sweet.	She smiled sweetly.

Practice B

Write each bold word on your paper. Next to each word, write whether it is an adjective or an adverb.

1. The sea was very **calm** today.
2. The boy **quietly** watched the movie.
3. "This is an **extremely** difficult case," the lawyer said.
4. "This is an **extreme** case," the lawyer said.
5. The hikers ate lunch **hungrily**.

You can change some nouns into adverbs by adding the ending -*ly*.

▶ **EXAMPLE 4**

Noun	Adverb
May I have part of that?	He is partly finished.
I have the receipts for the year.	I check the receipts yearly.

Write each bold word on your paper. Next to each word, write whether it is a noun or an adverb.

1. The books were in alphabetical **order.**
2. Please exit in an **orderly** fashion.
3. The family shops **weekly.**
4. The bills arrive every **month.**
5. We pay our bills **monthly.**

Adverbs and Adjectives Ending in *-ly*

Not all words ending in *-ly* are adverbs. Some common adjectives end in *-ly*, too.

▶ **EXAMPLE 5**

Mr. Baines gave Elizabeth some fatherly advice.
(*Fatherly* is an adjective that describes the noun *advice.*)

Other words that end in *-ly* can be adjectives or adverbs. You must look at the way the word is used in each sentence.

▶ **EXAMPLE 6**

Adjectives	Adverbs
He did the daily report.	He reported daily.
We left in the early afternoon.	We left early.

Practice D

Reading Strategy:
Inferencing

After reading this page, what inference can you make about words that end in *-ly*? What words helped you make your inference?

Write each bold word on your paper. Next to each word, write whether it is an adjective or an adverb.

1. New cars are very **costly.**
2. That is an **ugly** cut.
3. They sat **quietly** and waited.
4. Mr. Santos missed his **early** class.
5. They **easily** won first prize.

Good and Well

Good is always an adjective and describes a noun. Do not use *good* to answer questions about a verb.

▶ **EXAMPLE 7**

Incorrect	They worked good together.
	(Do not use the adjective *good* to tell how they worked.)
Correct	We had a good day.
	(What kind of day?)

Well is often an adverb. It means to do something correctly.

▶ **EXAMPLE 8**

She speaks well.
(How does she speak?)

Well is an adjective when it describes someone's health. *Good* and *well* can follow state-of-being verbs. Either *good* or *well* will work in the following example sentence.

▶ **EXAMPLE 9**

I feel good today.　　(describes emotions)

I feel well today.　　(describes health)

Reading Strategy:
Inferencing

What do you already know about the words *good* and *well*?

The string orchestra plays well.

Complete each sentence with *good* or *well*.

1. Carol is _____ at arithmetic.

2. Dan dances very _____.

3. She did her _____ deed for the day.

4. Larry isn't feeling _____ today.

5. Ashley sings _____.

BUILDING RESEARCH SKILLS

Organizing Research Information

Organize your notes and sources as you research your topic. If a source has relevant facts, begin by recording information about the publication. This includes the author, title, publisher, and copyright date. Record information from the source in a number of ways:

- Write each fact, statistic, or quote on a note card.
- Organize important details from a source using an outline.
- Arrange information in a table using spreadsheet software. You may also make a graphic organizer.
- Record information that helps you answer your research question.

Imagine that your research question is *what dolphins and humans have in common.* Find a source about dolphins, and answer the questions that follow.

1. Draw a note card on your paper. Record the following information for the source.

   Author last name, Author first name.
   "Article Title". Magazine, Journal or Book title
   Publishing Information (publisher, place of
    publication, date of publication)
   Page numbers

2. Draw a second note card on your paper. List a fact from your source about dolphins that could help to answer the research question.

3. **CRITICAL THINKING** Why is it important to organize your notes and sources as you research?

REVIEW

Write each word in bold on your paper. Next to each word, write whether it is an adverb, a noun, or an adjective.

1. This **deadly** poison will get rid of all kinds of bugs.

2. Mr. Ozawa prepared his **yearly** report.

3. We receive a newspaper every **day.**

4. Please try to come to class **early.**

Find the mistake in each sentence. Write each sentence correctly.

5. Yo-Yo Ma plays the cello very good.

6. Owen and I are well friends.

7. "I am doing very good," the student responded.

Write two sentences for each word. In the first sentence, use the word as an adjective. In the second sentence, use the word as an adverb.

8. fast

9. late

10. hard

PUTTING IT ALL TOGETHER

Write directions telling a friend how to do a task that you know how to do. Use at least four adverbs in your directions. Include an adverb of degree, an adverb of negation, and an adverb used to compare. Underline each adverb.

⬤ **Six Traits of Writing:**

Word Choice vivid words that "show, not tell"

Radio Broadcaster

Hannah Atwell is a radio broadcaster for a local radio station. She does more than introduce programs and music. She researches and prepares for interviews that she has with people. She also reads news, sports, and advertisements on the air. Many times during the year, she hosts events such as community events and competitions.

Ms. Atwell will read the following advertisement about Taylor's General Store. Read the advertisement, and answer the questions below.

Taylor's General Store is rapidly slashing prices on all summer products. Come quickly to get the best deals on lawn chairs and shade umbrellas. Find a set of glasses in the season's hottest summer colors at extremely cool prices. Sprinklers are now just $14.99. Taylor's General Store knows your summer needs better than anyone! Don't miss out on this sizzling sale today!

1. Identify five adverbs in the advertisement.

2. What adverb is used to compare in this advertisement? What is the positive form?

3. **CRITICAL THINKING** What effect do the adverbs in the advertisement have on the reader?

VIEWING AND SPEAKING

Facts are information that can be proven. Opinions are different from person to person. Describe a sports event by answering questions such as *who, where,* and *when.* Give an oral report to your class about this event. How did your report compare with your classmates' reports? When two people attend the same event, how might their descriptions of the event differ?

SUMMARY

- Adverbs answer questions such as *how, when, how often, how long, how many,* and *where*. Adverbs answer these questions about verbs.

- Adverbs of degree answer *how much, how little, how often,* and *to what degree*. These questions help to describe adjectives and other adverbs.

- *Never* and *not* are adverbs of negation. Use *not* with a verb and an apostrophe to form a contraction.

- When you use a contraction with the word *not*, do not use another negative word in the sentence.

- Adverbs can be in the positive, comparative, or superlative form.

- Use *more* and *most* to form the comparative and superlative forms for most adverbs. You can also use *less* and *least*.

- Look at the way a word is used in a sentence. Many adverbs end in *-ly*, but some adjectives also end in *-ly*.

- *Good* is always an adjective. *Well* can be either an adjective or an adverb.

Word Bank

adverb

adverb of degree

adverb of negation

Part A Find the word or words in the Word Bank to complete each sentence. Write the answer on your paper.

1. An _____ tells that an action in a sentence will not happen. It also could tell that a state of being is not present.

2. An _____ answers questions about a verb, an adjective, or another adverb.

3. An _____ answer questions about adjectives and other adverbs.

Part B Complete each sentence with the correct adverb Write the letter of the answer on your paper.

4. The class did _____ on the test.

    A good   **B** well   **C** bad   **D** gooder

5. This truck is moving _____ than that one.

    A faster   **B** fastly   **C** more fast   **D** quick

6. Russ spoke _____ to the reporter.

    A calm   **B** calmlier **C** calmly   **D** more calm

7. You shouldn't _____ drive fast through an intersection.

    A never   **B** ever   **C** not   **D** nowhere

8. He runs _____ than any other player on the team.

    A fastly   **B** fastest   **C** faster   **D** more fast

Part C Write the adverbs in each sentence on your paper. A sentence may have more than one adverb. Underline the adverbs of degree.

9. The lines at the store were awfully long today.

10. A heavy snowfall arrived very early in December.

11. At home Hisham was not so pleased.

12. He went to work anyway.

13. He knew the roads would be extremely slippery.

14. He drove slower than he usually did.

Part D Write each word in bold on your paper. Next to each word, write *adjective* or *adverb*. Write the correct form of any adverb or adjective used to compare.

15. The **stronger** man won the race **easily.**

16. I don't swim **better** than she does.

17. They went to Winnipeg on the **late** train.

18. We **never** listened to the **daily** weather report.

19. Dan plays the guitar very **well.**

20. Carmen's desk is in **order.**

Part E Complete each sentence with an adverb that answers the question in parentheses.

21. Gordon is going fishing (when?).

22. Put the paper (where?).

23. Fran has been to the restaurant (how many times?).

24. Keisha plays the piano (how?).

25. I will call you (when?).

Test Tip

Count the number of answers on your paper. Make sure the number of answers matches the number of items on the test.

Prepositional Phrases

The waterfall in the photograph is *in* the woods. It runs *over* the rocks, and leaves from the trees lay *upon* the rocks. Many branches are sitting *on top of* each other. The sun hides *behind* the trees. Words such as *in*, *over*, *from*, *on*, *of*, and *behind* are prepositions. What other sentences can you form about this photograph using these words?

A preposition shows a relationship between a noun or pronoun and other words in a sentence. A preposition is the first word of a prepositional phrase. A prepositional phrase is a group of words with a preposition and an object. It also includes adjectives and adverbs that describe the object.

In Chapter 7, you will learn about prepositions, prepositional phrases, and their purposes. Knowing how a preposition works in a sentence will help you understand relationships among ideas.

GOALS FOR LEARNING

- To identify prepositions and prepositional phrases in sentences
- To recognize the object of a preposition and to identify the form of pronouns used as objects of prepositions
- To identify adjective phrases in sentences
- To identify adverb phrases in sentences
- To use subject-verb agreement in sentences with prepositional phrases
- To tell prepositions apart from other words in a sentence

Reading Strategy: Metacognition

Metacognition means "thinking about your thinking." Use metacognition to become a better reader:

- Preview the text.
- Make predictions and ask yourself what you already know about the topic.
- Write the main idea, details, and any questions you have.
- Visualize what is happening in the text. If something does not make sense, go back and read it again.
- Summarize what you have read and make inferences about the meaning.

Key Vocabulary Words

Preposition A word that shows a relationship between a noun or pronoun and other words in a sentence

Object of the preposition The noun or pronoun that follows the preposition in a prepositional phrase

Prepositional phrase A group of words made up of a preposition and an object

Compound object Two or more objects in a sentence connected by a conjunction

Compound preposition A preposition made up of more than one word

Adjective phrase A prepositional phrase that answers the question *which one, what kind,* or *how many* about the noun or pronoun in a sentence

Adverb phrase A prepositional phrase that answers the question *how, when, where, how much,* or *how long* about the verb in a sentence

What Is a Prepositional Phrase?

A **preposition** shows a relationship between a noun or pronoun and other words in a sentence. The noun or pronoun that follows the preposition is the **object of the preposition.**

The preposition and the object of the preposition make up a **prepositional phrase.** Other words such as adjectives and adverbs may be included in the phrase.

▶ **EXAMPLE 1**

Michael put his notebook in his locker. (The preposition *in* shows the relationship of *locker* to *notebook.*)

Carl read the note from Maria. (The preposition *from* shows the relationship of *Maria* to *note.*)

When the preposition changes, the relationship between the words in the sentence changes. Notice how the relationship between *spoke* and *Alexis* changes in the following sentences.

▶ **EXAMPLE 2**

Charles spoke to Alexis.

Charles spoke about Alexis.

Common Prepositions

about	around	beneath	for	near	out	to
above	at	beside	from	of	over	under
across	before	down	in	off	past	until
after	behind	during	into	on	through	with

Compound object

Two or more objects in a sentence connected by a conjunction

Reading Strategy:
Metacognition

Before you read, what can you do that will help you understand the text?

Practice A

Write the preposition that completes each sentence.

1. The apples _____ the tree are ripe.

2. The story _____ pirates was exciting.

3. The girl _____ the picture is my sister.

4. The boots _____ the chair are mine.

5. The girl _____ Ken is a good dancer.

Compound Objects

In a prepositional phrase, the preposition may have a **compound object.** A compound object is two or more objects connected with a conjunction.

▶ **EXAMPLE 3**

Austin works with Noah and Yuri. (*Noah* and *Yuri* is the compound object of the preposition *with.*)

Other Words in a Prepositional Phrase

In a prepositional phrase, the object may be a noun. A noun can have adjectives that describe it.

▶ **EXAMPLE 4**

across the muddy grass

Because adverbs can answer questions about adjectives, a prepositional phrase can also have an adverb.

▶ **EXAMPLE 5**

after the very long appointment

The object of the preposition can be a pronoun. When the object is a pronoun, no words come between the preposition and the object.

▶ **EXAMPLE 6**

to him   beside it   between you and me

A sentence may have more than one prepositional phrase.

▶ **EXAMPLE 7**

We bought vegetables for supper at the market.

Practice B

Write the prepositional phrases in each sentence. Draw one line under the preposition and two lines under the object or objects.

1. Write your name in the left-hand corner.
2. They live near a very busy highway.
3. Would you please sit on the bench with Laura and me?
4. Give this book about Mexico to him.
5. Early in the day, the sun shines through the windows.

Compound Prepositions

A **compound preposition** is made up of more than one word.

Compound Prepositions

according to	in spite of	because of	instead of
in addition to	out of	in front of	as far as
in place of	along with		

▶ **EXAMPLE 8**

I want vegetables instead of potatoes.

Juan took the camera out of the box.

Practice C

Write each prepositional phrase. Then underline the compound preposition.

1. According to Jorge, the party was fun.
2. I am going instead of Tim.
3. Jorge will speak in place of Judy.
4. In spite of the heavy rain, they played the soccer game.
5. Jack traveled as far as the Pacific Ocean.

Practice D

Write a sentence on your paper using each preposition.

1. during
2. under
3. through
4. in front of
5. in addition to

In spite of the heavy rain, we went for a walk.

REVIEW

Write each prepositional phrase on your paper. Underline the preposition once and its object or objects twice. A sentence may have more than one prepositional phrase.

1. My dog, Honey, was sleeping in the shade under a tree.

2. Suddenly, a loud noise in the street frightened her.

3. Honey ran around the bush and the tree wildly.

Fill in each blank with a compound preposition. More than one compound preposition may make sense. Choose a different compound preposition for each sentence.

4. The chair _____ the window is yellow.

5. _____ the loud music, Kelly fell asleep.

SPELLING BUILDER

Spelling Demons
The preposition *across* is often misspelled. Words that are often misspelled are "spelling demons." Here are some examples:

beneath　　past　　through　　since

Practice spelling *beneath, past, through,* and *since* to learn how to spell them. Then look at the following words. Say each word and spell it aloud. Then write each word on your paper.

1. surprise　　　4. once
2. false　　　　5. library
3. doctor

More About Objects of Prepositions

The object of the preposition is a noun or a pronoun.

▶ **EXAMPLE 1**

Timothy threw the ball into the basket. (*Basket* is a noun.)

The players cheered for him. (*Him* is a pronoun.)

Practice A

Write each object of the preposition. Identify it as a *noun* or a *pronoun*.

1. Kevin plays the drums in the band.
2. He practices every night before dinner.
3. Hoshi looked at her coin collection.
4. She checked some Web sites for information.
5. Is Berto sitting with you?

If the object of the preposition is a pronoun, it must be in the object form.

▶ **EXAMPLE 2**

Incorrect   She sat between Gabriela and I.

Correct   She sat between Gabriela and me.

Reading Strategy:
Metacognition

Remember to look at the photographs and illustrations. Note descriptive words. This will help you visualize what you are reading.

Possessive nouns and pronouns cannot be objects of prepositions.

▶ **EXAMPLE 3**

Incorrect	Rashid went home with his.
	Rashid went home to Justin's.
Correct	Rashid went home with him.
	Rashid went home with his friend.

Practice B

Write each sentence on your paper. Correct any mistakes.

1. Please bring coats for Pete and I.

2. Sam bought an apple for his.

3. Susan passed out papers to theirs.

4. Let's keep this a secret between you and I.

5. Jennifer sat between Sara and she.

Tyrone passed the papers to them.

Location of Objects of the Preposition

The object of the preposition usually comes after the preposition. However, sometimes the preposition and its object are separated in sentences that ask questions.

▶ **EXAMPLE 4**

Object Preposition

What did you do that for?

Practice C

Write each preposition and its object on your paper.

1. Whom are you talking about?

2. Whom are Dionne and Len with?

3. What is that book about?

4. What was she thinking of?

5. Whom will you give it to?

Practice D

Write the prepositional phrases in each sentence. Underline the object of the preposition.

1. Have you ever heard of Mary Lyon?

2. She was a pioneer in the education of women.

3. Mary Lyon was born in 1797. She died in 1849.

4. She taught in schools in New Hampshire and in Massachusetts.

5. In 1837, she opened a school in Massachusetts. The name of the school was Mount Holyoke.

REVIEW

Find each object of the preposition and write it on your paper. Identify each one as a *noun* or a *pronoun*.

1. Rishi hoped to sing with them.

2. Tamara tossed the ball over the fence.

3. We walked through the exhibit.

4. Whom are you studying with?

5. In the springtime, we travel to the park for a picnic.

Write each sentence. Correct any mistakes.

6. Jeff gave the present to hers.

7. Will you come with Trina and I?

8. Bob gave a card to she.

9. Rosa took a picture of he and I.

10. For he, I bought a scarf.

VOCABULARY BUILDER

Among and *Between*

Use *among* to discuss three or more people or things. *The boys whispered* among *themselves.* Use *between* to discuss two people or things. Between *you and me, I didn't like that band.*

Write the correct word in each sentence on your paper.

1. Please arrive (among, between) one and two o'clock.
2. (Among, Between) milk and juice, I prefer juice.
3. You may choose (among, between) all of these dishes.
4. I have (among, between) six and ten pet goldfish.
5. We spotted Lee (among, between) the ten dancers.

Adjective Phrases

Objectives

- To identify adjective phrases and the words they describe
- To use adjective phrases in sentences

Adjective phrase

A prepositional phrase that answers the question *which one, what kind*, or *how many* about the noun or pronoun in a sentence

Reading Strategy:
Metacognition

Make a prediction about what will be covered in this lesson.

A prepositional phrase is either an **adjective phrase** or an adverb phrase.

An adjective is a word that describes a noun or pronoun. An adjective phrase does the same thing as an adjective. The phrase tells *which one, what kind*, or *how many* about the noun or pronoun in a sentence.

▶ **EXAMPLE 1**

The store across the road is open.
(*Which* store is open? The one *across the road* is open.)

This book by Katherine Paterson is popular.
(*Which* book is popular? The one *by Katherine Paterson* is popular.)

An adjective usually comes before the noun it describes. An adjective phrase follows the noun it describes.

▶ **EXAMPLE 2**

| Adjective | The Wilson High band won. |
| Adjective Phrase | The band from Wilson High won. |

Practice A

Write each adjective phrase in bold on your paper. Next to each phrase, write the noun or pronoun it describes.

1. The boy **with me** is my brother.
2. The flowers **on the table** are beautiful.
3. We built a house **of bricks and stone.**
4. None **of the girls** left early.
5. The poem **by Maya Angelou** was beautiful.

NOTE

Beside is a preposition
that means "next to." *He
sat* beside *her. Besides* is
a preposition that means
"except." *Everyone went*
besides *her.* Be sure not
to confuse the two words.

Phrases Describing an Object of the Preposition

An adjective phrase can describe the object of another
preposition.

▶ **EXAMPLE 3**

The woman at the front of the store is Mrs. Jackson.
(The adjective phrase *of the store* describes the noun *front.*)

Practice B

Write the adjective phrases in each sentence. Next to each
phrase, write the noun or pronoun it describes.

1. The woods beside the lake near our house are dark.
2. Elvin's dad owns a shoe store in the mall beside Jones
   River.
3. The woman with the baby in her arms is my aunt.
4. The lamp on the table beside your bed needs a new
   lightbulb.
5. All of the people in the auditorium cheered.

Practice C

Write each sentence on your paper. Add an adjective
phrase after each noun or pronoun in bold.

1. **Everyone** enjoys the football **games.**
2. Several **friends** are coming to the **party.**
3. The **dish** fell from the **counter.**
4. The **man** bought a new **car.**
5. The **teacher** liked that **book.**

REVIEW

Write the adjective phrases in each sentence. Next to each phrase, write the noun or pronoun it describes.

1. Vitus Bering was the first explorer of Alaska.

2. Other people from Russia also explored Alaska.

3. European settlers in Alaska formed a community on Kodiak Island.

Write each sentence on your paper. Add an adjective phrase after each noun or pronoun in bold.

4. The **dog** ran under the **porch.**

5. The **students** liked that **teacher.**

BUILDING RESEARCH SKILLS

Using Periodicals

Periodicals are publications such as journals or magazines. They are issued regularly (daily, weekly, monthly, or quarterly). A journal records experiences, current research, or ideas about a topic for a target audience. A magazine includes articles, stories, photos, and graphics of general interest.

Magazines and journals often have a front cover that lists the date for the periodical. You can usually find a table of contents on the first or second page. It tells you the section and page number for the articles. Advertisements often sell products and services in periodicals.

Find a magazine or journal and review three articles. Answer the questions below on your paper.

1. What are some text features of the articles? (For example, pictures or headings.)

2. Who do you think is the periodical's target audience? Explain.

3. CRITICAL THINKING Look at the kinds of advertisements in the magazine or journal. How might advertisements vary depending on the periodical? Explain.

The Prepositional Phrase Used as an Adverb

Objectives

Objectives

- To identify adverb phrases in sentences
- To use adverb phrases in sentences

Adverb phrase

A prepositional phrase that answers the question *how, when, where, how much,* or *how long* about the verb in a sentence

Reading Strategy:
Metacognition

Note the main idea and important details on this page. Summarize what you have read to make sure you understand it.

An adverb is a word that answers questions about a verb. You can use a prepositional phrase as an adverb. An **adverb phrase** does the same thing as an adverb. It is a group of words that tells *how, when, where, how much,* or *how long* about the verb in a sentence.

▶ **EXAMPLE 1**

Adverb	They shopped rapidly.
Adverb Phrase	They shopped in a hurry.
	(*How* did they shop? They shopped *in a hurry.*)

An adverb phrase may appear in different places in a sentence.

▶ **EXAMPLE 2**

After lunch we napped.

We napped after lunch.

Practice A

Write each adverb phrase in bold on your paper. Next to each, write the question the adverb phrase answers about the verb. Write *how, when, where, how much,* or *how long*.

1. **For three hours** the band played.
2. Ling ironed her dress **with great care.**
3. Dad put the roast **into the oven.**
4. **Before midnight** Parker wrote the report.
5. She beat the record **by 30 seconds.**

An adverb phrase can answer the question *why* about a verb.

▶ **EXAMPLE 3**

They were crying because of the sad story.
(*Why* were they crying? *Because of the sad story*.)

Practice B

Write the adverb phrase on your paper that answers the question *why* in each sentence.

1. I ran inside because of the rain.

2. She shopped for dinner.

3. Will you sing for me?

4. Because of his fever, Jeff stayed home.

5. Janet bought a gift for her aunt.

An adverb phrase can describe an adjective or an adverb.

▶ **EXAMPLE 4**

Miti is taller by two inches. (*Taller* is an adjective. The adverb phrase *by two inches* tells how much taller Miti is.)

Lea ran faster by one minute. (*Faster* is an adverb. The adverb phrase *by one minute* tells how much faster Lea ran.)

Practice C

Reading Strategy:
Metacognition

Think about how adverb phrases are used. Do any of the uses surprise you? Which uses did you expect?

Write the adverb phrase in each sentence on your paper.

1. Put the paper in the trash can.

2. Constance stayed longer than Zach by two hours.

3. She shopped with her mother at the store.

4. Carol wrote for the school newspaper.

5. Because of the weather, officials ended the game.

REVIEW

Write the adverb phrases in each sentence on your paper. A sentence may have more than one adverb phrase. Next to each phrase, write the question the adverb phrase answers about the verb.

1. Evan studies computer technology at Hanover Community College.

2. He will attend classes there for two years.

3. Someday Evan might use computers in a bank.

4. At school Evan studies in a computer lab.

5. Because of the programmer's directions, the computer performs its job without a problem.

Identify the prepositional phrase in bold as an adjective phrase or an adverb phrase. Write *adjective phrase* or *adverb phrase*.

6. **At the concert** the orchestra played the music **of Brahms.**

7. Both boys go **to Hanover Community College.**

8. Bess plays soccer **in the spring.**

9. The gift **from my aunt** arrived **before my birthday.**

10. A girl **in my class** wrote a short story **during her summer vacation.**

Prepositional Phrases and Subject-Verb Agreement

Objectives

- To identify prepositional phrases that describe the subject of a sentence
- To use subject-verb agreement in sentences with prepositional phrases

Reading Strategy:
Metacognition

What strategies will you use to understand the information in this lesson?

Remember that the verb or verb phrase in a sentence agrees with the main noun or pronoun in the subject. Use the singular form of the verb with a singular noun. Use the plural form of the verb with a plural noun.

Sometimes a prepositional phrase comes after the main noun in the subject. This prepositional phrase is part of the subject. The verb or verb phrase still must agree with the main noun or pronoun.

▶ **EXAMPLE 1**

The books arrive in the mail.
(*Books* is the subject. *Arrive* is the verb.)

The books from the catalogs arrive in the mail.
(*Books* is the plural subject. *Arrive* is the verb. *From the catalogs* is the prepositional phrase describing *books*.)

Practice A

Write the prepositional phrase that describes each subject.

1. The players on the other team talked to us.
2. His book of poems makes a thoughtful gift.
3. The company's team of engineers created the product.
4. The singers in the musical rehearse each day.
5. The woman with the grocery bags needs help.

The verb does not agree with the noun or pronoun in the prepositional phrase. Notice that the verb *were* is plural, even though *park* is singular. The subject *jobs* is plural and the verb must agree.

▶ **EXAMPLE 2**

| Incorrect | The jobs at the park was listed last. |
| Correct | The jobs at the park were listed last. |

Cover up the prepositional phrase to help you decide if you need a singular or plural form of the verb.

▶ **EXAMPLE 3**

His list of possible answers fills the whole page.

His list fills the whole page.

Practice B

Complete each sentence with the correct verb.

1. The papers on this table (is, are) very important.
2. The coach of the golf team (talk, talks) to her players.
3. The board of trustees (makes, make) a decision.
4. The men in the crowd (watches, watch) the game.
5. The pancakes on the stove (is, are) for breakfast.

Practice C

Correct the subject-verb agreement error in each sentence. If a sentence does not have an error, write *correct*.

1. One of my sisters sing very well.
2. The reporters on the scene ask many questions.
3. The oranges in the basket is spoiled.
4. Two buttons on the coat are missing.
5. The restaurant near the stores have closed.

Reading Strategy:
Metacognition

What are some of the details on this page that help you understand prepositional phrases?

REVIEW

Complete each sentence with the correct verb.

1. Pine trees in the forest (grows, grow) taller each year.

2. The singers in the choir (travels, travel) together each winter.

3. Which woman from the movies (comes, come) to your town?

4. The leaders of the other group (agrees, agree) with us.

5. The couch near the windows (needs, need) to be cleaned.

Complete each sentence with a verb that agrees with the subject. Write the sentence.

6. The doctors at the hospital _____ with patients.

7. A man with two trays _____ the medicine.

8. The phones in the hallway _____ all of the time.

9. The basket of cards _____ overflowing.

10. The nurses at the hospital _____ twelve-hour shifts.

Preposition or Not?

Some words can be either a preposition or an adverb. A preposition always has an object. An adverb does not.

▶ **EXAMPLE 1**

Adverb	Estella climbed aboard. (*Aboard* is not followed by a noun or a pronoun.)
Preposition	Estella climbed aboard the bus. (*Aboard* relates its object, *bus,* to the rest of the sentence.)

Practice A

Write each bold word on your paper. Next to it, write *adverb* or *preposition*.

1. Please come **in.**

2. Howard walked **in** the woods.

3. Turn the lights **off** when you leave.

4. Jane jumped **off** the stage.

5. I will come **by** later.

Practice B

Write two sentences for each word. In the first sentence, use the word as a preposition. In the second sentence, use the word as an adverb.

1. in

2. on

3. inside

4. near

5. below

Reading Strategy:
Metacognition

What questions do you still have after reading about prepositions and infinitives?

Preposition or Infinitive?

An infinitive is *to* plus the present tense of a verb. Do not confuse a prepositional phrase with an infinitive. The word that follows *to* in a prepositional phrase is a noun. The word that follows *to* in an infinitive is a verb.

▶ **EXAMPLE 2**

Infinitive	He wants to leave early.
	He hopes to have a party.
Prepositional Phrase	Nidal went to the store.
	Amber wrote to her uncle.

Practice C

Write whether *to* is used as a preposition or part of an infinitive. Write *preposition* or *infinitive* on your paper.

1. Jake hopes to swim on the team this year.
2. I went to the store for apples.
3. Lindsay gave the card to her son.
4. Ricardo wanted to ski near the lodge.
5. Ting raced to the cafeteria after class.

Technology Note

When giving a presentation, provide a handout. Many software programs allow you to print slides from your presentation to use as a visual aid. Handouts allow people to pay better attention to your presentation.

Practice D

Write five sentences using the word *to*. Next to each sentence, write whether *to* introduces a prepositional phrase or an infinitive.

REVIEW

Write each word in bold on your paper. Next to it, write *adverb* or *preposition*.

1. The dog sat **outside** and barked all afternoon.

2. Leave the package **outside** the door.

3. Haven't we met **before?**

4. The elephant disappeared **before** our eyes!

5. The old car rumbled **down** the highway.

Write whether the phrase in bold is an *infinitive* or a *prepositional phrase*.

6. Chris went **to his class.**

7. He likes **to work** with computers.

8. "Turn **to page 8,**" the teacher said.

9. Chris began **to read** his lesson.

10. He wanted **to ask** the teacher a question.

PUTTING IT ALL TOGETHER

Draw a diagram of a place (such as your room). Then write five sentences about your diagram. Use prepositions in your sentences. Underline all the prepositions, and draw two lines under their objects. List one example of an adjective phrase from your sentences. List one example of an adverb phrase from your sentences.

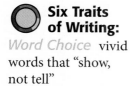

Six Traits of Writing:

Word Choice vivid words that "show, not tell"

Writing a Speech

A speech may be used to inform, describe, teach, compare, persuade, or tell a story. A good speaker uses nonverbal communication, such as eye contact, gestures, and tone of voice. Visual aids make a speech more interesting. Think about your purpose and audience. This will help you choose a good topic for your speech.

A good speaker keeps the attention of the audience. Grab their attention with an interesting opening. Keep their attention by using detail. Prepositional phrases used as adjective and adverb phrases help to add this detail.

With a partner, choose one of the purposes for giving a speech. Your audience will be other students. Choose a topic that your audience will enjoy. Write down the main idea of your speech and three supporting details.

1. Underline three prepositional phrases in your main idea or supporting details. If you do not have three prepositional phrases, add them to your speech.

2. Identify each prepositional phrase as an adjective or an adverb phrase.

3. **CRITICAL THINKING** With your partner, write three opening sentences using prepositional phrases. Decide which one is the most interesting and best fits the purpose of your speech.

LISTENING AND SPEAKING

Critical listeners evaluate the messages they hear. They often respond verbally to a speech. The speaker may encourage a discussion, ask for feedback, or answer questions. After hearing a speaker, give feedback on how the message could be better. Ask questions about something you did not understand. Ask the speaker to explain something in more detail.

- The preposition and the object of the preposition make up a prepositional phrase. A compound preposition is made up of more than one word.

- An object of the preposition may have adjectives and adverbs in front of it. An object of the preposition can be a noun or pronoun.

- Sometimes the preposition and its object are separated in sentences that ask questions.

- Adjective phrases answer the question *which one, what kind*, or *how many*. They can describe the object of another preposition.

- The object of a preposition can be compound.

- Adverb phrases answer the question *how, when, where, how much, how long,* or *why*. Adverb phrases can describe a verb, an adjective, or another adverb.

- Sometimes a prepositional phrase comes after the main noun in the subject. The verb or verb phrase still must agree with the main noun or pronoun.

- A preposition always has an object. An adverb does not.

- The word that follows *to* in a prepositional phrase is a noun. The word that follows *to* in an infinitive is a verb.

Word Bank

adjective phrase

adverb phrase

compound object

compound
 preposition

object of the
 preposition

preposition

prepositional
 phrase

Part A Find the word or words in the Word Bank to complete each sentence. Write the answer on your paper.

1. A group of words made up of a preposition and an object is a _____.

2. A _____ is a preposition made of more than one word.

3. A _____ shows a relationship between a noun and other words in a sentence.

4. An _____ answers the question *how, when, where, how much,* or *how long* in a sentence.

5. Two or more objects in a sentence connected by a conjunction form a _____.

6. An _____ follows the preposition in a prepositional phrase.

7. An _____ answers the question *which one, what kind,* or *how many* about the noun.

Part B Complete each sentence with a preposition. Write the object of each preposition. Write *noun* or *pronoun*.

8. The books _____ the shelf are heavy.

9. Play the CD _____ dinner.

10. Walk _____ Janet and me to the beach.

Part C Write *infinitive, prepositional phrase,* or *adverb* for each word in bold. Next to each prepositional phrase, write *adjective phrase* or *adverb phrase*.

11. **Inside** we were ready **to cook.**

12. Carol waited **to leave.**

13. Jiro traveled **across the country in a bus** last summer.

14. I put my homework **for math class inside my book.**

15. Manuel wanted **to go to the concert.**

Part D Choose the answer that completes each sentence. Write the letter of the answer.

16. Nathan watched TV _____.
    A with he father   **C** with him's father
    B with his father   **D** with he's father

17. Mario wrote a letter _____.
    A to Alex and me   **C** to he and I
    B to I and him   **D** to Alex and I

18. _____ did Elsa talk to?
    A Who   **B** What   **C** Whom   **D** Which

19. The girls from the shop _____ lunch outside each day.
    A eat   **B** eats   **C** eaten   **D** been eaten

20. The boy with the newspapers _____ his bike each morning.
    A riding   **B** ride   **C** rides   **D** been riding

Part E Write each sentence on your paper. Add at least one prepositional phrase to each one to make the sentence more interesting. Then write the word each prepositional phrase describes.

21. Everyone was happy.

22. The weather was good.

23. The family went out.

24. They came home.

25. The family was tired.

Test Tip

Make sure you understand what is being asked in a question. When taking a test, read each question twice.

Conjunctions and Interjections

The arch in the photograph connects one rock formation to another. Conjunctions work the same way in sentences. They help you link words and ideas together. Words such as *and*, *but*, and *for* can connect words, phrases, or ideas. Conjunctions can help you create sentences that are smooth and easy to understand.

A person first seeing this arch might say "Wow!" or "My goodness!" He or she would be using an interjection. Interjections are words or phrases that express strong feeling.

In Chapter 8, you will learn about conjunctions and interjections. Each lesson focuses on recognizing and using conjunctions and different kinds of interjections in sentences.

GOALS FOR LEARNING

- To identify and write sentences using coordinating conjunctions
- To identify and write sentences using correlative conjunctions
- To identify and write sentences using subordinating conjunctions
- To use interjections in sentences

Reading Strategy: Summarizing

Summarizing is taking a larger amount of information and restating it in a few sentences. When you summarize, be sure that you only include the information in the text. Do not add your own opinions. Follow these guidelines when summarizing:

- Use your own words.
- Capture the main ideas rather than all the details.
- Make a summary shorter than the text that you are summarizing.

Key Vocabulary Words

Conjunction A word that connects parts of a sentence

Clause A group of words with a subject and a verb

Coordinating conjunction A word that connects two or more equal parts of a sentence

Series A group of three or more words, phrases, or clauses

Correlative conjunctions A pair of conjunctions that connect words or groups of words

Subordinating conjunction A word that connects a dependent clause to an independent clause in a sentence

Independent clause A clause that expresses a complete thought

Dependent clause A clause that does not express a complete thought

Interjection A word or phrase that shows strong feeling

Coordinating Conjunctions

Objectives

- To identify and use coordinating conjunctions in sentences
- To punctuate sentences with coordinating conjunctions
- To tell prepositions and conjunctions apart

Conjunction
A word that connects parts of a sentence

Clause
A group of words with a subject and a verb

Coordinating conjunction
A word that connects two or more equal parts of a sentence

Reading Strategy:
Summarizing

In one sentence, explain the purpose of a conjunction.

A **conjunction** is a word that connects parts of a sentence. A conjunction can connect words, phrases, or clauses. A **clause** is a group of words with a subject and a verb.

A **coordinating conjunction** connects words, phrases, or sentences that are equal.

▶ **EXAMPLE 1**

Connect Words   Robert will play hockey or soccer.

Connect Phrases   He ran down the street and into the yard.

Connect Sentences   I'd like to help you, but I'm busy.

Here are the most common coordinating conjunctions.

Common Coordinating Conjunctions

and	but	nor	so
as well as	for	or	yet

Practice A

Write the coordinating conjunction in each sentence on your paper.

1. We can have chicken salad or tuna salad.
2. All night the winds blew and the snow fell.
3. The referee blew her whistle and stopped the game.
4. Micah is coming to the party as well as Gregor.
5. The actor sang well, but he could not dance.

Series

A group of three or more words, phrases, or clauses

 NOTE

To coordinate means to bring into proper order or relation. When you use a coordinating conjunction, you are bringing ideas into proper order.

Practice B

Complete each sentence with a coordinating conjunction.

1. I will have milk _____ water with my dinner.

2. Paco hits well, _____ he cannot throw a curve ball.

3. Vic tried hard _____ he made the team.

4. Louisa studies hard, _____ she has time for her friends.

5. After school we played CDs _____ relaxed.

Practice C

Use a coordinating conjunction to connect each pair of sentences. You may need to change the verb form.

1. Lena likes oranges. Andy likes oranges.

2. Lloyd plays football. Lloyd plays baseball.

3. Langston Hughes wrote short stories. He wrote plays.

4. I grew okra in my garden. I grew beans in my garden.

5. Laura plays basketball. Her sister plays basketball.

Punctuating a Series

Use a comma (,) to separate words, phrases, or clauses in a series. A **series** is three or more words, phrases, or clauses. Place the comma after each item in the series except the last one.

▶ **EXAMPLE 2**

Words in a Series   Rajeev, Ann, and Phil arrived late.

Phrases in a Series   Tamika jogged down the street, across the park, and around the lake.

Technology Note

When you save a file on a computer, keep the file name short. Use a name that will help you identify the file later. A file called *Justin saves money to go to college* could have the name *College Fund.*

Practice D

Write each sentence on your paper. Add commas where they are needed. Underline the conjunctions.

1. We planted bushes trees and flowers around the yard.

2. Later we showered changed our clothes and ate lunch.

3. I ordered a salad and soup.

4. My brother sister father and mother ordered the soup.

5. We talked about going to a movie playing golf or walking around the lake.

Using the Coordinating Conjunctions

Rule 1 Use *and* to connect two items when both are true. Lisa **and** Kylie entered the race. (Both entered.)

Rule 2 Use *but* to point out a difference between two ideas.
Lisa entered the race, **but** Ethan did not. (Only Lisa entered.)

Rule 3 Use *or* to connect ideas that are choices or differences.
Lisa **or** Kylie will enter the race. (One of them will enter. We do not know which one.)

Rule 4 Use *nor* when neither of the subjects did the action.
Ethan did not enter the race, **nor** did Leon. (Ethan did not enter. Leon did not enter.)

Practice E

Use each conjunction in a sentence. Write two sentences that contain items in a series. Use correct punctuation.

1. and

2. but

3. or

4. nor

5. yet

Reading Strategy:
Summarizing

Summarize the rules of using coordinating conjunctions in your own words.

Punctuating Sentences with Conjunctions

Sentences with *and, but, nor, for, so, or, yet,* or *as well as* need a comma before the coordinating conjunction.

▶ **EXAMPLE 3**

Natasha went to California, and I met her there.

I wanted to visit the beach, but she prefers the museum.

Sentences with *also, however, otherwise, besides, instead, therefore, consequently,* or *moreover* need a semicolon (;) before the conjunction and a comma after it.

▶ **EXAMPLE 4**

Grace plays the violin; however, she does not practice.

Graham worked all weekend; nevertheless, he didn't finish.

Coordinating Conjunction or Preposition?

The words *but* and *for* can be either conjunctions or prepositions. Remember that a conjunction connects items in a sentence. Prepositions show a relationship between words.

▶ **EXAMPLE 5**

| Conjunction | Trevor brought the CDs, for he was the DJ. |
| Preposition | Lee would work hard for the group. |

Practice F

Add the missing punctuation to each sentence. Then write whether the bold word is a preposition or a conjunction.

1. Everyone liked the story **but** Yolanda.

2. We wanted to go shopping **instead** we stayed home.

3. Last night Lisa read Marco did math **and** Jill relaxed.

4. Karl rode the bus to school **but** Kyle walked there.

5. The students cheered loudly **for** their team.

REVIEW

Write each sentence on your paper. Underline the coordinating conjunctions. Add any missing punctuation.

1. Sue is hard of hearing but she signs reads lips and notices the feelings on people's faces.

2. She learned sign language and lip reading in a class.

3. Lisa learned sign language for she wanted to communicate with Sue.

Write *conjunction* or *preposition* for each bold word.

4. Paul played tennis well **for** he practiced every day.

5. The apartment is beautiful, **but** the rent is high.

6. Everyone was on time **for** work **but** her.

Use a coordinating conjunction to connect the ideas in each pair of sentences. You may need to change the verb.

7. Mary likes to play soccer. Ricky likes to play golf.

8. Clara plays the tuba in the band. Clara plays the flute.

9. Rocky wants a new hat. Towanda wants a new hat.

10. Jovan wants to sing. Reggie wants to dance.

PUTTING IT ALL TOGETHER

Write a letter to a friend telling about a time when you were surprised. Include an example of a coordinating conjunction, subordinating conjunction, and correlating conjunction.

When you finish writing your letter, go back and underline the conjunctions. Draw two lines under the interjections. Trade your paper with a classmate. Check each other's punctuation.

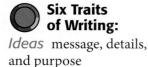

Six Traits of Writing:

Ideas message, details, and purpose

Correlative Conjunctions

Objectives

■ To identify correlative conjunctions in sentences

■ To use the correct verb form in sentences with correlative conjunctions

Correlative conjunctions express a shared relationship by connecting words or groups of words. Use correlative conjunctions in pairs.

▶ **EXAMPLE 1**

Neither Ethan nor Leon enjoyed that book.

Both the characters and the plot were weak.

Correlative Conjunctions

both . . . and	neither . . . nor	whether . . . or
either . . . or	not only . . . but also	

Correlative conjunctions

A pair of conjunctions that connect words or groups of words

Practice A

Write the correlative conjunctions in each sentence.

1. Ann will write her report on either Polk or Harrison.

2. Both Polk and Harrison were United States presidents.

3. Not only Ann but also Sue must write a report.

4. Sue does not know whether to study Arthur or Pierce.

5. She had heard of neither Arthur nor Pierce before.

Reading Strategy:
Summarizing

What type of conjunction is being introduced in this lesson?

Correlative Conjunctions and Subject-Verb Agreement

Subjects are often joined with correlative conjunctions. The verb agrees with the subject closer to the verb.

▶ **EXAMPLE 2**

Neither Jay nor Mark has signed up for a class. (singular)

Not only the deck but also the shed needs repair. (singular)

Either fruit or vegetables are a good snack. (plural)

Reading Strategy:
Summarizing

What details in this lesson help you to understand correlative conjunctions?

The correlative conjunctions *both* and *and* take a verb in the plural form.

▶ **EXAMPLE 3**

Both Lisa and Chris take photography classes.

Practice B

Write the verb on your paper that completes each sentence. Then say the sentences aloud to hear correct usage.

1. Either a pencil or a pen (is, are) all right to use.
2. Neither the coat nor the shoes (is, are) on sale.
3. Neither the car nor the truck (is, are) working today.
4. Both Yvette and her brother (loves, love) cooking.
5. Not only Juan but also Para (is, are) going to Florida.

Practice C

Write a sentence using each correlative conjunction. Be sure to make the subject and verb agree in your sentence.

1. both, and
2. either, or
3. neither, nor
4. whether, or
5. not only, but also

Both Jai and Reggie love snowboarding.

REVIEW

Write the correlative conjunctions in each sentence.

1. Ron won not only the game but also the tournament.

2. Would you like either milk or juice?

3. Both Chandra and her sister speak three languages.

4. She bought neither the dress nor the suit.

5. Inez and Dwight are not only in French class together but also math class.

Complete each sentence with correlative conjunctions. Be sure the subject and verb agree.

6. _____ Mark _____ Justin (have) part-time jobs.

7. Salma thinks _____ the skirt _____ the shirt (fit) her.

8. _____ Estelle _____ her brother (be) talented artists.

9. Mr. Wu _____ (drive) to work _____ (take) the bus.

10. Ann knows _____ the reports _____ the outlines (be) finished.

SPELLING BUILDER

Dropping the Final *e*
Many words have suffixes, or endings. To add an ending, you may need to change the spelling. Follow these rules when adding endings to words with a silent final *e*.

- Keep the *e* before adding an ending that starts with a consonant: safe + ty = safety
- Drop the *e* before adding an ending that starts with a vowel: choose + ing = choosing

Put the word and ending together. Write the new word.

1. surprise + ing =   3. care + less =
2. use + ful =   4. bake + er =

Subordinating Conjunctions

Objectives

- To identify dependent clauses introduced by subordinating conjunctions
- To connect independent and dependent clauses with subordinating conjunctions
- To tell prepositions and conjunctions apart in a sentence

Subordinating conjunction

A word that connects a dependent clause to an independent clause in a sentence

Independent clause

A clause that expresses a complete thought

Dependent clause

A clause that does not express a complete thought

A **subordinating conjunction** connects an **independent clause** to a **dependent clause.** An independent clause expresses a complete thought. A dependent clause is a group of words that has a subject and a verb. However, it does not express a complete thought. A dependent clause cannot stand alone as a sentence. A dependent clause depends on the main, or independent, clause to make sense.

A dependent clause may begin or end a sentence.

▶ **EXAMPLE 1**

When the cheers stop, we can continue the game.

We can continue the game when the cheers stop.
(*When* connects the incomplete idea *the cheers stop* to the clause *we can continue.* It is the subordinating conjunction.)

Common Subordinating Conjunctions

after	in order that	when	while
although	since	whenever	until
as	so that	where	if
because	unless	wherever	

Practice A

Write the dependent clause in each sentence on your paper. Underline the subordinating conjunctions.

1. If you want to play better, you have to practice.

2. I plan to study until I finish.

3. Justin saves money because he wants to go to college.

4. When Lisa gets here, we will leave.

5. They ate popcorn while they watched the movie.

Reading Strategy:
Summarizing

What are some details that help you understand when to use a comma?

Punctuating Subordinating Clauses

When a dependent clause begins a sentence, you use a comma. Separate the dependent clause from the independent clause. Do not use a comma when the dependent clause comes after the independent clause.

▶ **EXAMPLE 2**

Dependent Clause
After the game was over,

Independent Clause
we went to Tim's house.

Independent Clause
We went to Tim's house

Dependent Clause
after the game was over.

A subordinating conjunction introduces an adverb clause. Like adverbs, these clauses answer the questions *when*, *where*, *why*, and *how*.

Practice B

Add a dependent clause to each sentence. Underline the subordinating conjunction. Add commas where needed.

1. Dan would like to visit California.

2. Duane saved 25 dollars a week.

3. Ari's report was late.

4. The storm forced people to stay home.

5. The front door slammed shut.

Before the movie, Lisa bought popcorn to share with her friends.

Practice C

Connect each pair of sentences with a subordinating conjunction. Add commas where they are needed.

1. Zack is lifting weights. He wants to join the team.
2. Pavi went to the library. He needed a book.
3. I was asleep. A storm blew down our tree.
4. Lisa wants to see a movie. We will buy tickets in advance.
5. The team won the tournament. The town celebrated.

Reading Strategy:
Summarizing

Summarize the difference between a subordinating conjunction and a preposition.

Subordinating Conjunction or Preposition?

You can use some words as subordinating conjunctions or prepositions. If the word is followed by a subject and a verb, it is a conjunction.

▶ **EXAMPLE 3**

| Conjunction | The test was put off until we finished our projects. |
| Preposition | The test was put off until Friday. |

 Writing Tip

Use subordinating conjunctions to connect two short sentences. Use a mixture of short and long sentences to add variety to your writing.

Practice D

Write whether the word in bold is a conjunction or a preposition.

1. We went home **after** school was over.
2. **Since** last week, we have won every game.
3. I would like that coat **since** it is cold outside.
4. I haven't heard **from** her since Monday.
5. **Before** lunch, I have Spanish class.

REVIEW

Write each sentence on your paper. Add commas where needed. Underline each subordinating conjunction.

1. Kathy will hold dinner until everyone gets here.

2. If you will help we can finish early.

3. When spring arrives Marco and Tony will go fishing.

4. Until the team scored the fans were quiet.

5. Everyone cheered as the band played the school song.

Connect each pair of sentences with a subordinating conjunction. Add commas where needed.

6. Mai got a good grade on her test. She studied hard.

7. I will clean the house. You do the shopping.

8. Juan got hungry at three o'clock. He ate an apple.

9. The weather is too cold. I cannot go outside.

10. He lost the election. He did not have enough help.

VOCABULARY BUILDER

As, Because, and Since

As is used to create a time relationship in a sentence. *We waved to her* as *she drove away. Because* and *since* describe causes and effects. *We left* because (since) *the party was over*.

Write the word that completes each sentence.

1. We went swimming (as, because) it was hot outside.

2. (As, Since) Harriet arrived at school, it began to rain.

3. I let her borrow money (as, since) she forgot her wallet.

4. I arrived at the game (as, because) Levi hit a home run.

5. (As, Because) I was 18, I could vote in the election.

Interjections

Objectives

- To identify interjections
- To punctuate sentences with interjections
- To add interjections to sentences

Reading Strategy:
Summarizing

How can you find the main idea in the first paragraph on this page?

An **interjection** is a word or phrase that expresses a strong feeling. Always separate the interjection from the rest of the sentence with a punctuation mark. Use a comma, a question mark, or an exclamation mark. Use an exclamation mark after a strong interjection.

▶ **EXAMPLE 1**

Hurry! I'll be late again.   Oh? I didn't know that.

Say, could you help me?   Hey, don't ask me again.

Common Interjections

ah	hurrah	oh, boy	stop
alas	hurry	ouch	terrific
fine	hush	please	thanks
gosh	listen	quick	well
great	look out	quiet	what
ha	my goodness	really	whew
hello	nonsense	so	wow
hey	oh	so what	yes

Practice A

Write the interjection in each sentence on your paper.

1. Hush! The baby is sleeping.

2. Really? Jack wants to go to the movies.

3. Hello, my name is Carlotta.

4. Thanks, I needed some help.

5. Hey, do you know where to find the crossword answer?

Reading Strategy: Summarizing

Explain in your own words when you need to capitalize the word after an interjection.

Punctuation and Capitalization

When end punctuation comes after an interjection, capitalize the first word that follows.

▶ **EXAMPLE 2**

So? Who wants to drive?

Wow! That is lovely.

Whew! I'm glad that I am finished!

If you use a comma, do not capitalize the next word of the sentence. However, if the next word after an interjection is a proper noun, capitalize the word.

▶ **EXAMPLE 3**

Ah, that project looks great!

Oh, Amanda has not heard the news.

Practice B

Write each sentence. Add the missing punctuation and capitalization to each sentence.

1. quick I need help fast
2. wow what a great party this is
3. really I was surprised
4. well adam finally got here
5. gosh that was fun

Practice C

Write five sentences that use interjections on your paper. Punctuate each sentence correctly.

REVIEW

Add punctuation after each interjection and at the end of each sentence. Capitalize words when necessary.

1. no I cannot help you

4. whew that sure smells bad

2. ouch that hurts

5. hey I had better get home

3. well what is new

Add an interjection to each sentence. Also include the correct punctuation.

6. Isn't that beautiful?

9. I ripped my best shirt.

7. We are having a test.

10. That book is going to fall.

8. I won!

BUILDING RESEARCH SKILLS

Paraphrasing and Summarizing Findings

Use your own words to write ideas you find in sources. To summarize, take multiple sentences and restate the main idea in one sentence. To paraphrase, take one or two sentences and put them in your own words. You should include specific details when you paraphrase.

Do not plagiarize, or steal and pass off another's words as your own words.

You can write an author's exact words for a direct quotation. However, you must use quotation marks and give credit to the source.

Get a copy of your school newspaper. Find an article that interests you. Read it and follow the directions below.

1. Choose one paragraph in the article. Paraphrase the paragraph.

2. What are the differences between summarizing and paraphrasing?

3. CRITICAL THINKING Why is it so important to write an author's exact words as a direct quotation using quotation marks?

COMMUNICATING ON THE JOB

Service Advisor

James Swope is a service advisor for an automobile repair company. He greets customers and recommends services.

Mr. Swope uses terms related to cars. However, he must explain these terms in a way that customers will understand. Customers come to his store frustrated. He must show concern for their problems and ask thoughtful questions. Below are notes that Mr. Swope took while listening to a customer. Read his notes and follow the directions below.

> Customer: Judy and Mike Smith
>
> Phone Number: 651-555-6789
>
> Customer Notes:
>
> The car both shakes and rattles over 55 miles per hour. Customer wants the tire pressure wheel balance and suspension checked. Customer wants the oil changed. Neither Mr. Smith nor Mrs. Smith have a cell phone. Call home phone and leave a message.

1. What types of conjunctions are used in the customer notes?

2. Find the punctuation and subject-verb agreement errors in the notes. Write these sentences correctly.

3. **CRITICAL THINKING** Imagine a dialogue between Mr. and Mrs. Smith and Mr. Swope. What might Mr. Swope say to show his concern for the couple? What interjections might he use?

LISTENING

Be an active listener. Maintain eye contact and do not be distracted. Write important facts or ideas as you listen. Respond with questions and comments. Practice being an active listener. Listen to a classmate's story. After listening, paraphrase the story. Your classmate can evaluate you on how well you listened.

- Use coordinating conjunctions to connect words, phrases, or sentences that are equal.

- Use a comma to separate words, phrases, or clauses in a series.

- Use coordinating conjunctions and a comma to join complete sentences. Other conjunctions need a semicolon before the conjunction and a comma after it.

- Use correlative conjunctions in pairs to express a shared relationship.

- Subjects are often joined with correlative conjunctions. The verb agrees with the subject closer to the verb, except when using *and*.

- A subordinating conjunction connects an independent clause to a dependent clause.

- Use a comma after a dependent clause that appears at the beginning of a sentence.

- A subordinating conjunction introduces an adverb clause. These clauses answer the questions *when*, *where*, *why*, and *how*.

- Some words that look like conjunctions may be prepositions in a sentence. Look at the sentence meaning to decide if a word is a conjunction or preposition.

- An interjection is a word or phrase that expresses a strong feeling. Use a comma, a question mark, or an exclamation mark to separate an interjection from the sentence.

Word Bank

clause

conjunction

coordinating
   conjunction

correlative
   conjunction

dependent clause

independent clause

interjection

series

subordinating
   conjunction

Part A Find the word or words in the Word Bank to complete each sentence. Write the answer on your paper.

1. A clause that does not express a complete thought is a _____.

2. A _____ is a pair of conjunctions that connects words or groups of words.

3. A word that connects parts of a sentence is a _____.

4. A group of more than two words or phrases is a _____.

5. An _____ is a word or phrase that shows strong feeling.

6. A word that connects two or more equal parts of a sentence is a _____.

7. A _____ connects a dependent clause to an independent clause in a sentence.

8. A _____ is a group of words with a subject and a verb.

9. A clause that expresses a complete thought is an _____.

Part B Decide whether each word in bold is a *coordinating conjunction*, *subordinating conjunction*, or *correlating conjunction*. Write the answers on your paper.

10. They were hungry, **but** they were not tired.

11. **Both** Liang **and** Anthony ordered sandwiches.

12. Lisa wanted something hot, **so** she ordered soup.

13. **Neither** Lisa **nor** Tamara wanted dessert.

14. They talked about the dance **since** it was this weekend.

Part C Write each sentence. Use correct punctuation.

15. Lisa Anthony Tamara and Liang went to the dance together.

16. Because the night was warm they opened a window.

17. "The dance committee wanted a band however they got a disc jockey," Lisa said.

18. Hurry we are going to miss the bus.

Part D Decide which sentence is written correctly. Write the letter of your answer on your paper.

19. **A** Paul bought a coat, he bought a scarf, He bought some gloves.
B Paul bought a coat. A scarf. Some gloves.
C Paul bought a coat, a scarf, and some gloves.
D Paul bought a coat, He bought a scarf, he bought some gloves.

20. **A** It rained on Monday, it rained on Tuesday.
B It rained on Monday while it rained on Tuesday.
C It rained on Monday, nor it rain on Tuesday.
D It rained on Monday and Tuesday.

21. **A** Dan was absent, nor Abby was absent.
B Dan and Abby were absent.
C Dan but Abby was absent.
D Dan or Abby are absent.

Part E Write each sentence. Add an interjection and correct punctuation and capitalization.

22. What a funny story that was.

23. I ran a mile in less than eight minutes.

24. I bumped my elbow again.

25. The traffic light is changing.

Test Tip

Do not wait until the night before a test to begin studying for it. Get a good night's sleep the night before the test.

Sentences

The two deer in this photograph travel together. Subjects and predicates work the same way. They travel together. However, while a deer can stand alone, a subject or predicate cannot. You need both to express a complete thought. They work together to form a sentence.

Every sentence has a subject and a predicate. The subject of a sentence is who or what the sentence is about. For example, you might comment about the deer in this photograph. You might say, "The deer walked along the side of the pond." *Deer* is the subject. The predicate tells what the subject did or what happened to the subject. *Deer* and *walked* work together to form a complete thought.

In Chapter 9, you will study the different kinds of sentences. In doing so, you will also open up new ways of expressing yourself.

GOALS FOR LEARNING

- To tell the difference between sentences and sentence fragments
- To identify the simple subject and complete subject in a sentence
- To identify the simple predicate and the complete predicate in a sentence
- To identify the purpose of a sentence
- To write simple and compound sentences

Reading Strategy: Questioning

Asking questions is an important part of reading a text. Questioning allows you to think about what you are reading. You are able to identify those details that interest you. You can also figure out what you may need to read again. As you read, ask yourself:

- How well do I understand what I just read?
- What experiences have I already had with this topic?
- How might this information be useful in my life?

Key Vocabulary Words

Sentence A group of words that expresses a complete thought

Capital letter The uppercase form of a letter such as *A, B, C*

End punctuation A mark at the end of a sentence that tells the reader where a sentence ends: a period (.), a question mark (?), or an exclamation point (!)

Simple subject The main noun or pronoun that the sentence is about

Complete subject The simple subject and all of the words that describe it

Compound subject Two or more simple subjects connected by a conjunction

Simple predicate The main verb or verb phrase in the sentence

Complete predicate The simple predicate and all of the words that describe it

Compound predicate Two or more simple predicates connected by a conjunction

Declarative sentence A sentence that makes a statement

Interrogative sentence A sentence that asks a question

Imperative sentence A sentence that gives a command

Exclamatory sentence A sentence that shows strong feeling

Simple sentence A sentence with one subject and one predicate; an independent clause

Compound sentence Two independent clauses joined by a coordinating conjunction

What Is a Sentence?

Objectives

- To tell the difference between a sentence and a sentence fragment
- To write complete sentences from fragments

A **sentence** is a group of words that expresses a complete thought. Every sentence begins with an uppercase form of a letter, or **capital letter.** It ends with **end punctuation** such as a period, question mark, or exclamation point.

▶ **EXAMPLE 1**

Mr. Okada sold his truck to Reggie.

What did he pay for the truck?

Stop right there!

A group of words may look like a sentence. However, if it does not express a complete thought, it is not a sentence.

▶ **EXAMPLE 2**

Not a Sentence	The bicycle with the wide tires. (This group of words does not express a complete thought. What happened to the bicycle with the wide tires?)
Sentence	The bicycle with the wide tires is fast.
Not a Sentence	Looked all over school for Latasha. (This group of words does not express a complete thought. Who looked all over school for Latasha?)
Sentence	Mario looked all over school for Latasha.
Not a Sentence	Before Ming bought the scooter. (This group of words does not express a complete thought. What happened before Ming bought the scooter?)
Sentence	Before Ming bought the scooter, her brother looked it over.

Sentence
A group of words that expresses a complete thought

Capital letter
The uppercase form of a letter such as *A, B, C*

End punctuation
A mark at the end of a sentence that tells the reader where a sentence ends:
- a period (.)
- a question mark (?)
- an exclamation point (!)

Reading Strategy:
Questioning

Ask yourself: What do I already know about writing sentences?

Practice A

Read each group of words. Write *S* if the group of words is a sentence. Write *NS* if it is not a sentence.

1. Stop for the red light!

2. Before the storm was over.

3. In the house across the street.

4. Searching for a new job.

5. Where does he work?

Practice B

Each group of words is not a sentence. Write a sentence using each group of words. Use correct capitalization and end punctuation.

1. because of the cold weather

2. each day before the sun rises

3. after we ate lunch

4. when four inches of snow fell

5. during the last quarter of the basketball game

David searched the newspaper for a job.

REVIEW

Write *S* if the group of words is a sentence. If the words are not a sentence, add words to make a sentence.

1. Our neighbors in the house across the street.

2. They painted the house a light shade of brown.

3. The whole family picked out the color.

4. They needed a two-story ladder.

5. When dark clouds appeared in the sky.

Add words to make each group of words a complete sentence. Begin each sentence with a capital letter and finish it with end punctuation.

6. the papers on my desk

7. seen in the woods near the lake

8. walking to the game with friends

9. the girl on the bus

10. if anyone calls while I am out

VOCABULARY BUILDER

If and **Whether**

Use *if* to mean "in the event that." *I will go* if *you need me.*
Use *whether* to mean that choices are available. *I will go* whether *you need me or not.*

Complete each sentence by adding either *if* or *whether.*

1. Gregory does not know _____ to call Sarah or not.
2. The room will be dark _____ the candle burns out.
3. My umbrella will be wet _____ I go out in the rain.
4. You choose _____ we study now or later.
5. You will see new exhibits _____ you go to the museum.

Subjects of a Sentence

Simple subject
The main noun or pronoun that the sentence is about

Complete subject
The simple subject and all of the words that describe it

Reading Strategy:
Questioning

What is the difference between the simple subject and the complete subject?

Every sentence has two parts: the subject and the predicate. You will learn more about the predicate in the next lesson. The **simple subject** tells what the sentence is about. It often tells who or what does the action. The simple subject is usually a noun or pronoun.

▶ **EXAMPLE 1**

Amir opened the door. (Who opened the door? *Amir* did.)

The man became captain. (Who became captain? The *man*.)

The simple subject and all the words that describe it make up the **complete subject.** The complete subject may be one word or many words.

▶ **EXAMPLE 2**

The test in history was easy. (The simple subject is the noun *test.* The complete subject is *the test in history.*)

Mr. Torres is our principal this year. (The simple subject is the proper noun *Mr. Torres.* The complete subject is *Mr. Torres.*)

Practice A

Write the complete subject of each sentence. Underline the simple subject. A complete subject may be only one word.

1. Mr. Rojas comes from Mexico City, Mexico.
2. The entire class speaks in Spanish every day.
3. The teacher asks the questions in Spanish.
4. They must answer him in Spanish.
5. The students in this class learn quickly.

Simple Subjects and Prepositional Phrases

The simple subject cannot be the object of the preposition. Prepositional phrases act as adjectives and adverbs that can describe the simple subject.

▶ **EXAMPLE 3**

The lake by my house has many fish. (*The lake by my house* is the complete subject. *By my house* is a prepositional phrase describing the simple subject *lake.*)

Practice B

Write the complete subject in each sentence on your paper.

1. I am going to the store.
2. A friend of Mr. Torres visited from Mexico.
3. Three of our classmates went on the field trip.
4. The car with the flat tire pulled off the road.
5. Everyone in the band practiced for the concert.

Subjects in Sentences with *Here* and *There*

The subject of a sentence usually comes before the verb, but it may come after the verb. When a sentence begins with the words *here* or *there*, the subject comes after the verb.

▶ **EXAMPLE 4**

There will be a train at noon. (What will be there? A *train*)

Here comes Anton now. (Who comes now? *Anton* does.)

Practice C

Write the simple subject in each sentence on your paper.

1. There is a good program on TV tonight.
2. Here is the bus stop.
3. There are no sandwiches left.
4. There is my school.
5. Here is the correct answer.

Reading Strategy:
Questioning

Ask yourself: Do I understand where to find simple subjects in questions? If the answer is no, read the material again.

Simple Subjects in Questions

In a question, the subject may come between a helping verb and a main verb. Or it may come between parts of a verb phrase.

▶ **EXAMPLE 5**

When does Margot have class?
(The simple subject *Margot* is between the helping verb *does* and the main verb *have.*)

Are you leaving soon?
(The subject *you* comes between the verb phrase *are leaving.*)

Sometimes the interrogative pronoun *what*, *who*, or *which* begins a sentence that asks a question. The interrogative pronoun may be the simple subject of the sentence.

▶ **EXAMPLE 6**

Who called? What is happening?

Which of these backpacks is yours?

Practice D

Write the simple subject in each sentence on your paper.

1. Will you be going to the meeting?
2. Which of the members will speak?
3. Who will lead the discussion?
4. Has this group ever met before?
5. Who is going to the meeting?

Simple Subjects in Commands

In a command or a request, the subject is *you*. Although the word *you* does not appear in the sentence, it is understood. The subject is the person spoken to.

▶ **EXAMPLE 7**

(You) Please help me arrange the flowers.

Practice E

Write the simple subject in each sentence on your paper.

1. Help me carry these bags into the house.
2. Open your books to page 45.
3. Please come home right after school.
4. Don't touch that!
5. Please hurry!

Compound Subjects

The subject of a sentence can be compound. A **compound subject** is two or more simple subjects connected by a conjunction.

▶ **EXAMPLE 8**

David and Brittany went to the park.

The boy and his cousin went skating.

Practice F

Write the compound subject in each sentence.

1. Neither Freddie nor Tricia went to the concert.
2. Both my hat and my gloves are blue.
3. Spring and summer are my favorite seasons.
4. Are my books or my papers in your locker?
5. There are enough sandwiches and juice for everyone.

REVIEW

Write the simple subject in each sentence on your paper. The subject *you* may be understood.

1. Christa and Jim looked at CD players in the store.

2. Her birthday is in two weeks.

3. Who is coming to Christa's party?

Write each sentence. Underline the complete subject once. Underline the simple subject twice. Some of the subjects may be compound.

4. Baseball season begins soon.

5. Are James and Darren on the team?

BUILDING RESEARCH SKILLS

Using Internet Search Engines

Internet search engines find Web sites on a topic.

- Type in the Internet address of a search engine.

- Enter keywords in the search window. A keyword is a word that the engine uses to find sites. Put quotation marks around words to search for a specific phrase. Use *and* in between keywords to find sites with both words. Use *or* to find sites with at least one of the words. Use *not* before a word to avoid a word on a site.

- Read the summaries to pick the best Web site for your topic.

Use a search engine to gather information about a topic that interests you. Search your topic using different keyword combinations.

1. Which keywords found the most useful sites? Explain.

2. Which keywords found the least useful sites? Explain.

3. CRITICAL THINKING Use three search engines to find information. Which search engine do you prefer to use? Explain.

Predicates of a Sentence

Objectives

- To identify the complete predicate
- To identify the simple predicate
- To identify compound predicates

Simple predicate
The main verb or verb phrase in the sentence

Complete predicate
The simple predicate and all of the words that describe it

Reading Strategy:
Questioning

What do you already know about predicates in a sentence?

Simple Predicate

The **simple predicate** of a sentence is the main verb or verb phrase. It tells what the subject does, did, or will do. It can also tell the condition of the subject.

▶ **EXAMPLE 1**

We studied.

Andy will look at the videotapes this weekend.

Practice A

Write the simple predicate in each sentence on your paper.

1. Lena lost her earring yesterday.
2. Denise found the earring today.
3. One of the stones was lost.
4. Someone had stepped on it.
5. A jeweler replaced the stone in Lena's earring.

Complete Predicate

The **complete predicate** includes the simple predicate. It also includes all of the words that describe the simple predicate. Words found after the simple predicate are often part of the complete predicate.

Each simple predicate is underlined in Example 2. The complete predicate is in blue.

▶ **EXAMPLE 2**

Jessica helped her mother in the kitchen.

Latasha will meet us at the mall.

Practice B

Write the complete predicate in each sentence on your paper. Underline the simple predicate.

1. Mrs. Barry gave Christa a surprise birthday party.
2. Christa's brother Will invited her friends.
3. Her friends had decorated the house.
4. Christa was arriving home at six-thirty.
5. Everyone yelled "Surprise!"

Finding the Simple and Complete Predicates

Usually the predicate comes after the subject in a sentence. In a question, part of the predicate comes before the subject.

▶ **EXAMPLE 3**

Did **you** bring Sita the tapes?   Are **you** having fun?

Practice C

Write each sentence. Underline the complete predicate in each sentence once. Underline the simple predicate twice.

1. Did you talk to Christa?
2. Why did Elena leave early?
3. Maybe she was feeling sick.
4. Her mother needed her at home.
5. What was wrong?

Adverbs and Prepositional Phrases in the Predicate

Adverbs and prepositional phrases in the complete predicate may come at the beginning of the sentence.

NOTE

The word *o'clock* is a contraction of the words *of the clock.*

▶ **EXAMPLE 4**

At twelve o'clock **everyone** went to lunch.

Then **Akira** helped his sisters clean up.

Compound predicate

Two or more simple predicates connected by a conjunction

Practice D

Write the complete predicate in each sentence on your paper. Underline each simple predicate.

1. In the morning, Julio walked his dog.

2. After their walk, Julio gave the dog a bath.

3. Then he called Mandy and Diego.

4. Later, they all watched a movie about sharks.

5. The next day Julio bought a book about sharks.

Compound Predicates

A predicate can be compound. A **compound predicate** is two or more simple predicates joined by a conjunction such as *and*, *but*, or *or*. The subject of both predicates is the same.

▶ **EXAMPLE 5**

The deer moved behind the trees and disappeared.

The parents clapped and cheered.

The actors looked calm but were very nervous.

Practice E

Write each sentence on your paper. Underline the compound predicate in each sentence.

1. Andy looked at new cars but did not buy one.

2. The big cars cost too much and used too much gas.

3. The small cars got good gas mileage but remained out of his price range.

4. The used cars showed rust spots and needed repairs.

5. Will he buy that car or look some more?

Reading Strategy:
Questioning

Ask yourself: What have I learned about predicates after reading this lesson?

REVIEW

Write each sentence on your paper. Underline the complete predicate in each sentence.

1. Will you come to an apple picking party this Sunday?

2. When does it start?

3. Around two o'clock, all of my relatives will arrive.

4. Usually we walk around the orchard and pick apples.

5. Bring a big appetite!

Write the simple predicate or simple predicates in each sentence. For those sentences with a compound predicate, write *compound predicate*.

6. I always enjoy the first day of spring.

7. My neighbor Matt takes out his fishing gear.

8. He cleans his gear and practices his casting.

9. Each year he goes on a fishing trip and returns with many fish.

10. He has already invited us to a fish dinner.

SPELLING BUILDER

Doubling the Final Consonant

Read these words: hopping, bigger, hottest. Note the double consonants before the –*ing*, -*er*, and -*est* endings. The endings –*ing*, -*er*, and -*est* begin with vowels. To add an ending that begins with a vowel to a consonant-vowel-consonant word, first double the final consonant. Then add the ending.

1. Add -*ing* to *dig*.

2. Add -*er* to *win*.

3. Add -*est* to *red*.

4. Add -*ed* to *jog*.

5. Add -*ing* to *hum*.

Then use each word in a sentence.

Purposes of Sentences

Declarative sentence

A sentence that makes a statement

Interrogative sentence

A sentence that asks a question

Imperative sentence

A sentence that gives a command

Exclamatory sentence

A sentence that shows strong feeling

Reading Strategy: Questioning

Ask yourself: Why is it important to know the purposes of sentences?

Every sentence has a purpose. A **declarative sentence** makes a statement. An **interrogative sentence** asks a question. An **imperative sentence** gives a command or makes a request. An **exclamatory sentence** shows strong feeling.

▶ **EXAMPLE 1**

Declarative (Statement)	They went to the game.
Interrogative (Question)	Are you going to the game?
Imperative (Command)	Go to the game with them.
Exclamatory (Exclamation)	What a great game that was!

Declarative Sentence

A sentence that makes a statement usually begins with the subject. A statement ends with a period.

▶ **EXAMPLE 2**

The play began at seven o'clock.

Interrogative Sentence

A sentence that asks a question begins with either a helping verb or an interrogative pronoun or adverb. A question ends with a question mark.

▶ **EXAMPLE 3**

Did you like the play?

Where are my books?

Reading Strategy:
Questioning

What is the difference between an interrogative and an exclamatory sentence?

 Writing Tip

A sentence that expresses a command can add excitement to your writing. It can also allow you to speak directly to the reader. Use a command when you want readers to take action. For example: *Save the park!*

"Should we eat here for lunch?" Mark asked.

Imperative Sentence

A sentence that makes a command or request begins with a verb. The subject *you* is understood. A command ends with a period or an exclamation point.

▶ **EXAMPLE 4**

(You) Please give me two CDs.   (You) Do it now!

Exclamatory Sentence

A sentence that shows strong feeling or excitement ends with an exclamation point.

▶ **EXAMPLE 5**

I cannot believe we won!   What a great race!

Practice A

Write *S* on your paper if the sentence makes a statement. Write *Q* if it asks a question. Write *C* if it states a command or request. Write *E* if the sentence is an exclamation.

1. Are you hungry?

2. I am starved!

3. We can eat at this restaurant.

4. Melissa and her parents had lunch here last week.

5. Please order something for both of us.

REVIEW

Write each sentence on your paper. Add the correct end punctuation. Next to each sentence, write its purpose: *declarative*, *interrogative*, *imperative*, or *exclamatory*.

1. Listen to this new CD

2. What a terrific sound that is

3. Where do you buy your CDs

4. The music store at Crosstown Mall has the best prices

5. What is the price of a CD at the store near our school

Write an example of each kind of sentence. Add the correct capitalization and punctuation.

6. a statement (declarative sentence)

7. a question (interrogative sentence)

8. a request (imperative sentence)

9. a command (imperative sentence)

10. shows strong feeling (exclamatory sentence)

Simple and Compound Sentences

A **simple sentence** has one subject and one predicate that work together. A simple sentence is an independent clause. An independent clause expresses a complete thought.

Objectives

- To find subjects and predicates in simple and compound sentences
- To tell the difference between simple and compound sentences
- To write compound sentences

► **EXAMPLE 1**

```
  S     P
Julian smiled.

      S        P
The stars were shining.
```

Simple sentence

A sentence with one subject and one predicate; an independent clause

Compound sentence

Two independent clauses joined by a coordinating conjunction

Practice A

Identify the simple subject and simple predicate in each sentence. Write them on your paper.

1. Logan was sick on Thursday.
2. Emma brought him chicken soup.
3. Isabella caught his cold.
4. Everyone washed their hands well.
5. The clinic opened at noon.

A **compound sentence** has two or more independent clauses joined together with a coordinating conjunction. Common coordinating conjunctions are *and*, *but*, *or*, *nor*, *for*, *so*, *yet*, and *as well as*. Each independent clause has a subject and a predicate and expresses a complete idea. A comma comes before the coordinating conjunction in a compound sentence.

Reading Strategy:
Questioning

What details on this page are important in order to understand simple sentences?

► **EXAMPLE 2**

```
       S              P      Conj.  S      P
Jennifer went to the party, and Sue met her there.
```

Practice B

Write each compound sentence. Underline the complete subject in each independent clause once. Underline the complete predicate in each independent clause twice.

1. They were hungry, but all the restaurants were closed.

2. Alice has a cat, Mike has a gerbil, and Amit has a dog.

3. Mr. Barry likes apples, but Mrs. Barry prefers pears.

4. Lori plays the piano, and her sister plays the flute.

5. Ms. Ray gives a lot of homework, but her tests are easy.

A compound sentence tells about two or more related events.

▶ **EXAMPLE 3**

Incorrect   Jeni went to the party, but I like grapes.

Correct   Jeni went to the party, but Alex stayed home.

Practice C

Decide whether each compound sentence tells about two related events. Write *correct* or *incorrect* for each sentence.

1. Conner went to the store, but it was closed.

2. The workers towed the car, but cherries are expensive.

3. My mom read a book, and our house is painted blue.

4. The leaves on the trees turned red, and we admired them.

5. Winter is a cold time of year, but I still find plenty to do outside.

Simple or Compound Sentence?

Remember that a simple sentence may still have a compound subject or a compound predicate. A compound sentence has at least two complete ideas. Each complete idea has its own subject and verb that work together.

▶ **EXAMPLE 4**

Simple	Nell mowed the lawn and painted the fence. (Two simple predicates: *mowed* and *painted.* It is one complete idea, not two.)
Simple	Nell and I mowed the lawn and painted the fence. (Two simple subjects: *Nell, I;* and two simple predicates: *mowed, painted.* It is not two independent thoughts.)
Compound	Nell mowed the lawn, and I painted the fence. (Two independent clauses, or two complete thoughts.)

Reading Strategy:
Questioning

Ask yourself: What can I do to better understand the difference between simple and compound sentences?

Practice D

Write each sentence on your paper. Write *S* if the sentence is simple. Write *C* if it is compound.

1. Andrea and Michelle signed up for the play.
2. He fishes every spring but has never caught a big one.
3. The phone rang three times, and then it stopped.
4. The girls hurried, but they were late anyway.
5. After school, we came home and did our homework.

Practice E

Write five compound sentences. Be sure the ideas in each sentence are related. Punctuate each sentence correctly.

REVIEW

Write *S* if the sentence is simple. Write *C* if it is compound.

1. Riley plays on the basketball team and works part time at the grocery store.

2. The store manager hired him as a bagger, but Riley wanted more responsibility.

3. After two months, Mr. Alvarez and Riley talked.

4. Mr. Alvarez offered Riley the job in the deli, and Riley accepted it.

5. It meant more responsibility, but also a raise in pay.

Write the number of independent clauses in each sentence. Then list the simple subject and simple predicate for each independent clause.

6. Latasha called me after school and asked for help with her project.

7. I met her at the library, and we reviewed the project.

8. Andrea spotted us and came over to our table.

9. Andrea, Latasha, and I are in the same math class.

10. Andrea lives close to the library, so she walked home.

PUTTING IT ALL TOGETHER

Create a travel brochure for a place that you have been. Include both pictures and words. Use at least three compound sentences in your brochure. Underline complete subjects once and complete predicates twice in each compound sentence. Use an example of a declarative, interrogative, imperative, and exclamatory sentence in your brochure.

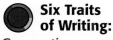

Six Traits of Writing:

Conventions correct grammar, spelling, and mechanics

Giving Instructions

Many instructions have more than one step. Before you write a set of instructions, think about the correct order of steps. Visualize the supplies that a person will need. Think of the actions that need to be performed. Assume the person who will read your instructions does not know what to do.

When writing instructions, you will often use imperative sentences. These are sentences that give a command or make a request. Instructions are usually written in the present tense. However, sometimes the future tense can be used. Be sure to use specific words in your sentences. Choose action verbs that will help a person understand what he or she needs to do. Sometimes instructions are numbered to help a person follow each step carefully.

Write technical instructions for assembling, repairing, or replacing something. Then answer the questions.

1. Give an example of an imperative sentence in your instructions. What is the subject of the sentence?

2. Underline all of the simple predicates used in your instructions. Did you use compound predicates?

3. CRITICAL THINKING Do you think simple sentences or compound sentences are better to use when giving instructions? Explain.

SPEAKING AND LISTENING

Practice following verbal directions that have several steps. Take notes, make a list, or draw a diagram while listening. Ask questions about anything that is confusing. Ask for help if you need it. Give verbal driving directions to your house while a partner takes notes. Check your partner's notes. Correct any mistakes.

- Sentences begin with a capital letter, end with end punctuation, and express a complete thought.

- Sentences have a subject and a predicate. The simple subject tells who or what the sentence is about.

- The simple subject and all the words that describe it make up the complete subject. Some sentences have compound subjects.

- The subject of a sentence usually comes before a verb. However, some sentences are exceptions.

- The simple predicate is the main verb or verb phrase in a sentence. Some sentences have compound predicates.

- The complete predicate includes the simple predicate and the words that describe it. Part of the predicate can come before the subject.

- Sentences can have one of four purposes: statement, question, command or request, or exclamation. Sentences can be declarative, interrogative, imperative, or exclamatory.

- A simple sentence is one independent clause. A simple sentence may have a compound subject or a compound predicate.

- A compound sentence has two or more independent clauses joined with a coordinating conjunction. A comma comes before the coordinating conjunction.

Word Bank

capital letter

complete predicate

complete subject

compound
   predicate

compound
   sentence

compound subject

declarative
   sentence

end punctuation

exclamatory
   sentence

imperative sentence

interrogative
   sentence

sentence

simple predicate

simple sentence

simple subject

Part A Find the word or words in the Word Bank to complete each sentence. Write the answer on your paper.

1. The uppercase form of a letter such as *A* is a _____.

2. A period, a question mark, and an exclamation point are all examples of _____.

3. A _____ is a sentence that makes a statement.

4. The simple predicate and all of the words that describe it is the _____.

5. Two independent clauses joined by a coordinating conjunction form a _____.

6. Two or more simple predicates connected by a conjunction form a _____.

7. An _____ is a sentence that asks a question.

8. A _____ is a group of words that expresses a complete thought.

9. The _____ is the noun or pronoun that the sentence is about.

10. An _____ is a sentence that gives a command.

11. A _____ tells the condition or what the subject does, did, or will do.

12. Two or more simple subjects connected by a conjunction form a _____.

13. A _____ is the simple subject and all the words that describe it.

14. An _____ is a sentence that shows strong feeling.

15. A _____ is one independent clause.

Part B Write the letter of the word that describes the purpose of each sentence.

16. Listen to this.
   A declarative sentence   C imperative sentence
   B interrogative sentence   D exclamatory sentence

17. Do you want to be a stand-up comic?
   A declarative sentence   C imperative sentence
   B interrogative sentence   D exclamatory sentence

18. Experience and talent are the keys to success.
   A declarative sentence   C imperative sentence
   B interrogative sentence   D exclamatory sentence

Part C Write *S* if the group of words is a sentence. If it is not a sentence, add other words to make it a sentence.

19. The ball landed in the field.

20. As usual, each of the boys on the team.

21. Practicing at four o'clock instead of three on Monday.

Part D Write each sentence on your paper. Underline the simple subject once and the simple predicate twice. Then write *simple* or *compound*.

22. The car sputtered and came to a stop.

23. His parents and the mechanic at the garage had warned him.

24. That strange noise scared the dog.

25. He did not listen to his parents, and he bought the car anyway.

Test Tip

Restate test directions in your own words. Think about what you are expected to do. Your answer is more likely to be complete and correct.

Sentence Patterns

L ook at the autumn forest in this photograph. Can you find a pattern in the colored treetops? Many things in nature, such as a rainbow or the shape of a honeycomb, follow patterns. You can also see patterns in things that people do, such as patchwork quilts. What patterns do you see in nature or in your daily life?

Sentences have patterns, too. Understanding those patterns can help you write sentences that will improve your writing. The English language has many kinds of sentences. Chapter 10 focuses on six kinds of sentences that are commonly used.

GOALS FOR LEARNING

- To identify intransitive verbs in sentences
- To diagram sentences with intransitive verbs
- To identify direct objects in sentences
- To diagram sentences with direct objects
- To identify indirect objects in sentences
- To diagram sentences with indirect objects
- To identify object complements in sentences
- To diagram sentences with object complements
- To identify predicate nouns in sentences
- To diagram sentences with predicate nouns
- To identify predicate adjectives in sentences
- To diagram sentences with predicate adjectives

Reading Strategy: Predicting

Predicting allows you to think before and after you read. Before you read, think about what a text might be about. After reading, think about how your ideas have changed. Keep these things in mind as you make predictions:

- Ask yourself what you already know about a topic.
- After reading some of the text, decide if you need to change your prediction.
- Ask yourself how well you were able to make a correct prediction.

Key Vocabulary Words

Intransitive verb A verb that does not pass an action from the subject to another person or thing

Transitive verb A verb that shows action passed from the subject of the sentence toward another person or thing

Direct object The noun or pronoun that receives the action from a transitive verb

Indirect object A noun or pronoun that tells who receives the direct object of the verb

Complement A word that completes the meaning of the verb

Object complement A noun or an adjective that follows the verb and refers to a direct object

Linking verb A verb that joins the subject with a noun, pronoun, or adjective in the predicate; it is always a state-of-being verb

Predicate noun A noun or pronoun that follows a linking verb and renames the subject

Predicate adjective An adjective that follows a linking verb and tells about the subject

Intransitive Verbs

Intransitive verb

A verb that does not pass an action from the subject to another person or thing

NOTE

Sometimes people use abbreviations in place of longer words. Take a look at these abbreviations. You will see them in this lesson. S = subject, V = verb, Adj. = adjective, Adv. = adverb.

The most basic kind of sentence is one with an **intransitive verb.** An intransitive verb does not pass the action from a subject to another person or thing. It does not need an object to complete the meaning in a sentence. This kind of sentence expresses a complete thought with a subject and a verb (or predicate).

▶ **EXAMPLE 1**

   S   V   S   V
She is laughing.   The rowboat sank.

Adjectives and Adverbs with Intransitive Verbs

Sentences with intransitive verbs may have adjectives and adverbs. An adjective describes the subject. An adverb tells more about the verb. An adverb may come at the beginning of a sentence or between the helping verb and the main verb.

▶ **EXAMPLE 2**

Adj. Adj.   S   V Adv.
The newborn baby cried loudly.

Practice A

Write each sentence on your paper. Write *S* above the subject and *V* above the verb or verb phrase. Write *Adj.* above any adjectives and *Adv.* above any adverbs.

1. Victor can run fast.

2. That little baby is always smiling.

3. Alison practices often.

4. The old radio works.

5. Yesterday it rained hard.

Reading Strategy:
Predicting

Recall your knowledge
of verbs. Use what
you know to make
a prediction about
intransitive verbs.

Prepositions in Intransitive Verb Sentences

A sentence with intransitive verbs may have a prepositional phrase. The prepositional phrase may be an adjective phrase that describes the subject. It may be an adverb phrase that tells more about the verb.

▶ **EXAMPLE 3**

       S   Adj. Phrase   V
The woman behind me coughed. (Which woman coughed?)

       S   V   Adv. Phrase
Carlos is walking to the library. (Where is Carlos walking?)

Practice B

Write each sentence on your paper. Draw a line between the complete subject and complete predicate. Underline the prepositional phrase or phrases in each sentence.

1. Madison went to school.

2. Mr. DeLeo works at the post office.

3. The gas station on the corner closed.

4. Our friends from Ohio are visiting for two weeks.

5. The basket of flowers fell from the porch.

Questions and Commands with Intransitive Verbs

A sentence with an intransitive verb can ask a question. Part of the verb phrase can help form the question. It comes before the subject. A sentence with an intransitive verb can also be a command or request. The subject *you* is understood. The entire sentence in a command or a request is the complete predicate.

▶ **EXAMPLE 4**

V   S   V   S   V
Is the actor crying?   (You) Come to the park.

Reading Strategy:
Predicting

Think about your prediction. What changes can you make to it?

Practice C

Write the subject and simple predicate for each sentence.

1. Is Annette practicing?

2. Are you listening to the radio?

3. Did anyone call?

4. Come with me to the movie.

5. Listen to the teacher.

Compound Subjects, Predicates, and Sentences

A sentence with an intransitive verb may have a compound subject or a compound predicate.

▶ **EXAMPLE 5**

Compound Subject	Alma and Hector will go next.
Compound Predicate	He will sit and wave in a parade.

Join two sentences with intransitive verbs to form a compound sentence. Use a coordinating conjunction and a comma.

▶ **EXAMPLE 6**

Dr. Taylor laughed loudly, but Mr. Wilson only smiled.

Practice D

Each sentence has a compound subject or a compound predicate. Write each sentence. Underline the simple subject once. Underline the simple predicate twice.

1. The book and the pencil fell on the floor.

2. Marilyn laughed first and then cried.

3. Lisa and Rico were on time, but Alex was not on time.

4. Clarissa studied, and then she read for an hour.

5. The actors and director bowed on the stage, but the writer stayed behind the curtain.

Sentence Diagrams with Intransitive Verbs

Subjects and Predicates

Objectives

■ To identify the subject and predicate in sentences with intransitive verbs
■ To identify adjectives, adverbs, and prepositional phrases in sentences
■ To diagram sentences with intransitive verbs

A sentence diagram is a picture of a sentence. It helps you see the parts of the sentence more clearly. When you diagram, you identify the parts to see how they work together.

To diagram a sentence with an intransitive verb:

1. Find the simple subject (noun or pronoun) and the simple predicate (verb or verb phrase) in the sentence.

▶ **EXAMPLE 1**

The daring woman in the blue jumpsuit skied expertly down the mountain.

2. Write the simple subject and the simple predicate on a horizontal line.

3. Draw a short vertical line between the subject and predicate.

▶ **EXAMPLE 2**

woman | skied

Reading Strategy:
Predicting

Preview the lesson title and the diagrams in this lesson. What do you think this lesson is about?

Practice A

Diagram each sentence with an intransitive verb.

1. Snow fell.

2. Susan is smiling.

3. Dogs are barking.

4. Jennifer will dance.

5. Rain is falling.

Adjectives, Adverbs, and Prepositional Phrases

To add other words to a diagram with an intransitive verb:

1. Below the subject, write the adjectives and prepositional phrases that describe the subject.

2. Place adjectives (including articles) on slanted lines.

3. Below the verb, write the adverbs and prepositional phrases that describe the verb.

▶ **EXAMPLE 3**

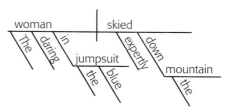

Compound Subjects and Compound Predicates

A sentence with an intransitive verb can have a compound subject and a compound predicate. Some sentences with intransitive verbs are compound sentences.

▶ **EXAMPLE 4**

Compound Subject   Maria and Kaitlin sang.

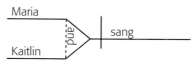

Reading Strategy:
Predicting

Think about your prediction at the beginning of this lesson. What details about diagramming can you now add to make your prediction more specific?

▶ **EXAMPLE 5**

Compound Verb   He arrived late and is sitting in the kitchen.

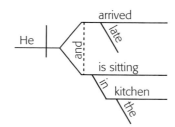

▶ **EXAMPLE 6**

Compound Sentence   Nat walks fast, so we ran ahead.

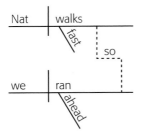

Practice B

Diagram each sentence with an intransitive verb. Follow the directions for diagramming that begin on page 264.

1. The school band went on a trip.

2. Everyone on the bus was laughing and singing.

3. Students and parents had been gone for a week.

4. Photographers were everywhere, and reporters wrote quickly.

5. Band members beamed happily into the camera.

VOCABULARY BUILDER

Unique and *Unusual*
People often confuse the words *unique* and *unusual*. Use *unique* when you mean "one of a kind."
     Each snowflake is *unique*.
Use *unusual* when you mean "out of the ordinary."
     The warm weather is *unusual* for December.
Complete each sentence by writing *unique* or *unusual*.

1. Each human being in the world is _____.
2. The sunset last evening was _____.
3. Every person's fingerprints are _____.
4. What an _____ choice—to wear boots in June!
5. It is _____ to live in the same town one's whole life.

REVIEW

Lesson 10-1

Write each sentence on your paper. Draw a vertical line between the complete subject and the complete predicate.

1. The ball bounced over the fence.

2. My best friend from school moved to California.

3. They were singing and dancing in the musical.

Write each sentence. Write *S* above the subject and *V* above the intransitive verb or verb phrase. Underline the complete subject once and the complete predicate twice.

4. Which students are in the band room?

5. Everyone in the band will ride on the bus.

Lesson 10-2

Diagram each of the sentences with an intransitive verb.

6. We were giggling about a silly joke.

7. Kira just smiled, but Jovan laughed loudly.

8. The little boy knocked on our door.

9. Tina and Louie work for their father after school.

10. Suddenly, the man arose and left.

Direct Objects

Objectives

- To identify direct objects
- To identify subjects and predicates in sentences with direct objects
- To identify adjectives, adverbs, and prepositional phrases in sentences with direct objects
- To write sentences with transitive verbs and direct objects

Transitive verb

A verb that shows action passed from the subject of the sentence toward another person or thing

Direct object

The noun or pronoun that receives the action from a transitive verb

Reading Strategy:
Predicting

Now that you know about intransitive verbs, predict what you think transitive verbs are.

Transitive Verbs and Direct Objects

The two main kinds of verbs are transitive and intransitive. A **transitive verb** transfers action from a sentence's subject to another person or thing. The person or thing that receives the action is the **direct object.**

▶ **EXAMPLE 1**

Jake mowed the backyard. (What did Jake mow?)

A sentence with a transitive verb has a direct object. The direct object of the predicate is a noun or pronoun. The direct object answers *what* or *whom* about the predicate.

▶ **EXAMPLE 2**

      S   V   DO

Dr. Ramirez made breakfast.

Practice A

Write each direct object. The transitive verb is in bold.

1. He **found** the book.
2. Rosa **took** notes.
3. The teacher **praised** him.
4. The farmer **planted** corn.
5. Len **raised** his hand.

NOTE

Sometimes people use abbreviations in place of longer words. Take a look at this abbreviation. You will see it in this lesson. DO = direct object.

Adjectives and Direct Objects

Use adjectives to describe nouns used as direct objects.

▶ **EXAMPLE 3**

S   V   Adj.Adj.DO
David sold his old car.

Practice B

Write the direct object in each sentence on your paper. The verb is in bold. Do not include adjectives.

1. Len **lost** his wallet.
2. They **ate** an early supper.
3. He **is washing** his mom's car.
4. The next-door neighbors **are painting** their house.
5. She **sang** a beautiful song.

Pronouns and Direct Objects

When a pronoun is the direct object, use the object form. Personal pronouns in the object form include *me, you, him, her, it, us,* and *them.* Refer to the chart on page 39 for help.

▶ **EXAMPLE 4**

S   V   DO
Susan drove them to the park.

Practice C

Write the correct pronoun on your paper. Remember, when a pronoun is a direct object, use the object form.

1. Did you see (he, him)?
2. Fred saw (she, her) at the library.
3. Before he put on his sneakers, he cleaned (they, them).
4. Tina helped (we, us) with our math homework.
5. He likes (I, me).

Reading Strategy:
Predicting

Think about your earlier prediction. How well did you predict what transitive verbs are?

Adverbs in Sentences with Direct Objects

A sentence with a direct object must have a subject and a transitive verb. It may also have an adverb.

▶ **EXAMPLE 5**

Adv.   S   V   DO
Luckily, Julie found her backpack.

S   V   DO   Adv.
David read an interesting article yesterday.

Prepositional Phrases with Direct Objects

A sentence with a direct object may have a prepositional phrase. The phrase may tell about the subject, the transitive verb, or the direct object.

▶ **EXAMPLE 6**

S   V   DO Adv. Phrase
Matt ate an apple at lunch. (*At lunch* is an adverb phrase that describes the transitive verb *ate.* When did Matt eat an apple?)

S   V   DO Adj. Phrase
Matt ate both apples in his lunch. (*In his lunch* is an adjective phrase that describes *apples.* Which apples?)

Practice D

Write each complete predicate. Write *V* above transitive verbs and *DO* above direct objects. Write *Adj. phrase* above adjective phrases, and *Adv. phrase* above adverb phrases.

1. Carol wrote a letter to her Uncle Albert.
2. Sara bought the sneakers with very small trim.
3. He carried the two bags of toys into the house.
4. We fed the fish in the tank before school.
5. We filled the fish tank in the hall today.

Direct Objects in Questions and Commands

Sentences with direct objects and transitive verbs can be questions or commands. Part of the verb may come before the subject to help form the question. To find the subject in a question, change the question to a statement.

▶ **EXAMPLE 7**

   V S V   DO   Adv. phrase
Did I see a cat on your porch? (I did see a cat.)

   DO V S   V   Adv.
What is he doing today? (He is doing what today.)

Remember that the subject of a command or request is understood to be *you*.

▶ **EXAMPLE 8**

   S   V   DO
(You) Finish your homework.

   S   V   DO
(You) Take the cat inside the house.

Practice E

Write the simple subject, the simple predicate, and the direct object in each sentence. Write your answers on your paper.

1. Have you read that article?
2. Take this book to the library.
3. Complete your essay at home.
4. What will he do after graduation?
5. Which of these do you want?

The word *compound* comes from a French word that means "put together." It has many meanings that all share the idea of blending several things into one.

Compound Predicates, Compound Objects, and Compound Sentences

A sentence with a direct object can have a compound predicate and a compound object. A compound object is two or more objects in a sentence. The direct objects are connected by a conjunction. You may also join sentences with direct objects together using a conjunction. This makes a compound sentence.

▶ **EXAMPLE 9**

Compound Predicate	We cooked and served lunch.
Compound Direct Object	She will play golf or hockey.
Compound Sentence	I saw Brad, but he did not have my coat.

Each part of a compound predicate may have its own direct object.

▶ **EXAMPLE 10**

         S   V   DO   V   DO
We arranged the flowers and put them on the table.

Practice F

Decide whether each sentence has a compound predicate or compound object. Write *compound predicate* or *compound object* on your paper.

1. Are you reading that book or this one?
2. Tim has a part-time job and takes classes at a community college.
3. They returned the wallet and its contents to the owner.
4. Virginia plays the piano and the violin.
5. Alex fed and walked his dog.

Sentence Diagrams with Direct Objects

Objectives

- To identify the subject and predicate in sentences with direct objects
- To identify adjectives, adverbs, and prepositional phrases in sentences
- To diagram sentences with direct objects

To diagram a sentence with direct objects:

1. Identify the subject, predicate, and direct object.
2. Place the object on a line with the subject and predicate.
3. Draw a short vertical line to separate the predicate and the direct object.
4. Put each adverb, adjective, or prepositional phrase under the word it describes or tells about.

▶ **EXAMPLE 1**

Amber baked potatoes for dinner.

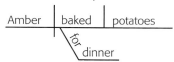

Reading Strategy:
Predicting

Make a prediction about what you will learn in this chapter. What details did you use to make your prediction?

5. If a sentence is a question, change the question to a statement. Then draw the diagram.

▶ **EXAMPLE 2**

Question	Statement
Did you find your backpack?	You did find your backpack.

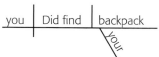

6. In a command or request the subject *you* is understood. Put it in parentheses.

▶ **EXAMPLE 3**

Change that dirty shirt immediately.

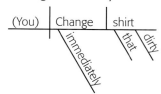

7. Diagram a sentence with a direct object and a compound predicate this way.

▶ **EXAMPLE 4**

Abigail bought a new sweater and wore it to the game.

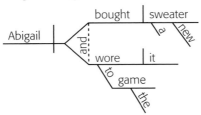

8. Diagram a sentence with compound objects this way.

▶ **EXAMPLE 5**

Jack left his notebook and pen in his locker.

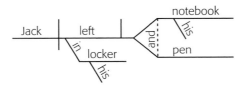

9. Diagram a compound sentence with direct objects this way.

▶ **EXAMPLE 6**

Kaitlin wrote a poem, and Devon painted a mural.

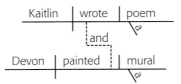

Practice A

Diagram each sentence. Refer to the examples on pages 273–274.

1. Stop that noise immediately!

2. Brayden left his jacket and gloves in the car.

3. Have you seen Sally?

4. He fixed the car, but it still had a problem.

5. Bill and Mary bought tickets for the early show.

REVIEW

Lesson 10-3

Create three columns on your paper with the headings *Subject, Predicate*, and *Direct Object.* Identify the simple subject, simple predicate, and direct object in each sentence. Write them in the correct column. Some have a compound direct object or are compound sentences.

1. Sign the contract on Tuesday, and fax it on Wednesday.

2. Did Eva purchase a new CD at the mall?

3. Our family likes apples and oranges for dessert.

Write each sentence. Write *S* above the subject, *V* above the verb, and *DO* above the direct object.

4. Evan's dad sold an expensive computer yesterday.

5. Laura described her new dress to her friends.

Lesson 10-4

Diagram each of the sentences with a direct object.

6. Have you seen that movie?

7. We bought a ticket for the early show.

8. First, read the book, and then see the movie.

9. He bought a book and read a story about UFOs today.

10. Otis recited the long poem and the story without a single mistake.

Indirect Objects

Objectives

- To identify indirect objects in sentences
- To identify subjects, predicates, and direct objects in sentences with indirect objects
- To identify adjectives and prepositional phrases in sentences with indirect objects
- To write sentences with indirect objects

Indirect object

A noun or pronoun that tells who receives the direct object of the verb

 NOTE

Sometimes people use abbreviations in place of longer words. Take a look at this abbreviation. You will see it in this lesson. IO = indirect object.

Some sentences have a transitive verb, a direct object, and an **indirect object.** An indirect object is a noun or pronoun. It tells who will receive the direct object of the verb.

The indirect object comes after the simple predicate and before the direct object. An indirect object answers the question *to whom* or *for whom* about the predicate. It can also answer *to what* or *for what*.

▶ **EXAMPLE 1**

    S   V   IO   DO
Christa wrote Paul a note. (Christa wrote a note *to whom?*)

Practice A

Write the indirect object in each sentence on your paper.

1. Joanna gave her mother a gift.
2. I wrote myself a reminder.
3. The school mailed students their final report cards.
4. I offered Chan some assistance.
5. Mrs. Lopez brought me my homework.

Indirect Object or Object of a Preposition?

An indirect object is never part of a prepositional phrase.

▶ **EXAMPLE 2**

| Indirect Object | He sent me an e-mail message. |
| Object of the Preposition | He sent an e-mail message to me. |

Reading Strategy:
Predicting

Think about the title of this lesson. Predict what this page will be about.

Practice B

Decide whether the word in bold is an indirect object or the object of the preposition. Write *indirect object* or *object of the preposition* on your paper.

1. Lou gave his **dog** a treat.

2. Helena poured some milk for her **cat.**

3. The store sent coupons to its best **customers.**

4. The server brought **us** lunch.

5. Mrs. Jenkins handed my paycheck to **me.**

Practice C

Create four columns on your paper. Write the headings *Subject, Predicate, Indirect Object,* and *Direct Object.* Identify the simple subject, simple predicate, indirect object, and direct object in each sentence. Write each in the correct column.

1. The director gave the band members their music.

2. Fred asked Mr. Smith a question.

3. The music company sent the school a bill.

4. Mrs. Arloff offered the students her help.

5. She taught her friend sign language.

Pronouns as Indirect Objects

When the indirect object is a pronoun, the pronoun must be in the object form. Remember that the object pronouns are *me, you, him, her, it, us,* and *them.*

NOTE
A sentence cannot have an indirect object unless it has a direct object.

▶ **EXAMPLE 3**

```
       S       V    IO      DO
His teacher offered him some help.
```

Practice D

Complete each sentence with the correct pronoun.

1. Tom gave (I, me) the message.
2. Fred sent (he, him) a letter.
3. Martha told (she, her) the answer.
4. That teacher taught (we, us) Spanish.
5. We served (they, them) dinner.

Adjectives and Adjective Phrases in Sentences with Indirect Objects

Sentences with indirect objects can have adjectives and adjective phrases that describe indirect objects.

▶ **EXAMPLE 4**

    S   V   Adj. IO   DO
Amanda wrote her boss a memo.

    S   V Adj. IO   Adj. Phrase DO
She gave her cousin from Idaho a necklace.

Writing Tip

When writing, you may want to mix indirect objects and prepositional phrases. This will add variety to your writing. For example, *Dad gave me his old car. I did not expect him to give it to me.*

Practice E

Write each sentence on your paper. Add an adjective or adjective phrase to describe the indirect object in bold.

1. Pat sent her **friend** from school a message.
2. Marcus offered the **woman** his seat.
3. The teacher told the **boy** the answer.
4. We made our **neighbor** an offer.
5. We asked the **mechanic** a question about the car.

Indirect Objects in Questions and Commands

A sentence with an indirect object can be a question. Part of the verb phrase can come before the subject. The question can begin with an interrogative pronoun.

▶ **EXAMPLE 5**

V S V IO   DO
Will you give Dana a present?

S   V IO   DO
Who sent you that sweater?

A command or request can have an indirect object.

▶ **EXAMPLE 6**

S   V   IO   DO
(You) Show the doctor your cut.

S   V IO   DO
(You) Give me his new coat.

Practice F

Write the indirect object in each sentence on your paper.

1. Tell him the answer.

2. Did Amanda give Jeff the volleyball?

3. Would you lend me your sweater for the evening?

4. Please teach me Spanish.

5. When did Anna write you that note?

Compound Objects

Sentences can have more than one indirect object after a predicate. These are compound objects.

▶ **EXAMPLE 7**

Fix Tom and Lin a sandwich.

Will you give Greg and Sharon some milk?

Jorge read his cousin and his neighbor a folktale.

Practice G

Complete each sentence with a compound indirect object. Write each sentence on your paper.

1. Give _____ more time.

2. Please tell _____ the answer.

3. Uncle Fred made _____ a model airplane.

4. Would you lend _____ five dollars?

5. I offered _____ more juice.

Practice H

Arrange each group of words to make a sentence with an indirect object. Write each sentence on your paper.

1. them served we dinner the

2. gave rose Erica Julio a

3. the score told audience the announcer the

4. myself snack fixed I a

5. a him she handed dollar

Gabi is teaching her friend sign language.

Sentence Diagrams with Indirect Objects

To diagram a sentence with indirect objects:

1. Draw a slanted line and a horizontal line under the predicate.

2. Leave the slanted line blank.

3. Write the indirect object on the horizontal line.

▶ **EXAMPLE 1**

Emilio gave me a warm jacket.

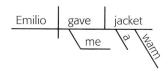

Maria gave Jason advice about CDs.

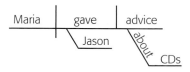

4. If a sentence with indirect objects is a question, change the question to a statement.

▶ **EXAMPLE 2**

Question

Can you give my brother and me part-time jobs?

Statement

You can give my brother and me part-time jobs.

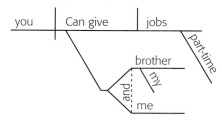

Diagram each sentence with indirect objects on your paper. Look at the examples on page 281.

1. Pass me the bread.

2. Did Jack lend Larry his car?

3. Jane made Yolanda an offer for her bike.

4. Lana sent her aunts and her uncles thank-you notes.

5. Will you bring Tina and me an apple?

BUILDING RESEARCH SKILLS

Preparing Citations and Bibliographies

A bibliography is a list of sources that you use to research a topic. It includes information such as the author, title, and publisher. One way to organize your sources is to list them by the authors' last names. This is one way to organize information for a book:

Author last name, First name. *Title of Book*. Place of Publication: Publisher, Year of Publication.

This is a way to organize information from an article on the Internet:

Author last name, First name. "Title of Article." *Title of Online Publication*. Date of Publication. Date you accessed the Web site <electronic address>.

Find a book and a Web magazine that could be used for research.

1. Look at the authors' last names for the book and the Web magazine. Write a bibliography entry for the source whose author's name is first alphabetically.

2. Write the bibliography entry for the source you did not use in Question 1.

3. CRITICAL THINKING What are some of the similarities between a book entry and a Web site entry on a bibliography? What are some of the differences?

REVIEW

Lesson 10-5

Write each sentence on your paper. Write *S* above the subject and *V* above the transitive verb. Write *IO* above the indirect object and *DO* above the direct object.

1. Sue brought Rita and Pam some books.

2. After dinner, Grandpa told the family some old stories.

3. Will you make Sam and me some lunch?

Write the indirect object in each sentence. If a sentence does not have an indirect object, write *none*.

4. Alicia paid me for the tickets.

5. She gave the money to me yesterday.

Lesson 10-6

Diagram each sentence with an indirect object on your paper.

6. Dan gave Meg and Lian a ride to work.

7. Who gave you that book?

8. Father prepared Danny and Anna their lunch.

9. Will you give Sean my phone number?

10. Nancy asked Joan a question.

Object Complements

Objectives

■ To identify object complements in sentences

■ To write sentences with object complements

Complement
A word that completes the meaning of the verb

Object complement
A noun or an adjective that follows the verb and refers to a direct object

Reading Strategy:
Predicting

What can you predict about the content of this lesson?

NOTE

Abbreviations are often used in place of longer words. This abbreviation is used in this lesson: OC = object complement.

A **complement** is a word that completes an idea expressed by a verb. Some sentences have a transitive verb, a direct object, and an **object complement.** An object complement is a noun or an adjective that follows the verb. It refers to the direct object. The object complement comes after the direct object in the sentence.

▶ **EXAMPLE 1**

       S   V   DO   OC
The Rands named their daughter Olivia.
(*Olivia* is a noun that renames the direct object *daughter*.)

Practice A

Write the object complement in each sentence.

1. The people elected him mayor of the city.

2. The frost turned the leaves bright red.

3. Happiness made the girl beautiful.

4. Everyone calls him a great actor.

5. Emilio considers Alison smart.

Practice B

Complete each sentence with an object complement.

1. Do not make the soup _____.

2. Students in Mr. Alvarez's class find his tests _____.

3. The hot oven turned the dough _____.

4. The new parents named their baby _____.

5. Andy considers the comic strip _____.

Reading Strategy:
Predicting

Based on past lessons, what do you predict the rest of this lesson will cover?

 Writing Tip

The words *complement* and *compliment* sound alike. *Compliment* is praise. When you write, be sure to choose the correct word. For example, *the noun* complements *the direct object. The boy gave his friend a* compliment.

Object Complements in Questions and Commands

A sentence with an object complement can be a question or a command.

▶ **EXAMPLE 2**

```
   V              S      V   DO  OC
Will that dark room make you sleepy?

   V     DO       OC
Make Alison the leader.
```

Practice C

Write the object complement in each sentence.

1. Will you make the cake chocolate?

2. Did the polls name him the winner?

3. Has Samantha found the instructions helpful?

4. Make the chili spicier, please.

5. Turn the heat in the oven down.

Compound Object Complements

The object complement can be compound. The object complements are joined together with a conjunction.

▶ **EXAMPLE 3**

```
  S    V       DO     OC        OC
They painted the garage beige and brown.
```

Practice D

Write each object complement. Not all sentences have one.

1. Riley and his friend Ted found the spring day perfect.

2. The sun had turned the air warm and inviting.

3. They judged the situation perfect for a fishing trip.

4. "I consider myself an outstanding fisherman," said Ted.

5. "I would call you a beginner," said Riley.

Object Complements with a Compound Direct Object or Compound Predicate

Sentences with a compound direct object can have an object complement after each direct object.

▶ **EXAMPLE 4**

    S   V   DO   OC   DO   OC
They elected Corey president and Vonetta treasurer.

In a sentence with a compound predicate, each predicate can have a direct object. Each direct object can have an object complement.

▶ **EXAMPLE 5**

    V   DO   OC   V DO OC
Do not make the dip spicy or serve it cold.

Practice E

Write each sentence on your paper. Write *DO* over each direct object and *OC* over each object complement.

1. The game made the players hot and tired.

2. We find computer studies fun and typing class easy.

3. The team named Jill the MVP and voted her captain.

4. The cool weather turned the leaves gold and orange.

5. The flight delay made him anxious and others angry.

Sentence Diagrams with Object Complements

Objectives

- To identify object complements in sentences
- To diagram sentences with object complements

Reading Strategy:
Predicting

Predict how an object complement may be added to a diagram.

1. Place the object complement on the baseline of the diagram next to the direct object.

2. Separate the object complement from the direct object with a line slanted toward the direct object.

▶ **EXAMPLE 1**

Jennifer dyed the yarn red.

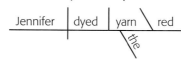

3. If a sentence with an object complement is a question, change it to a statement. Then draw the diagram.

▶ **EXAMPLE 2**

Question	Statement
Did Brittany find it fun?	Brittany did find it fun.

4. If a sentence with an object complement is a command or request, the subject *you* is understood. Put *you* in parentheses on the diagram.

▶ **EXAMPLE 3**

Make Sarah the leader.

5. Diagram sentences with a compound subject or compound predicate and an object complement this way.

▶ **EXAMPLE 4**

Runners and bikers consider the new trail excellent.

6. Diagram sentences with a compound direct object and an object complement this way.

▶ **EXAMPLE 5**

The city council chose Mrs. Ozawa president and Mr. Hemsi secretary.

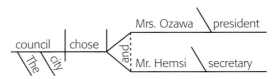

7. Diagram sentences with a compound object complement this way.

▶ **EXAMPLE 6**

Mr. Santos considered our project interesting and educational.

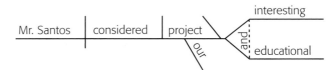

Practice A

Diagram each sentence with an object complement.

1. Jerry found his computer class helpful and enjoyable.

2. The students elected Jack treasurer.

3. Make this sauce thicker.

4. They named Mrs. Santiago "Woman of the Year."

5. Did Grace paint her room yellow?

REVIEW

Lesson 10-7

Write the object complements in each sentence.

1. They declared the young boy the winner.

2. We made Rashad group leader and declared Joe the secretary.

3. They call their hamster Swifty.

4. Old age has turned the dog's hair silver.

5. They dyed the wool brown.

Write each sentence. Write *S* above the subject and *V* above the transitive verb. Write *DO* above the direct object and *OC* above the object complement.

6. You made that meal delicious!

7. We named the white kitten Snowball and the black kitten Midnight.

8. Did you find that program interesting?

9. What makes him so shy and quiet?

10. Do you consider yourself an expert on the subject?

Lesson 10-8

Diagram each sentence with an object complement.

11. The wind turned the day cold.

12. The class will elect Carlotta president and Ethan vice-president.

13. Can we call the puppy Pooch?

14. Mya and Danzel found the play long and boring.

15. Paint the inside of your closet purple.

Predicate Nouns

Linking Verbs and Predicate Nouns

Sentences may have a **linking verb** and a **predicate noun.** A linking verb joins the subject to a word in the predicate of a sentence. A linking verb is always a state-of-being verb. *Feel, look, become, remain,* and *be* are linking verbs.

▶ **EXAMPLE 1**

| Action Verb | Hector studies art. |
| Linking Verb | Hector is an art student. |

A linking verb joins the subject to a predicate noun. The predicate noun is a noun or pronoun that renames the subject. It helps the sentence express a complete thought.

▶ **EXAMPLE 2**

          S   LV   PN
That neighborhood was once a farm.

Linking verb

A verb that joins the subject with a noun, pronoun, or adjective in the predicate; it is always a state-of-being verb

Predicate noun

A noun or pronoun that follows a linking verb and renames the subject

Reading Strategy:
Predicting

What details do you already know about the words *predicate* and *noun*? How can these details help you to predict what a predicate noun is?

Practice A

In each sentence, write *S* above the simple subject and *LV* above the linking verb. Write *PN* above the predicate noun.

1. She became my friend in first grade.

2. The song writer is also a poet.

3. The winner of the race was Emily.

4. The woman in the picture is a neighbor.

5. Charles will be the director.

Predicate Nouns and Adjectives

Adjectives often come before the predicate noun. The adjective describes the predicate noun.

▶ **EXAMPLE 3**

   S LV Adj. Adj.   PN
Ling is a good auto mechanic.
(The adjectives *good* and *auto* describe the noun *mechanic.*)

Practice B

Write the predicate nouns and adjectives that describe it.

1. George Washington was the first president.
2. Aunt Marie is a great cook.
3. Carol has always been a friendly, helpful person.
4. Ted has become an excellent soccer coach.
5. Ms. Marino is a popular teacher.

Predicate Noun or Direct Object?

Do not confuse a direct object with a predicate noun. Remember, a direct object receives the action of a transitive verb. A predicate noun follows an intransitive verb and renames the subject.

▶ **EXAMPLE 4**

Direct Object   Alicia introduced the new student.
                  (*Student* receives the action of the transitive verb *introduced*.)

Predicate Noun Alicia is a new student.
                  (*Student* renames the subject *Alicia*.)

Practice C

Decide whether the bold word is a *direct object* or a *predicate noun*. Write your answer on your paper.

1. James plays **baseball** in the spring.

2. He is the team **captain.**

3. Tony is the league's best **catcher.**

4. He can also hit the **ball** a mile.

5. He is a good **hitter.**

NOTE

Do not confuse a predicate noun with an object of the preposition. A predicate noun is never the object of a preposition.

Adverbs and Prepositional Phrases

Sentences with predicate nouns can have an adverb or a prepositional phrase. Adverbs and prepositional phrases can answer questions about the linking verb.

▶ **EXAMPLE 5**

    S   LV   PN   Adv. phrase
She has been my neighbor for years.
(How long has she been a neighbor? She has been a neighbor *for years.*)

Sentences can have a prepositional phrase that describes the predicate noun.

▶ **EXAMPLE 6**

    S   LV   PN   Adj. phrase
She became the captain of our team.
(She became the captain of what? She became the captain *of our team.*)

Practice D

Write each sentence. Write *S* above the subject and *LV* above the linking verb. Write *PN* above the predicate noun.

1. Uruguay is a country in South America.

2. My cousin was a very popular actor.

3. Pasta is a common food in the United States.

4. Tina is my cousin from Winnipeg.

5. *Star Wars* is still Andy's favorite movie.

A sentence with a predicate noun can be a question. It can also be a command or a request.

▶ **EXAMPLE 7**

   LV   S   PN
Were you the one in the newspaper photo?

   LV   PN
Be a good neighbor.

Practice E

Write each sentence. Write *S* above the subject and *LV* above the linking verb. Write *PN* above the predicate noun. If the subject *you* is understood, write it in.

1. Was Franklin Pierce a U.S. president?

2. Canada is a country in North America.

3. Please be my friend.

4. Picasso is a famous Spanish artist.

5. Is that your house?

Compound Nouns and Sentences

A sentence with a predicate noun can have compound parts.

▶ **EXAMPLE 8**

> S   S LV   PN   PN
> Alvaro and Sita are excellent musicians and talented artists.

Combine two sentences with a conjunction to form a compound sentence.

▶ **EXAMPLE 9**

> S   LV   PN   S LV PN
> Deshawn is a defender now, but last year he was goalie.

Practice F

Write each sentence. Write *S* above the subject and *LV* above the linking verb. Write *PN* above the predicate noun. Sentences may be compound or have compound parts.

1. Joyce Carol Oates is a poet and a novelist.
2. Are those trees oaks or maples?
3. Gavin and his father are the night owls in the family.
4. Is that title a movie or a book?
5. Phil is a student, but he will be an architect some day.

SPELLING BUILDER

Practice with Contractions

Sometimes we combine a pronoun and a verb into a contraction. A contraction is a word made from two words by replacing one or more letters with an apostrophe.

Example

you + have = you've   he + will = he'll
she + would = she'd   I + have = I've

Combine each pair of words into a contraction. Use apostrophes to replace the letters you take out. Write the letters you take out.

1. he + is = _____
2. let + us = _____
3. they + have = _____
4. we + are = _____
5. I + would = _____

Sentence Diagrams with Predicate Nouns

To diagram a sentence with a predicate noun:

1. Write the predicate noun on the baseline of the diagram.

2. Separate the predicate noun from the linking verb with a line slanted toward the verb.

▶ **EXAMPLE 1**

Mr. Stamos is an excellent principal.

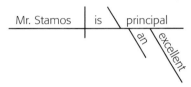

3. Some sentences with predicate nouns are questions. Change the question to a statement. Then draw the diagram.

▶ **EXAMPLE 2**

Question	Statement
Is that your brown jacket?	That is your brown jacket.

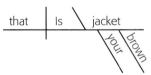

4. In a command or request, the subject *you* is understood. Put *you* in parentheses.

▶ **EXAMPLE 3**

Be a good student.

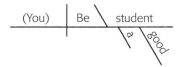

5. To diagram a compound predicate noun:

▶ **EXAMPLE 4**

Janine is a musician and an artist.

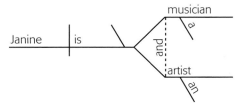

6. To diagram a compound sentence with predicate nouns:

▶ **EXAMPLE 5**

New York is my favorite city, but my home is Los Angeles.

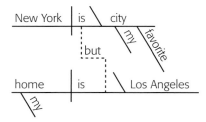

Practice A

Diagram each of the sentences with a predicate noun.

1. Who is she?

2. Kim became our class secretary.

3. Sue and Kelly have become good friends.

4. Two popular sports are soccer and baseball.

5. Annie has always been a great speaker, but she has never been a good listener.

REVIEW

Lesson 10-9

Write whether the verb in bold is a linking verb or action verb. Write *linking verb* or *action verb* on your paper. Remember, a linking verb never has a direct object.

1. **Be** a good friend.

2. Later I **am going** to the movies.

3. **Taste** this stew for me.

4. You **are** a good cook.

5. I **like** dinner at your house.

Write each sentence on your paper. Write *S* above the subject and *LV* above the linking verb. Write *PN* above the predicate noun.

6. Two popular Mexican foods are tacos and burritos.

7. Jupiter is the largest planet in the solar system.

8. Is Dan a friend of yours?

9. Who was that?

10. Lima is the capital of Peru.

Lesson 10-10

Diagram each of the sentences with a predicate noun.

11. Janelle is a good artist.

12. Be a responsible student and worker.

13. I am an unemployed singer, and Sal is the owner of a small theater.

14. Are they the champions?

15. Jack is a friend of mine.

Predicate Adjectives

Objectives

- To identify predicate adjectives
- To write sentences with predicate adjectives

Predicate adjective

An adjective that follows a linking verb and tells about the subject

 NOTE

Sometimes people use abbreviations in place of longer words. Take a look at this abbreviation. You will see it used in this lesson. PA = predicate adjective.

Predicate Adjectives and Linking Verbs

Some sentences have a linking verb and a **predicate adjective.** When an adjective appears after a linking verb, the adjective describes the subject. This adjective is called a predicate adjective. It is part of the complete predicate, but it describes the subject of the sentence.

▶ **EXAMPLE 1**

       S   LV PA   PA

The orange is juicy and sweet.

(*Juicy* and *sweet* are adjectives. What is juicy and sweet?)

Practice A

Decide whether the bold word is a predicate noun or predicate adjective.

1. Jim looks **old.**

2. That painting is a **work** of art.

3. The fish tastes **fresh.**

4. The music sounds **loud.**

5. Amanda is a **teacher** at a school.

Predicate Adjectives and Adverbs

A sentence with predicate adjectives may have adverbs that tell about the predicate adjectives. Adverbs of degree answer questions about adjectives.

▶ **EXAMPLE 2**

    S   LV   Adv. PA

Her plan sounded very risky.

Practice B

Write each sentence on your paper. Add an adverb of degree that tells about the predicate adjective in bold.

1. She looks **happy.**

2. He sounds **tired.**

3. The day turned **cold.**

4. They appeared **calm.**

5. You seem **worried.**

Prepositional Phrases

A sentence with a predicate adjective can have prepositional phrases that act as adverbs. They give more information about the predicate adjective.

▶ **EXAMPLE 3**

    S LV Adv.   PA Adv. phrase
She is always busy on Saturday.
(When is she always busy? She is always busy *on Saturday*.)

Practice C

Write each sentence. Underline the predicate adjectives. Add adverbs and prepositional phrases.

1. Yvonne looks amused.

2. The sky grew dark.

3. This salad tastes delicious.

4. Lydia seems quiet.

5. His notebook is neat.

Reading Strategy:
Predicting

Predict what other parts of a sentence may help to describe a predicate adjective.

Predicate Adjectives in Questions and Commands

A sentence with a predicate adjective may be a question. The predicate adjective may come right after the subject. Use the verb or part of a verb phrase to form the question.

▶ **EXAMPLE 4**

```
LV        S    LV   PA
```
Did his speech seem short?

A sentence with a predicate adjective may be a command or request. Commands are always in the present tense.

▶ **EXAMPLE 5**

```
LV   PA
```
Be quiet.

Practice D

Write each sentence on your paper. Underline the linking verb once and the predicate adjective twice.

1. Look friendly during the job interview.
2. Does the school day seem longer to you?
3. Was she excited about the play?
4. Will these flowers stay fresh until Friday?
5. Remain loyal and true to your friends.

Compound Predicate Adjectives

In a sentence, the predicate adjective may be compound.

▶ **EXAMPLE 6**

```
       S    LV   PA      PA
```
Roberto's speech was short and funny.

Reading Strategy:
Predicting

How do the details on this page help support your prediction?

NOTE

Remember that a compound sentence has two complete thoughts.

Practice E

Add compound predicate adjectives to the sentences.

1. The new curtains were _____ and _____.

2. The win was not _____ or _____.

3. Michael's new bike is _____ but not _____.

4. The month of May is _____ and _____.

5. After a big dinner, I am usually _____ and _____.

Compound Sentences with Predicate Adjectives

Add a conjunction to two sentences with predicate adjectives to form a compound sentence.

▶ **EXAMPLE 7**

S	LV	PA		S	LV	PA

Mrs. Cruz is usually serious, but Mr. Santos is always funny.

Practice D

First, write two related sentences with predicate adjectives. Then use one of these conjunctions—*and, for, or, but*—to create a compound sentence.

Lila's old car is clean but not dry.

Sentence Diagrams with Predicate Adjectives

To diagram a sentence with a predicate adjective:

1. Place the predicate adjective on the baseline.

2. Separate the predicate adjective from the verb with a line slanted toward the verb.

▶ **EXAMPLE 1**

The lilacs smelled sweet.

3. Place an adverb of degree under the adjective on a slanted line.

▶ **EXAMPLE 2**

The salad was very tasty.

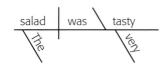

4. Some sentences with predicate adjectives are questions. Change the question to a statement. Then draw the diagram.

▶ **EXAMPLE 3**

Question	Statement
Was the movie exciting?	The movie was exciting.

5. In a command or request, the subject *you* is understood. Put *you* in parentheses.

Reading Strategy:
Predicting

Predict what you think
this next section will be
about.

▶ **EXAMPLE 4**

Be kind.

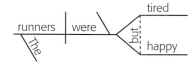

6. Diagram a compound predicate adjective this way.

▶ **EXAMPLE 5**

The runners were tired but happy.

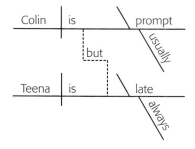

7. Diagram a compound sentence with predicate adjectives this way.

▶ **EXAMPLE 6**

Colin is usually prompt, but Teena is always late.

Practice A

Diagram each sentence with predicate adjectives on your paper. See the examples on pages 302–303 for help.

1. This morning was very windy, but the air was warm.

2. Stay quiet and absolutely still.

3. Is your puppy afraid of loud noises?

4. Is Emily usually calm during a thunderstorm?

5. He is tall, but I am strong.

Lesson 10-11

Complete each sentence with a predicate adjective.

1. My mom's cookies taste _____ and _____.

2. That couch appears _____, but it is actually _____.

Write *S* above the subject and *LV* above the linking verb. Write *PA* above the predicate adjective.

3. The lemon tasted sour.

4. Have they always been so active?

5. That computer is small but powerful.

Lesson 10-12

Diagram each sentence with predicate adjectives.

6. Does the air feel unusually chilly today?

7. Everyone seemed happy and carefree.

8. Be careful on that ladder!

9. Was my speech too long?

10. Ari looked serious, but Teresa seemed bored.

PUTTING IT ALL TOGETHER

1. Find a piece of your own writing.
2. In that piece, find an example of each sentence part listed. Write the abbreviation above each example.

Intransitive verb (IV)	Object complement (OC)
Direct object (DO)	Predicate noun (PN)
Indirect object (IO)	Predicate adjective (PA)

3. Review your writing. Which part of speech do you use most often in sentences? Which do you use least often?

Six Traits of Writing:
Organization order, ideas tied together

SENTENCE DIAGRAM REVIEW

Diagram each sentence on your paper.

1. Is Mrs. Simpson your math teacher?
2. The Smiths named their puppy Fluffy.
3. The blue van skidded right suddenly.
4. Sara ate a sandwich for lunch.
5. Did Rebecca seem nervous?
6. Send Jake a birthday card today and tell him about the party.
7. Janna painted the wall blue.
8. The football team will travel to Columbus and will play for the championship.
9. That house looks shabby and old.
10. Teresa won a set, but Jack won the match.
11. Did Rico send you an e-mail message?
12. Be nice to your sister!
13. After lunch, we played basketball for two hours.
14. Give me the hammer and then hand me some nails.
15. Her speech was lively and entertaining.

Athletic Trainer

Mia Cruz is an athletic trainer for a high school. She helps injured athletes and teaches them to prevent new injuries.

To provide the best care for athletes, Ms. Cruz takes notes on the players. These notes include details on the injuries and treatments of each player. Ms. Cruz uses both transitive and intransitive verbs when taking notes.

Read Ms. Cruz's notes and follow the directions.

HEALTH RECORD FORM

Trainer's Name: Mia Cruz

Player's Name: Cody Durham

Date of Injury/Illness: September 15, 2006

Description of Injury/Illness: During a soccer game, Cody fell to the ground. His right knee is very swollen and bruised. His injury is a sprain.

Rehabilitation Program: I gave him crutches and an air cast. He should ice and elevate his knee every hour.

Current Physical Restrictions: Limit movement. Use crutches for three days. Return to the trainer for further evaluation.

1. List an example of a linking verb in the notes. Write the predicate noun or predicate adjective that follows the linking verb. Then label it *predicate noun* or *predicate adjective*.

2. List two examples of transitive verbs in the notes. Write the direct object next to each verb on your paper.

3. **CRITICAL THINKING** What is the difference between the sentences in the rehabilitation and restriction sections? Explain your answer.

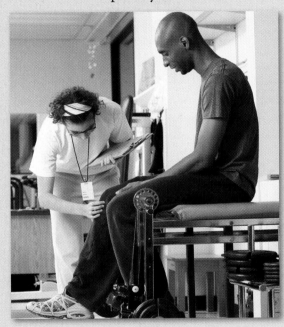

VIEWING

Visual aids or images often accompany word messages. Sometimes visuals can explain or show something better than words can. Think of a visual aid that an athletic trainer might use in his or her work. Share your ideas with a partner.

- An intransitive verb does not have a direct object.

- A transitive verb has a direct object. Direct objects can be nouns or object pronouns.

- Some sentences with direct objects have indirect objects before them. Indirect objects tell who or what receives the direct object.

- An indirect object can be a noun or object pronoun. An indirect object can never be the object of the preposition.

- An object complement gives more information about the direct object. An object complement can be a noun or an adjective.

- An object complement appears after a direct object.

- A linking verb is a state-of-being verb. It links the subject to another word in the predicate.

- A predicate noun is a noun or pronoun that renames the subject. It comes after a linking verb in a sentence.

- A predicate adjective is an adjective that describes the subject. It comes after a linking verb in a sentence.

- Direct objects, indirect objects, object complements, predicate nouns, and predicate adjectives can be compound. They can all be used in questions and commands.

Word Bank

complement

direct object

indirect object

intransitive verb

linking verb

object complement

predicate adjective

predicate noun

transitive verb

Part A Find the word or words in the Word Bank to complete each sentence. Write the answer on your paper.

1. A _____ shows action passed from the subject toward a person or thing.

2. An _____ does not pass action from the subject to an object.

3. A _____ is a noun or pronoun that receives the action from a transitive verb.

4. An _____ tells who receives the direct object of a verb.

5. A _____ is a word that completes the meaning of the verb.

6. An _____ follows the verb and refers to a direct object.

7. A _____ links the subject to a noun, pronoun, or adjective in the predicate.

8. A _____ follows a linking verb and renames the subject.

9. A _____ follows a linking verb and tells about the subject.

Part B Decide whether the verb in bold is transitive or intransitive. Write *transitive* or *intransitive*.

10. Mr. and Mr. Ellis **shopped** for weeks.

11. One day Mr. Ellis **bought** a computer.

12. The child **stared** at the computer screen.

13. That program **ran** all evening.

14. Mrs. Ellis **keeps** a daily journal on the computer.

15. Her friend from Ohio is **eating** at my favorite cafe.

Part C Write each sentence. Write *S* above the simple subject and *V* above the transitive verb. Write *DO* above any direct objects and *IO* above any indirect objects. Write *OC* above any object complements.

16. We gave Jiro a CD and a stereo for his birthday.

17. Elect John president.

18. The band raised money for the trip.

19. Have you read that book?

20. The band played that song, and I bought the record.

Part D Identify the *kind* of sentence: *intransitive verb, direct object, indirect object, object complement, predicate noun,* or *predicate adjective.* Write the letter of the answer on your paper.

21. Try it for yourself.
    A object complement   **C** indirect object
    B direct object   **D** predicate noun

22. Tamika and Andrea asked their mother a question.
    A object complement   **C** indirect object
    B direct object   **D** predicate noun

23. Their mother is a well-known lawyer and businesswoman.
    A object complement   **C** indirect object
    B direct object   **D** predicate noun

24. In the classroom, we called our coach Mr. Thompson.
    A direct object   **C** object complement
    B predicate noun   **D** predicate adjective

25. The message was short, but it was very important.
    A direct object   **C** object complement
    B predicate noun   **D** predicate adjective

Test Tip

Put a check mark beside questions you do not know. After you finish the test, return to the check-marked questions. Try again to answer them.

Complex Sentences

As you look at the photograph, how might you finish these sentences? "We went to the national park because . . ." "We went during the time of year when. . ." You might say, "We went during the time of year *when the flowers were blooming.*" "We went during the time of year" is a clause that can stand alone. However, "when the flowers were blooming" cannot stand alone. In a complex sentence, some sentence parts can work independently and others cannot.

In Chapter 11, you will learn how to write complex sentences.

GOALS FOR LEARNING

- To recognize words, phrases, and clauses in a sentence
- To identify adverb clauses
- To recognize noun clauses
- To identify appositives and nouns of direct address
- To recognize adjective clauses
- To identify complex sentences
- To identify compound-complex sentences

Reading Strategy: Text Structure

Figuring out how information is organized is an important part of understanding a text. You know what to expect in a text when you preview it before reading. You can find information more easily when you know a text's structure.

- Look at how a text is broken into paragraphs.
- Skim any charts, graphs, or boxes on a page.
- Use a graphic organizer (such as a chart or word web) to help you organize information visually as you read.
- Notice subheads and words that are in bold or italics.

Key Vocabulary Words

Word A set of letters that has meaning

Phrase A group of words without both a subject and a predicate

Adverb clause A dependent clause that works like an adverb in a sentence

Noun clause A dependent clause that works like a noun in a sentence

Appositive A noun, noun phrase, or noun clause that renames or explains another noun

Noun of direct address The name of a person addressed or spoken to in a sentence

Adjective clause A dependent clause that describes a noun or pronoun

Complex sentence A sentence with one independent clause and one or more dependent clauses

Compound-complex sentence A sentence that has two or more independent clauses and one or more dependent clauses

Phrases and Clauses

Objectives

- To decide if a group of words in a sentence is a phrase or a clause
- To decide if a clause is dependent or independent

In this chapter, you will learn about complex sentences. It is important to understand the meanings of three important terms: *word, phrase,* and *clause*. A **word** is a set of letters that has meaning. A **phrase** is a group of words without both a subject and a predicate.

▶ **EXAMPLE 1**

| Prepositional Phrase | across the street |
| Verb Phrase | has been |

Word

A set of letters that has meaning

Phrase

A group of words without both a subject and a predicate

A clause is a group of words with both a subject and a predicate. An independent clause is a sentence. It has a subject and a predicate and expresses a complete thought. A dependent clause has a subject and a predicate, but it is not a sentence. It is not a complete thought.

▶ **EXAMPLE 2**

| Independent Clause | James was happy. (complete thought) |
| Dependent Clause | Because he passed the test. (incomplete thought) |

Reading Strategy:
Text Structure

As you read this lesson, use a graphic organizer to compare dependent and independent clauses.

Practice A

Decide whether each group of words is a phrase or a clause. Write *phrase* or *clause* on your paper.

1. over the river

2. if he leaves

3. will have been late

4. the youngest girl in school

5. whoever wants an apple

Dependent Clauses

Either a subordinating conjunction or a relative pronoun can introduce a dependent clause.

Subordinating conjunctions are words such as *because*, *if*, *when*, and *since*. Relative pronouns are words such as *that*, *which*, *who*, *whom*, *whose*, *what*, and *whoever*.

▶ **EXAMPLE 3**

Independent Clause	Felipe walked to school.
Dependent Clause	Because he missed the bus.

Practice B

Decide whether each group of words is a dependent or an independent clause. Write *dependent* or *independent* on your paper.

1. Whom you asked.
2. That girl is in my class.
3. Until he knows all the answers.
4. The team exercised before practice.
5. Whoever finishes first.

Practice C

Write each dependent clause. Underline the word that introduces the dependent clause in each sentence.

1. Because Shelly left school late, she missed the bus.
2. I will fix dinner if you are hungry.
3. Since he did not try out for a part, he will not appear in the play.
4. We will start the movie when Tony and Maria arrive.
5. Rick admires the man who coaches his team.

REVIEW

Write *phrase* or *clause* for each group of words in bold.

1. We huddled in the cabin **as the snow fell.**

2. She will not be back **until tomorrow.**

3. Everyone has arrived **except Jody and Bill.**

4. I cannot leave **until I finish my report.**

5. **When you know the answer,** raise your hand.

Write *independent clause* or *dependent clause* for each clause in bold. For each dependent clause, write the word that introduces the clause.

6. **After the party ended,** we cleaned and went to bed.

7. Please take this to the woman **who lives next door.**

8. **I am so glad** that you made the team.

9. **Ask the girl** who is standing by the fence.

10. **Because the store closed,** people lost their jobs.

VOCABULARY BUILDER

Marmalade, Jam, and Jelly
What is the difference between these three breakfast spreads?
Use a dictionary to look up definitions that you do not know.

Match each word with its definition.

1. jam
2. marmalade
3. jelly
A A food made by boiling the pulp and rinds of fruit with sugar
B A food made by boiling fruit and sugar into a thick mixture
C A partly clear food made from boiling fruit juice and sugar

Adverb Clauses

Objectives

- To identify adverb clauses
- To tell an adverb phrase from an adverb clause in a sentence
- To identify missing words in an adverb clause
- To write sentences with adverb clauses

Adverb clause

A dependent clause that works like an adverb in a sentence

Reading Strategy:
Text Structure

Preview Lesson 11-2. Notice the headings, features, and bold words.

An **adverb clause** is a dependent clause that works like an adverb in a sentence. It answers questions about the verb.

▶ **EXAMPLE 1**

Adverb	Karli went home early.
Adverb Phrase	Karli went home after practice.
Adverb Clause	Karli went home when practice was over.

Practice A

Write *adverbs*, *adverb phrase*, or *adverb clause* on your paper for each group of words in bold.

1. Amy writes **well** and **often.**
2. Mom always knows exactly **where I put my things.**
3. **Except for you,** I have not told anyone the news.
4. **Until you find your pen,** you can borrow mine.
5. I can hardly wait **until my birthday.**

Like adverbs, an adverb clause answers questions like *where, when, why,* and *how much.*

▶ **EXAMPLE 2**

Where?	Kim smiled wherever she went.
When?	When Dale was a boy, he lived in Haiti.
Why?	Joy joined the club because she likes art.

Reading Strategy:
Text Structure

Study the examples on this page. How do the examples help you understand adverb clauses?

Practice B

Write the adverb clause in each sentence on your paper.

1. Enrique runs whenever he has time.
2. If he gets up early, he runs in the morning.
3. He runs because he enjoys it.
4. Unless it is raining hard, Enrique runs every day.
5. Because I injured my knee, I walk for exercise.

Adverb Clauses as Adverbs of Degree

An adverb clause can answer questions about an adjective or adverb. These adverb clauses can act like adverbs of degree. They answer questions such as *how much* or *how far*.

▶ **EXAMPLE 3**

S   V Adj.   S   V
Sean is taller than the other students are.
(How much taller is Sean? He is taller *than the other students.*)

Missing Parts in an Adverb Clause

Sometimes part of an adverb clause is missing. The missing part is understood.

▶ **EXAMPLE 4**

Sean is taller than the other students. (In the clause *than the other students,* the verb *are* is understood.)

NOTE
Remember, an adverb clause answers questions about a verb, an adverb, or an adjective.

Practice C

Write each adverb clause. Write any words that are understood.

1. My dog barks louder than any other dog around.
2. Irene practices longer than anyone else.
3. Is Vicky taller than Beth?
4. Enrique ran farther than the others ran.
5. Charlotte is as happy as she can be!

REVIEW

Decide whether the words in bold are an adverb phrase or an adverb clause. Write *adverb phrase* or *adverb clause*.

1. Sue has been hard of hearing **since birth.**

2. **Because she and Lisa became friends,** Lisa learned sign language.

3. **If you wish to learn,** Sue will help you.

Write the adverb clause in each sentence on your paper. Then write any words that are understood.

4. We will go to the beach when summer arrives.

5. Alexa bought a new car because her old one fell apart.

6. You should get some rest if you are tired.

7. That building is higher than any other city building.

Write each sentence on your paper. Add an adverb clause to each sentence.

8. Rain had been falling.

9. The field was wet.

10. The game began.

Noun Clauses

Objectives

- To identify a noun clause in a sentence
- To identify the function of a noun clause in a sentence

Noun clause
A dependent clause that works like a noun in a sentence

Reading Strategy:
Text Structure

Explain how the words in bold help to highlight important ideas in this lesson.

A **noun clause** is a group of words with a subject and a verb. A noun clause is a dependent clause that works like a noun in a sentence. A noun clause can be used as a subject, predicate noun, direct object, or indirect object. A noun clause can also be an object complement or the object of the preposition.

▶ **EXAMPLE 1**

Subject	S LV PA What you did was wonderful.
Predicate Noun	S LV PN That paper is what I need.
Direct Object	S V DO I remember what you said.
Indirect Object	S V IO DO I gave whoever wanted one an apple.
Object Complement	S V DO OC She can name the cat whatever she wants.
Object of the Preposition	S V DO Obj. Prep. We made dinner for whoever was hungry.

Write the function of each noun clause in bold. Write
*subject, predicate noun, direct object, indirect object, object
complement,* or *object of the preposition.*

1. The teacher said **that my answer was wrong.**

2. **Who will get the lead in the play** has not been
   decided.

3. They argued about **who should go first.**

4. This is **what I want.**

5. She offered **whoever was still around** a ride.

Noun Clauses and Relative Pronouns

A relative pronoun introduces a noun clause in a sentence.

Common Relative Pronouns

that	who (subject)
what	whom (object)
whatever	whoever (subject)
whichever	whomever (object)
	whose (possessive)

The pronouns *that* and *what* each have only one form.
They do not change, regardless of whether they are subjects
or objects. The pronoun *who* does change, however.

- Use *who* when the relative pronoun is the subject of
  the noun clause.

- Use *whom* when the relative pronoun is the direct
  object of the clause. Also use *whom* when it is the
  object of the preposition in the noun clause.

- Use *who* when the relative pronoun is the predicate
  noun in the noun clause.

► **EXAMPLE 2**

          S   V   DO

I remember who called me.

        DO   S   V

I remember whom you called.

       PN S LV

I remember who you are.

Practice B

Complete each sentence with *who* or *whom*.

1. I know _____ called you.

2. I know _____ you are.

3. I know _____ you saw.

4. I know _____ you invited.

5. I know to _____ you wrote.

The relative pronoun *that* often introduces a noun clause. Sometimes the pronoun *that* is left out of the sentence because it is understood. Either way is correct.

► **EXAMPLE 3**

Do you think that he is nice?

Do you think he is nice?

The other relative pronouns cannot be left out.

► **EXAMPLE 4**

Incorrect	Did you hear I said?
Correct	Did you hear what I said?

Reading Strategy:
Text Structure

Describe the organization of this page. Is it cause and effect? Description? Compare and contrast?

Practice C

Write each sentence on your paper. Underline the noun clause once. Underline the relative pronoun twice.

1. Do you know who found my book?

2. I remember that the book is on sale.

3. What I really need are my notes!

4. I am offering a reward to whoever finds them.

5. Do you think that Raitna found my notes, too?

Practice D

Write the noun clause in each sentence. Then write *subject, predicate noun, direct object, indirect object, object complement,* or *object of the preposition.*

1. I made supper for whoever wants some.

2. I knew that I would be late.

3. Some hot soup is what I need right now.

4. What you see is what you get!

5. The salesperson gave whoever was in the store a free CD-ROM.

NOTE

A CD-ROM stands for "Compact Disc-Read Only Memory." Many CD-ROM drives now allow you to "burn" a CD-ROM. "To burn a CD" means to add files to the CD-ROM.

George will give a ride to whoever needs one.

REVIEW

Underline the noun clause once and the relative pronoun twice. If the relative pronoun *that* is understood, add it.

1. She said she is tired.
2. When the paper is due is not clear.
3. He will go on an errand for whoever asks him.
4. Carl and George go to wherever they can swim.
5. Seth forgot whom he invited.

Write the noun clause in each sentence. Then write *subject, predicate noun, direct object, indirect object, object complement,* or *object of the preposition.*

6. We went shopping for whatever we needed.
7. That love conquers all is a common idea in films.
8. Mrs. Li gave whoever asked for it more time.
9. Is this what the dog brought home?
10. You can name the dog whatever you choose.

SPELLING BUILDER

Homonyms: Words That Sound Alike

Words such as *principle* and *principal* are homonyms. They sound the same, but they have different meanings and different spellings. Here are some other homonyms:

to, too, two	fare, fair	weak, week
hear, here	waist, waste	whether, weather

Write the correct homonym for each sentence.

1. Jamal does not like to (waste, waist) time.
2. We saw Carl last (weak, week).
3. I cannot (hear, here) you when you whisper.
4. Today's (whether, weather) looks perfect.
5. We were (to, too, two) tired to continue practice.

Appositives and Nouns of Direct Address

Objectives

- To identify appositives in sentences
- To identify nouns of direct address in sentences
- To punctuate sentences with appositive phrases and nouns of direct address

An **appositive** renames or explains another noun in the same sentence. An appositive may be a noun, a noun phrase, or a noun clause. In Example 1, the appositive is in blue. The noun the appositive renames is in italics.

▶ **EXAMPLE 1**

My *cousin* Helena has a bird.

Chiquita, a parakeet, belongs to her.

Chiquita's favorite *thing*, a small brass bell, is in its cage.

I have a secret *wish*—that I will someday be captain.

Appositive

A noun, noun phrase, or noun clause that renames or explains another noun

Practice A

Write the appositive in each sentence. Next to it, write the noun or nouns the appositive renames or explains.

1. Who wrote the line: "All the world's a stage"?

2. The committee members—Carlos, Jill, and Alma—met in the student lounge.

3. People liked Gwen's idea—a surprise party for Jill.

4. Galileo's invention, the telescope, changed people's views of the universe.

5. Friends since kindergarten, Rita and Marianne still enjoy each other's company.

Reading Strategy:
Text Structure

How effective are the examples on this page? Do they help you understand appositives?

Appositives are often set off from the rest of the sentence with punctuation. Use commas to set off an appositive phrase from the rest of the sentence.

▶ **EXAMPLE 2**

Melanie, an old friend of mine, will be in town tomorrow.

Jamal and Leigh made spaghetti, their favorite meal.

Nouns of Direct Address

Sometimes a person is addressed or spoken to by name in a sentence. This is called a **noun of direct address.** The name can be at the beginning or at the end of the sentence. It can also be in the middle of the sentence. Use commas to separate the person's name from the rest of the sentence.

▶ **EXAMPLE 3**

Tammy, can you help us?   Can you help us, Tammy?

I will be happy, Tammy, to help you.

Practice B

Write *appositive* or *noun of direct address* on your paper for each bold word.

1. My friend **Chen** wants to go for a walk.
2. **Marissa,** I will walk with you tomorrow.
3. We traveled with our son **Scott.**
4. Do you plan on mailing the letter today, **Kiki?**
5. I will take the letter, **Sam,** and drop it in the mailbox.

Practice C

Write each sentence on your paper. Add punctuation to set off the appositive phrase or noun of direct address.

1. Carolyn a girl in my class wants to go roller skating.
2. Eric please turn down the radio.
3. Will Jill attend West High a school close to her home?
4. I need two cups of brown sugar Maria.
5. The biggest challenge Chris is managing your time well.

Write each sentence on your paper. Underline the appositive once. Underline the word the appositive renames twice. Then, add commas where they are needed.

1. My neighbor Ms. Bell invited me over for dinner.

2. Soccer my favorite sport takes a lot of energy to play.

3. Kate told us her thoughts: that we should never give up.

4. We chased after Tyrese the boy with the basketball.

5. Mario the flight attendant helped me with my bags.

Write each sentence on your paper. Underline the noun of direct address. Then, add commas where they are needed.

6. Andrew please take out the trash.

7. Wouldn't it be fun Ben to ride our bikes to the park?

8. You told me that you wanted a red sweater Yusef.

9. Latoya can you work for me this weekend?

10. I do not know Wayne if we should go now or later.

Adjective Clauses

Objectives

- To identify adjective clauses in a sentence
- To identify words that adjective clauses describe in a sentence
- To write sentences with adjective clauses

Adjective clause

A dependent clause that describes a noun or pronoun

Reading Strategy:
Text Structure

Which words or phrases emphasize the important points in this lesson?

An adjective describes a noun or pronoun. Remember that adjectives answer questions like *what kind, which one, how many,* and *how much.* Use an **adjective clause** like an adjective in a sentence. An adjective clause is a dependent clause that describes a noun or pronoun.

▶ **EXAMPLE 1**

Adjective	The middle boy is Ted.
Adjective Phrase	The boy in the middle is Ted.
Adjective Clause	The boy who is in the middle is Ted.

Practice A

Write *adjective, adjective phrase,* or *adjective clause* for each group of words in bold.

1. Terry is the player **who scores the most.**

2. The **best** and **most popular** player on our team is Terry.

3. The player **with the most points** on our team is Terry.

4. Pam, **who has played soccer all her life,** is the coach.

5. The team **that I enjoy watching the most** is Terry's.

Like an adjective phrase, an adjective clause follows the noun or pronoun it describes.

▶ **EXAMPLE 2**

The present that I gave him was expensive. (What present was expensive? *The present that I gave him* was expensive.)

Practice B

Write the adjective clause in each sentence on your paper. Next to each clause, write the noun it describes.

1. A girl whom I know won first prize in a contest.
2. The present that Gayle gave Aaron was for his birthday.
3. The package that she sent was heavy.
4. The boy who sits in the first seat has been out all day.
5. We bought a new refrigerator that has an ice maker.

Adjective Clauses and Relative Pronouns

A relative pronoun can introduce an adjective clause. Some common relative pronouns are *who, whom, whose, which, what,* and *that.* You can also use the words *where* and *when* to introduce an adjective clause.

▶ **EXAMPLE 3**

The store where I bought my jacket has closed.

The woman who gave the presentation was from Ontario.

Practice C

Write each adjective clause on your paper. Underline the relative pronoun.

1. The band went to Ohio, where the contest took place.
2. The contest, which is for students, is an annual event.
3. The director, whose name is Mr. Smith, was happy.
4. The band, which had won before, performed well.
5. We took our coats to Ohio where the weather is sometimes cold.

Write each sentence. Underline each adjective clause once. Underline each relative pronoun twice.

1. Please get the bread that is baked at the grocery store.

2. Did you know the people who gave the party?

3. Mike is the one who plays right field.

Write the adjective clause in each sentence. Next to each clause, write the noun it describes.

4. The girl who was in line behind me got the last ticket.

5. The man who lived next door moved to Kansas.

BUILDING RESEARCH SKILLS

Using an Online Library Catalog

Some libraries use card catalogs, but many libraries also have an online catalog. Catalogs list a call number to help you find a source in the library.

Follow these steps to find a source on an online library catalog:

• Use a computer and find the library's Web site. Click on the catalog.
• Look for a source by keyword, title, subject, author, or call number. You may also do an advanced search.
• Write the call numbers of the sources you need. The online catalog may let you know if a source is checked out.
• Use the library's online catalog to search for nonfiction books about the ocean tide.

1. Use a keyword search to find sources. How many sources did you find? Explain the types of sources you have found.

2. Use a subject search to find sources. How many sources did you find? Explain the types of sources you have found.

3. CRITICAL THINKING Try using an advanced search. Look for sources published in the last 10 years. How do the results of this search compare with the results of your other searches? Explain.

Complex Sentences

Objectives

■ To identify complex sentences

■ To identify independent and dependent clauses in a complex sentence

Complex sentence

A sentence with one independent clause and one or more dependent clauses

Reading Strategy:
Text Structure

As you read the lesson, use a graphic organizer to compare and contrast simple and complex sentences.

One way to group sentences is according to purpose (statement, question, command, or exclamation). You can also group them according to structure. A sentence may be *simple, compound, complex,* or *compound-complex.*

A simple sentence has one independent clause.

▶ **EXAMPLE 1**

S   V
I will drive to work.

A **complex sentence** has one independent clause and one or more dependent clauses.

▶ **EXAMPLE 2**

S   V   S   V PA
I will drive if you are tired. (*I will drive* is the independent clause. *If you are tired* is the dependent clause.)

Practice A

Write each sentence. Label the subject and the verb of each clause as shown. Then write *simple* or *complex.*

                    S   V   S   V
Answer: The team was behind until Tim kicked
            a goal.—complex

  1. Every afternoon the baseball team practices.

  2. When practice is over, the players are tired.

  3. The team begins with warm-up exercises.

  4. If players do not warm up well, injuries are likely.

  5. Baseball teams do not usually play during storms.

Finding Clauses in a Complex Sentence

A complex sentence can have more than one dependent clause.

▶ **EXAMPLE 3**

Adj. Clause

Toni Morrison, who was born in Ohio, was a student at

Adv. Clause

Howard University before she became a writer.

To find an independent clause in a complex sentence:

- First identify the dependent clause or clauses in the sentence.

- Then read all the words that are not in the dependent clause or clauses. These words make up the independent, or main, clause of the sentence.

Practice B

Answer each question about the following sentence.

Toni Morrison, who was born in Ohio, was a student at Howard University before she became a writer.

1. What is the independent clause in the sentence?
2. What is the subject of the independent clause?
3. What is the predicate of the independent clause?
4. What noun does the adjective clause describe?
5. What question does the adverb clause answer?

NOTE

When typed, the titles of books, magazines, and movies always appear in italics. Underline these titles when writing them by hand. The titles of short stories, songs, and articles appear in quotation marks.

Quotations in Complex Sentences

Direct and indirect quotations within sentences are noun clauses. These noun clauses help make complex sentences.

▶ **EXAMPLE 4**

    S   V   DO

Mrs. Kwan said, "I enjoyed our tennis match."

    S   V   DO

Mrs. Kwan said that she enjoyed the tennis match.

Practice C

Change each indirect quotation to a direct quotation. Use proper punctuation. Underline each noun clause.

1. Mr. Kwan said that he wants a new tennis racket.

2. I told my boss that I could not come to work today.

3. Anita said that her mother was going back to college.

4. My brother Eli yelled that he had a surprise for me.

5. Tina told me that she had found my book in her desk.

Lena says that she wants a camera for her birthday.

REVIEW

Write each sentence on your paper. Underline the independent clause in each sentence once. Underline any dependent clauses twice.

1. Mrs. Huang planned a party for Kim because she was graduating from high school.

2. "It could be fun," Elena told the others.

3. Kim wanted a new watch for a graduation gift.

4. Kim and Angie shopped for a waterproof watch that was not too expensive.

5. Angie hoped to go to the graduation party next Friday.

Write whether each sentence is *simple* or *complex*.

6. Since the party, I have not had a chance to talk to her.

7. Do you think that we should call Sarah?

8. Pick up the cake that I ordered yesterday.

9. In the first part of the book, the hero fights a large monster.

10. Since it is a nice day, we should walk on the beach.

Compound-Complex Sentences

Objectives

- To identify compound-complex sentences
- To analyze sentence structure

Compound-complex sentence

A sentence that has two or more independent clauses and one or more dependent clauses

Reading Strategy:
Text Structure

How does the structure of this lesson compare with other lessons in this chapter?

The four sentence structures are simple, compound, complex, and compound-complex.

A compound sentence has two independent clauses.

▶ **EXAMPLE 1**

S   V   S V   PA
I would drive, but I am too tired.

A **compound-complex sentence** has two or more independent clauses and one or more dependent clauses.

▶ **EXAMPLE 2**

S   V   S V   PA   S V   PN
I will drive if you are too tired, but it is your decision.

Practice A

Find the independent and dependent clauses in each sentence. Write *complex* or *compound-complex* for each.

1. Mai and Jamal play golf, and I like to swim.

2. What I would like is a vacation, but you want to stay home.

3. Lea works at the cafe, and her sister works there, too.

4. Wildfires, which can start suddenly, destroy trees and plants, but they also can create regrowth.

5. We must study hard, or we will not get into college.

Analyzing Sentence Structure

To understand the construction of a sentence, analyze it. To analyze means to break something down into its parts. Analyze a sentence to find out whether it is compound, complex, or compound-complex. Study this sentence:

> Brady knows that college is important, and because he wants to go, he saves money.

Follow these steps to analyze a sentence. Use the sentence above as an example.

How to Analyze a Sentence

1. Identify the independent clauses in the sentence. In the example, the independent clauses are *Brady knows* and *he saves money*. They are joined by the conjunction *and*.

2. Identify the dependent clauses in the sentence. In the example, the noun clause *that college is important* is the direct object. It tells what Brady knows in the independent clause. *Because he wants to go* is an adverb clause. It answers why he saves money.

3. The example sentence has two independent clauses and two dependent clauses. It is a compound-complex sentence.

4. Here is a breakdown of each clause:

   S   **V**   **DO**
Brady knows that college is important,

 Conj.   **S**   **V**
and because he wants to go,

 S   **V**   **DO**
he saves money.

One idea may be expressed in different kinds of sentences.

▶ **EXAMPLE 3**

Simple	Rafael writes stories and poems.
Compound	Rafael writes stories, but he also writes poems.
Complex	Rafael, who writes stories, also writes poems.
Compound–Complex	Rafael writes stories, but he also has written poems that have been published.

Practice B

Answer each question about the examples above.

1. Which sentence provides the most information?

2. What is the independent clause in the complex sentence example?

3. What kind of dependent clause is *who writes stories* in the complex example? Noun, adjective, or adverb clause?

4. How many independent clauses are in the compound-complex example?

5. What kind of dependent clause is *that have been published*? Noun, adjective, or adverb clause?

Practice C

Write each sentence. Underline each independent clause once and each dependent clause twice. Write *simple, compound, complex*, or *compound-complex* for each.

1. After graduation, Emily hopes that she can find a job.

2. She asked Vic about a job, but he was not hiring.

3. She became upset about her job search.

4. Emily keeps looking since she needs money, and she knows a job is out there.

5. Emily, who does not quit easily, will find a job soon.

REVIEW

Find the independent and dependent clauses in each sentence. Write *simple, compound, complex,* or *compound-complex* for each clause.

1. We left the store, and then we picked up some lunch.

2. I hope that you can come because I miss you.

3. Ask her about when she can meet, and then call me.

Use the following sentence to answer questions 4–6.

Rafael decided he needed a break, so he went to the cafe.

4. Name the independent clauses in the sentence.

5. What kind of dependent clause is *he needed a break*? What word is missing in the sentence?

6. Is this a simple, compound, complex, or compound-complex sentence?

Write a sentence using each structure. Underline the independent clause once and the dependent clause twice.

7. simple

8. compound

9. complex

10. compound-complex

PUTTING IT ALL TOGETHER

Write a note to a friend. Explain why you cannot attend a party or school activity. Use an adverb clause, an adjective clause, and a noun clause. Underline and identify each of the dependent clauses. Use at least one compound-complex sentence. Underline the compound-complex sentence twice.

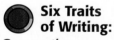

Six Traits of Writing:

Conventions correct grammar, spelling, and mechanics

Writing to Address a Problem or Express an Opinion

Think of a problem or issue in your school, home, community, or workplace. How should it be fixed?

Write a letter to complain about a problem or express your opinion on an issue. Who should receive your letter? State the main problem or issue. Support your opinion with details. End by telling the receiver to take a specific action.

Use a variety of sentences (simple, compound, complex, and compound-complex) in your letter. This adds interest and helps your writing flow smoothly.

Use the sample format below to write your letter. Then answer the questions.

Your address

Date

Person to receive letter
Person's title
Person's address

Salutation (*such as Dear Mr. Price:*)

Body of letter

Closing (*such as Sincerely,*)
Your signed name

1. Does your letter have a complex sentence? If not, add one. Underline each dependent clause. Decide what type of clause it is. Write *adjective*, *adverb*, or *noun clause.*

2. Does your letter have a compound-complex sentence? If not, add one. Underline the independent clause once and the dependent clause twice.

3. **CRITICAL THINKING** Find a place in your letter to add variety. Rewrite this section with a new sentence structure.

SPEAKING AND LISTENING

A speech must get a listener's attention. Read your letter to a partner. If your letter was a persuasive speech, what would you change? Could you make the opening line more interesting? How might you change the ending?

CHAPTER 11

SUMMARY

- A clause has a subject and a predicate, but a phrase does not.

- A clause can be either dependent or independent. A dependent clause begins with a subordinating conjunction or relative pronoun.

- Use an adverb clause to answer questions like *where, when, why, how much,* and *how far.*

- Sometimes part of an adverb clause is missing. The missing part is understood.

- A noun clause can be a subject, predicate noun, direct object, or indirect object. It can also be an object complement or an object of the preposition.

- Use a relative pronoun to introduce a noun clause. Sometimes the word *that* is understood.

- Use an appositive to rename or explain another noun.

- A noun of direct address is the name of a person spoken to in a sentence.

- Use an adjective clause to answer questions like *what kind, which one, how many,* and *how much.*

- A complex sentence has one independent clause and one or more dependent clauses. Sentences with quotations are often complex sentences.

- A compound-complex sentence has two or more independent clauses and one or more dependent clauses. Analyzing a sentence helps you figure out if a sentence is compound-complex.

Word Bank

adjective clause

adverb clause

appositive

complex sentence

compound-complex
   sentence

noun clause

noun of direct
   address

phrase

word

Part A Find the word or words in the Word Bank to complete each sentence. Write the answer on your paper.

1. A _____ is a dependent clause that works like a noun in a sentence.

2. An _____ is a dependent clause that works like an adverb in a sentence.

3. An _____ is placed next to a noun to rename or explain it.

4. A _____ has one independent clause and one or more dependent clauses.

5. A _____ is a group of words that does not contain a subject and predicate.

6. A _____ has two or more independent clauses and one or more dependent clauses.

7. An _____ is a dependent clause that describes a noun or pronoun.

8. A set of letters that has a meaning is a _____.

9. The name of a person addressed or spoken to in a sentence is a _____.

Part B Write whether each group of words is a *phrase*, an *independent clause*, or a *dependent clause*.

10. Before his senior year was over

11. To the party

12. You should go to bed

13. For Kim and her friends

14. Because Kim is graduating

15. Steve was sad

Part C Write the letter of the answer that tells the structure of each sentence.

16. Gordon made a present, but he also bought a book that Kim would like.
  A simple   **C** complex
  B compound   **D** compound-complex

17. Joyce said, "We had a wonderful time at the party."
  A simple   **C** complex
  B compound   **D** compound-complex

18. Who won the CD that Mrs. Huang bought?
  A simple   **C** complex
  B compound   **D** compound-complex

19. Carrie and Mark drove together, and they arrived first.
  A simple   **C** complex
  B compound   **D** compound-complex

20. Tell the clerk we need help.
  A simple   **C** complex
  B compound   **D** compound-complex

Part D Write *adjective clause*, *adverb clause*, or *noun clause* for each clause in bold. Then write any appositives or nouns of direct address in each sentence.

21. Tina, get Kim, **who has already graduated,** a present from Bermuda.

22. Mrs. Huang, Kim's mother, has planned a surprise for the person **who arrives first.**

23. **Whoever it is** will be surprised.

24. **Because the party is for Kim,** the guests will not expect a gift.

25. I did not know **that the party is on Saturday,** Kate.

Verbal Phrases

What caption would you write for this photograph? What might you say about the *fishing* bear? You might write "The brown bear likes *to fish*." You may also say, "*Fishing* is one way the bear gets its food." Each of the words in italic type is a verb form. However, these words do not act as verbs in these sentences. Instead, they act as nouns, adjectives, or adverbs. Verbs that you use as different parts of speech are called verbals. The three kinds of verbals are *infinitives, gerunds,* and *participles.*

In Chapter 12, you will learn about verbals and how to use them in sentences.

GOALS FOR LEARNING

- To identify and use infinitives and infinitive phrases in sentences
- To identify and use gerunds and gerund phrases in sentences
- To identify and use participles and participle phrases in sentences

Reading Strategy: Visualizing

Visualizing means to picture something in your mind. Think about how something looks and sounds as you read. Follow these tips to visualize a text:

- Pick out descriptive words that help to create a picture.
- Draw a picture in your mind after reading a section or paragraph.
- Write down or explain to someone what you think of as you read the text.

Key Vocabulary Words

Verbal A verb that is used as another part of speech

Verbal phrase A verbal, its complements, and any adjectives, adverbs, or prepositional phrases that describe it

Infinitive phrase An infinitive, its complements, and any adjectives or adverbs that describe it

Gerund A verb form that ends in -*ing* and acts as a noun

Gerund phrase A gerund and any adjective, adverb, prepositional phrase, or complement the gerund may have

Participle A verb form that is used as an adjective

Participle phrase A participle and an adverb or adverb phrase

Infinitives and Infinitive Phrases

Objectives

- To define *verbal* and *verbal phrase*
- To identify infinitives and infinitive phrases in sentences
- To determine how an infinitive or infinitive phrase acts in a sentence

Verbal

A verb that is used as another part of speech

Verbal phrase

A verbal, its complements, and any adjectives, adverbs, or prepositional phrases that describe it

A **verbal** is a verb that you use as another part of speech. A **verbal phrase** is a verbal and its complements. A verbal phrase also includes any adjectives, adverbs, or prepositional phrases that describe the verbal. The three kinds of verbals are infinitives, gerunds, and participles.

An infinitive is a verb form made up of *to* plus a verb. It is usually a noun, but it may be an adjective or adverb.

▶ **EXAMPLE 1**

Noun	I like to dance.
	(*To dance* is used as a direct object.)
Adjective	There was plenty of time to eat.
	(*To eat* explains what kind of time.)
Adverb	He practices to improve.
	(*To improve* explains why he practices.)

Infinitives and Tense

An infinitive is usually in the present tense. It can also be in the present perfect tense (*to* + *have* + a verb).

▶ **EXAMPLE 2**

| Present | Scott decided to go to Cedar Lake. |
| Present Perfect | He hoped to have caught six fish by noon. |

Practice A

Write the infinitive in each sentence on your paper.

1. Dan and Scott really like to fish.
2. They hoped to catch enough trout for lunch.
3. Dan agreed to clean the trout.
4. Scott said he wanted to cook the trout in a skillet.
5. They were ready to make their first cast by dawn.

Infinitives and Predicates

An infinitive is not a part of the simple predicate. However, it may be part of the complete predicate. The complete predicate is the verb and the words that answer questions about that verb.

▶ **EXAMPLE 3**

$$\text{V} \qquad \text{Inf.} \quad \text{Adv.}$$

Stefan decided to leave early.

P

Practice B

Write the complete predicate of each sentence. Underline the simple predicate once. Underline the infinitive twice.

1. Tamika appeared to be happy.
2. Our family likes to go during the summer.
3. Greg seems to be taller than Reggie.
4. Elizabeth hoped to get the lead in the play.
5. Do you want to use the laptop?

Reading Strategy:
Visualizing

What clues help you visualize the difference between a prepositional phrase and an infinitive?

Infinitives and Prepositional Phrases

Do not confuse infinitives with prepositional phrases. An infinitive is *to* + a verb. A prepositional phrase is *to* + a noun or pronoun.

▶ **EXAMPLE 4**

Infinitive	They want to leave. (*Leave* is a verb.)
Prepositional Phrase	Let's go to the park. (*Park* is a noun and the object of the preposition *to*.)

Practice C

Write each word in bold. Then write whether the group of words is an *infinitive* or a *prepositional phrase*.

1. When Scott got **to the lake,** he saw Dan ready **to fish.**
2. He carried his equipment **to the boat.**
3. Soon he was ready **to begin.**
4. Scott wanted **to be** the one **to catch** the first fish.
5. "I hope **to beat** the champion," Dan said **to Scott.**

Infinitives and Their Uses

An infinitive is a verb form that is used as a noun, an adverb, or an adjective in a sentence.

Study Example 5 to learn how to use an infinitive in a sentence. Ask yourself the same questions you ask to identify parts of speech and sentence parts.

▶ **EXAMPLE 5**

Noun	Tanya wants to catch a big trout. (What does Tanya want?)
Adverb	Christian will need a big fire to cook his trout. (Why does he need a big fire?)
Adjective	The best fishing rod to use is made of aluminum. (What kind of fishing rod?)

NOTE

The word *fish* can be a noun or a verb. As a noun, it has two plural forms—*fish* and *fishes.* Use *fishes* when you are describing more than one kind of fish: *I enjoy eating all kinds of fishes, but mackerel and sea bass are my favorite.*

Practice D

Write each bold infinitive. Then write whether it is used as a *noun,* an *adverb,* or an *adjective.* Remember that subjects, predicate nouns, and direct objects are nouns.

1. **To catch** a big fish was William's ambition.
2. William's favorite fishes **to eat** are trout and halibut.
3. After an hour, they decided **to move** to another spot.
4. They hoped **to find** a place with some fish.
5. The fish were hard **to catch.**

Reading Strategy:
Visualizing

What words on this page help you visualize how infinitive phrases are used in a sentence?

Infinitive Phrases

An **infinitive phrase** is an infinitive, its complements, and any adjectives or adverbs that describe it. An infinitive phrase is one type of verbal phrase.

An infinitive may have an adverb or an adverb phrase to answer questions about its action.

▶ **EXAMPLE 6**

    Inf. Adv.   Adv. Phrase
To leave early for Cedar Lake was their idea.
(The entire infinitive phrase is *to leave early for Cedar Lake*. *Early* is an adverb that answers the question *when*. The adverb phrase *for Cedar Lake* tells about *early*. It answers the question *where*.)

An infinitive may also have a complement such as a direct object, a predicate noun, or a predicate adjective.

▶ **EXAMPLE 7**

        Inf.   DO
He wants to buy a boat.
(*Boat* is the direct object of the infinitive *to buy*.)

        Inf.   PN
She wants to be the mayor.
(*Mayor* is a predicate noun. It follows the linking verb *to be*.)

        Inf.   PA
They wanted the trout to taste delicious.
(*Delicious* is a predicate adjective that follows the linking verb *to taste*. The infinitive *to taste* also acts as an object complement for the direct object *trout*.)

Practice E

Write each infinitive phrase. After it, write how it is used in the sentence. Write *noun*, *adjective*, or *adverb*.

1. Scott began to reel the fish into the boat.
2. The fish started to fight hard.
3. Scott's fish struggled to win the battle.
4. Dan got a net to help Scott.
5. To land that fish was their goal.

Sometimes the preposition *to* is missing from the infinitive.

▶ **EXAMPLE 8**

"Don't make me (to) laugh," shouted Jerome.

"Help me (to) reel it in," Scott said.

Practice F

Write the infinitive in each sentence. Add *to* if it is missing.

1. "Will you let me help you?" Dan asked.
2. They heard the other boaters cheer for Scott.
3. "Let us see the size of that fish," they all said.
4. They watched Scott hold his fish high in the air.
5. Their attention made Scott feel proud.

Dan and Scott fished until the sun began to set.

REVIEW

Write each infinitive phrase. Underline the infinitives.

1. Scott and Dan wanted to be home by dark.

2. They decided to stop at six o'clock.

3. Scott began to count the fish.

4. They had hoped to catch many fish.

5. To catch enough fish for dinner had been their goal.

Write the group of words in bold. Write whether it is an *infinitive* or a *prepositional phrase*.

6. Jerod wants **to work** at the hospital this summer.

7. He will go **to the hospital** three days a week.

8. Melanie and I are going **to the library** after school.

9. We need **to finish** our project.

10. "Look," Mel said, pointing **to Adam** at another table.

SPELLING BUILDER

Homographs

What is a round children's toy? A ball. What is a formal dance? A ball. Ball (the toy) and ball (the dance) are homographs. Homographs are words with the same spelling but different meanings. Look at the context to find a word's meaning. The context is the words and sentences around the word.

Match one word with each pair of meanings.

fleet   stroke   bear   rare
tire   light   story   school

1. large animal
   carry or support

2. place for learning
   group of fish

3. not heavy
   not dark

4. rapid
   group of ships

Gerunds and Gerund Phrases

Objectives

- To identify gerunds and gerund phrases in sentences
- To determine how a gerund or gerund phrase acts in a sentence
- To determine if a word in a sentence is a progressive verb or a gerund

Gerund

A verb form that ends in *-ing* and acts as a noun

Gerund phrase

A gerund and any adjective, adverb, prepositional phrase, or complement the gerund may have

A **gerund** is a verb form that ends in *-ing*. In sentences, gerunds act like nouns.

▶ **EXAMPLE 1**

Subject	Rock climbing is Mitsu's favorite activity.
Direct Object	Terrance enjoys fishing.
Predicate Noun	My favorite exercise is hiking.
Object of the Preposition	A hiker got in trouble for climbing the steep cliff.
Appositives	Jade loves two things: dancing and skiing. You might try these activities: walking, jogging, or skating. Her talents—writing and speaking—got her the job.

Practice A

Write the gerund in each sentence on your paper.

1. Riding a bicycle on back roads is great exercise.
2. I like running better.
3. Reggie enjoys reading and going to the movies.
4. Getting to school on time is not difficult.
5. They were sent to the office for running in the halls.

Gerund Phrases

A **gerund phrase** includes a gerund and any words that go with it. These words could be adjectives, adverbs, prepositional phrases, or complements.

Because a gerund acts like a noun, it may have an adjective that describes it.

Reading Strategy:
Visualizing

What words on this page help you visualize how to use gerund phrases?

▶ **EXAMPLE 2**

$$\text{Adj. \quad Gerund}$$

Meg asked for expert training in weight lifting. (Meg asked for what kind of training? She asked for *expert* training. The gerund phrase is the object of the preposition *for.*)

A gerund phrase may also include an adverb or adverb phrase.

▶ **EXAMPLE 3**

$$\text{Gerund \qquad Adv. Phrase}$$

He likes swimming after school. (When does he like *swimming*? After school. *After school* is a prepositional phrase used as an adverb. The entire gerund phrase is the direct object of the action verb *likes.*)

Because a gerund is a verb form, it may have complements.

▶ **EXAMPLE 4**

Gerund   DO

Rowing a boat is fun. (*Boat* is the direct object of the gerund *rowing.* The gerund phrase is the subject of the verb *is.*)

Practice B

Write each gerund phrase. Then write how the gerund phrase acts in the sentence. Write *subject, direct object, predicate noun, object of the preposition,* or *appositive.*

1. Kaitlin watched the running of the Boston Marathon.

2. One of her dreams was winning that race.

3. She began thinking about entering a marathon.

4. Practicing for the race took a lot of time.

5. Kaitlin enjoys two things: running and winning!

Gerunds and Progressive Verbs

Progressive verb forms and gerunds both end in *-ing*. Do not confuse progressive verb forms with gerunds. When the *-ing* form is the main verb, it is not a gerund.

▶ **EXAMPLE 5**

| Verb Phrase | Kaitlin has been running every morning. |
| Gerund | Kaitlin likes running every morning. |

Practice C

Decide whether the word in bold is a verb or gerund. Write *verb* or *gerund* on your paper.

1. They are **planning** a party for her birthday.

2. **Planning** a party can be a lot of work.

3. Jake has been **trying** to find the perfect gift.

4. Robert has stopped **trying** to call her.

5. Her favorite sport is **swimming.**

Practice D

Write a sentence for each gerund. Do not use it as a verb.

1. being   **4.** wishing

2. finding   **5.** singing

3. running

Running track is a popular school sport.

REVIEW

Write each gerund phrase. Underline each gerund. Write *subject, direct object, predicate noun, object of the preposition,* or *appositive* for each gerund phrase.

1. Flying an airplane must be a thrill.

2. My favorite activity, reading books, is a way to relax.

3. We enjoyed swimming in the lake.

Write *verb* or *gerund* on your paper for each word in bold.

4. Kaitlin enjoys **going** to the art museum.

5. Jamal will be **attending** the play next week.

BUILDING RESEARCH SKILLS

Formatting a Document

Teachers often require you to format a paper or a presentation in a certain way. Word-processing programs help you do this. Many teachers require a title page. A title page includes your name, your paper's title, and your teacher's name. It also includes the class and date.

Teachers may make specific requests about margins, line spacing, indents, and font. A teacher may also require a certain word or page count.

Use word-processing software to type a paragraph about technology. Explain the technology you use in your daily life. Use the Times New Roman font in size 12. Follow these directions to continue formatting your document:

1. Double space your paragraph. You may do this by choosing *Format* and then *Paragraph* in the tool bar.

2. Make all of the margins one-inch margins. You can often do this by choosing *File* and then *Page Setup.*

3. CRITICAL THINKING Why do teachers make certain formatting rules?

Participles and Participle Phrases

Objectives

■ To identify participles and participle phrases in sentences
■ To identify the word in a sentence that a participle describes
■ To determine if a word in a sentence is part of a verb phrase or a participle

Participle
A verb form that is used as an adjective

Reading Strategy:
Visualizing

Create a graphic organizer to illustrate the differences between participles used as adjectives and verbs.

A **participle** is a verb form. Use participles as adjectives in sentences. A participle may be in the present tense or in the past tense.

▶ **EXAMPLE 1**

Present Tense	The sleeping baby was peaceful.
Past Tense	The room looks smaller painted green.

Practice A

Write the participle in each sentence on your paper.

1. The setting sun turned the sky red and purple.

2. Those cooked carrots are mushy.

3. The girl reading that book is my sister.

4. Will you help that crying child find her mother?

5. My rumbling stomach told me I was hungry.

Participles and Verbs

Do not confuse a participle used as an adjective with part of a verb phrase.

▶ **EXAMPLE 2**

Participle	The stew simmering on the stove smelled delicious.
Verb Phrase	The stew was simmering on the stove.

Practice B

Decide whether each word in bold is used as a participle or a verb. Write *participle* or *verb* on your paper.

1. We will be **catching** the train.
2. The newly **painted** room was bright and cheery.
3. The wind was **howling** all night.
4. The **laughing** students enjoyed the funny story.
5. Everyone avoids **annoying** people.

Participle Phrases

A **participle phrase** is a participle and an adverb or adverb phrase. A participle comes right before or right after the noun or pronoun it describes.

▶ **EXAMPLE 3**

Running at full speed, she caught the taxi.
(The participle phrase *Running at full speed* describes *she.)*

Writing Tip

Practice C

Write each sentence. Underline the participle phrase once. Underline the noun or pronoun it describes twice.

1. Howling wildly, the wind frightened the child.
2. Dana gave her book to the girl seated in the first row.
3. Expecting the worst, Julian was pleasantly surprised with his grade.
4. The keys locked inside the car were of little use.
5. Concentrating on her notes, Mrs. Agnello did not hear Julian enter the room.

REVIEW

Write the participle or the participle phrase in each sentence on your paper. Then write the word that the participle or participle phrase describes.

1. We could see the boy running around the track.

2. Arriving early, we were first in line for tickets.

3. I wondered who the girl walking by the restaurant was.

4. Feeling lost, Susan stopped for directions.

5. The dog waving its tail happily stood and waited for its dinner.

Write whether each word in bold is used as a participle or a verb.

6. The dog was **barking** at every car.

7. The children cheered for the **marching** band.

8. The flowers in the centerpiece had **drooped.**

9. The lawyer wanted a **signed** contract.

10. Yesterday John raked all of the **fallen** leaves.

PUTTING IT ALL TOGETHER

Many people enjoy telling scary stories. Write down a scary story you have heard, or make up a new story.

1. Tell the scary story in two or three paragraphs. Think it through before you start writing.

2. Include verbals—infinitives, gerunds, and participles—in your sentences. Look at this example:
   Walking through the woods I heard a growling noise.

3. When you are finished, underline all the verbals.

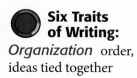

Six Traits of Writing:

Organization order, ideas tied together

Call Center Representative

Shawna Reynolds is a call center representative. She calls people to see if they are interested in the products her company provides. She answers questions about the products and shows them to customers.

Ms. Reynolds uses a script when she talks to possible customers. She follows a specific process for setting the appointments. The verbal phrases used in the script keep the listener interested. Read a section of the script below:

```
Hello,

My name is [Name], and I am
calling from [Company's
name]. To walk into a brand
new kitchen is a magical
feeling. Delivering this
experience to you is our
business. Currently, we are
running a special on our
kitchen cabinets. Our wide
selection will leave a
lasting impression on you.

Would you like to learn
more about our products?
```

1. List an example of a gerund phrase used in the script. Explain how it functions in the sentence.

2. List an example of a participle and an infinitive phrase.

3. **CRITICAL THINKING** How are gerunds and participles similar? How are they different? Explain your answer.

SPEAKING

To memorize a speech or script, practice it. Use devices such as an outline or note cards. Ask for feedback from a practice audience. Speak clearly and at a reasonable rate so that others can understand you. Also, keep an audience interested in what you are saying by sounding interested yourself. Practice the script on this page with a partner.

- A verbal looks like a verb but acts as another part of speech in a sentence. The three types of verbal phrases are infinitives, gerunds, and participles.

- An infinitive can act as a noun, adjective, or adverb in a sentence.

- An infinitive phrase includes the infinitive and the complements, adjectives, and adverbs with it.

- Do not confuse an infinitive with a prepositional phrase.

- A gerund ends in *-ing* and acts like a noun. It can be the subject, direct object, predicate noun, object of the preposition, or appositive.

- A gerund phrase includes the gerund and the adjectives, adverbs, prepositional phrases, and complements with it.

- Do not confuse progressive verb forms with gerunds.

- A participle ends in *-ing* or *-ed* and is used as an adjective. A participle phrase includes a participle and an adverb or adverb phrase.

- Do not confuse a participle used as an adjective with part of a verb phrase.

VOCABULARY BUILDER

Idioms

An idiom does not follow the usual patterns of a language. For example, you say "It is raining." Usually, a pronoun must have an antecedent. In this sentence, the noun that it replaces is not clear. You do not say, "The sky is raining" or "The clouds are raining." You understand idioms because you are familiar with them.

Write the meaning of each idiom on your paper.

1. He caught my eye.
2. The puppy went missing.
3. It is raining cats and dogs.
4. Sarah put up a good fight.
5. She means well.

Word Bank

gerund

gerund phrase

infinitive phrase

participle

participle phrase

verbal

verbal phrase

Part A Find the word or words in the Word Bank to complete each sentence. Write the answer on your paper.

1. A _____ is a verb form that is used like an adjective.

2. A _____ includes a participle and an adverb or adverb phrase.

3. An _____ includes an infinitive, its complements, and any adjectives or adverbs.

4. A _____ is a verb form that ends in *-ing* and acts like a noun.

5. A _____ includes a gerund and any adjective, adverb, prepositional phrase, or complement with it.

6. A _____ is a verb form that is used as another part of speech.

7. A _____ includes a verbal, its complements, and any words that describe the verbal.

Part B Write each infinitive or infinitive phrase. Then tell whether it acts as a *noun,* an *adverb,* or an *adjective.*

8. "Did you know that Sam wants to go to Peru this fall?" Val asked.

9. "To travel to Italy is my dream," Val said.

10. "Let's get together in 10 years to talk about our success," Sam suggested.

11. Sam and Val want to visit Oklahoma City next year.

12. They are meeting tomorrow to make their plans.

Part C Write *subject, direct object, predicate noun, object of the preposition,* or *appositive* for each gerund phrase.

13. "My favorite activity is playing cards at a party," Ella said.

14. For Elena, graduating from college was a big event.

15. After hugging, Al and Supta looked for their parents.

16. He stopped kicking the ball, and I asked him about it.

Part D Write each participle or participle phrase. Write the word the participle or participle phrase describes.

17. Sue received her well-earned diploma.

18. Holding back tears, the friends said their good-byes.

19. The chirping birds provided background noise.

20. "What a frightening movie that was!" exclaimed Mai.

21. The shimmering lake was a lovely sight.

Part E Decide if each phrase is an *infinitive phrase, gerund phrase, participle phrase,* or *prepositional phrase.*

22. <u>Standing before the school,</u> Mel had tears in her eyes.
   A infinitive phrase   **C** participle phrase
   B gerund phrase   **D** prepositional phrase

23. Sue turned <u>to take one last look at her school.</u>
   A infinitive phrase   **C** participle phrase
   B gerund phrase   **D** prepositional phrase

24. <u>Leaving school</u> was not easy for her.
   A infinitive phrase   **C** participle phrase
   B gerund phrase   **D** prepositional phrase

25. Ray thinks about <u>rowing to the middle of the lake.</u>
   A infinitive phrase   **C** participle phrase
   B gerund phrase   **D** prepositional phrase

Test Tip
Studying in small groups is one good way to review for tests. Take turns asking each other questions.

▼ SIX TRAITS OF GOOD WRITING

Good writing is not a miracle. It is not an accident either. Good writing is part science and part art. It is the result of careful thinking and choices. To write well, you need to know about six important traits that determine the quality of writing.

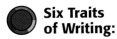

Six Traits of Writing:

Ideas message, details, and purpose

Ideas

What message do you want to get across? What details are important to get your message across clearly? Ideas are the heart of any writing. So begin the writing process by developing strong, clear ideas. Set off your ideas with details that stand out and catch attention.

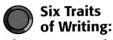

Six Traits of Writing:

Organization order, ideas tied together

Organization

A piece of writing has a structure or pattern, just like a building. Organize your ideas into a structure that makes sense and fits the ideas well. For example, you may tell about events or steps in order. You may compare two things or explain a solution or an effect. Organization holds writing together and gives shape to ideas.

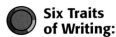

Six Traits of Writing:

Voice the writer's own language

Voice

Your writing should "sound like you." It should capture your thoughts and your point of view. This is your "voice." In writing, your voice shows that you are interested in and understand the subject. Your voice also gives a personal tone to your writing that is yours alone.

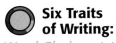

Six Traits of Writing:

Word Choice vivid words that "show, not tell"

Word Choice

Choose your words so that they are clear and interesting. Name things exactly. Use strong action verbs and specific adjectives. Good word choice helps you say exactly what you want to say. It helps your readers create a mental picture of what you want them to understand.

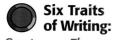

Six Traits of Writing:

Sentence Fluency
smooth rhythm and flow

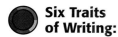

Six Traits of Writing:

Conventions correct grammar, spelling, and mechanics

Sentence Fluency

Well-made sentences make your writing easy to read. Aim for sentences that have the natural rhythms of speech. Vary sentence length and style. Then your sentences will flow. They will move your readers through your writing with ease.

Conventions

Once you have written something, ask yourself: Could this be published in a newspaper? Make sure your writing is free from mistakes in spelling, grammar, and mechanics. Mechanics includes things such as correct capitalization and punctuation.

The rest of Appendix A describes the writing process. As you follow this process, remember to include these six traits of good writing.

▼ STEPS IN THE WRITING PROCESS

When writers turn words into a paragraph or a report, they use a set of steps. These steps make up the writing process. The writing process helps you organize your ideas and form them into paragraphs. The five main steps in the writing process are prewriting, drafting, revising, editing, and publishing.

Prewriting

Prewriting is the planning stage. This is when you decide what to write about. You also think about your audience, your purpose for writing, and any assignment directions. You gather needed information, and then you organize your ideas about your topic.

Drafting

In the drafting step, you put your ideas into sentences. Then you build your sentences into paragraphs. You do not have to worry about mistakes in this step. You will find and fix them later.

Revising

When you revise, you improve your writing. You look for words and phrases that need to be changed. You may decide to add more information or take some information out. You may choose to arrange your ideas in a different way.

Editing and Proofreading

When you edit, you find and correct mistakes in spelling, grammar, punctuation, and capitalization. You also improve your word choice. The process of marking editing changes is called proofreading. After proofreading, you create the final draft.

Publishing and Presenting

There are several ways to publish, or share, your writing with others. One way is to read it to an audience. Other forms of publishing include giving someone a copy of your written work, or presenting it as a poster or in a slide show.

The five steps of the writing process are explained in more detail on the following pages.

 PREWRITING

Six Traits of Writing:

Ideas message, details, and purpose

Choosing Your Topic

Many writers find choosing a topic to be the hardest part of writing. Certainly, it is an important part. Without a good topic, you have nowhere to go with your writing. Here are some ways to look for a topic:

- Think about people you know, places you have seen, and activities you enjoy.
- Think about memories or experiences from your past.
- Read newspapers and magazines. Search the Internet. Listen to the radio. Think about what you have seen on TV recently. What is going on in the world around you?
- Write down anything that comes to mind. This is called *brainstorming*. When you brainstorm, you write down every idea as you think of it. You do not judge your ideas.
- Talk to other people. They may offer suggestions.

■ Think of questions about a subject. A question can become a good topic.

Once you have a list of possible topics, check them against your writing assignment. Cross off topics that do not fit the assignment. Then cross off topics that do not interest you. Look at the remaining topics. Choose one that you feel strongly about. It may be something you like or dislike.

Six Traits of Writing:

Organization order, ideas tied together

Choosing Your Main Idea

Now think more about your topic. What is the main idea you want to talk about? To help you decide on your main idea, use a graphic organizer such as a diagram, word web, or chart. Write your topic as the title of the graphic organizer. Write down subtopics, or different parts of the topic. Then write details related to each subtopic. For example, suppose your topic is "teenagers and cell phones." You might create this graphic organizer as you prewrite:

Teenagers and Cell Phones		
Problems	When Cell Phones Are Used	Popular Phone Features
cost of phone plan	to chat with a friend or family member	camera
use in school	to report an emergency	text messaging
losing your phone	to tell someone that your plans changed	games
remembering phone plan details	to ask a question	

A graphic organizer like this can help you organize your thoughts and see how ideas relate to each other. It can help you narrow your topic and choose your main idea. For example, after looking at the chart above, you might decide you want to write about why teenagers use cell phones. Your main idea might be: Besides talking with friends, teenagers use cell phones to make last-minute plans, to get information, to be entertained, and to call for help.

Six Traits of Writing:

Ideas message, details, and purpose

Developing Your Main Idea

Supporting details will make up the body of your writing. What details support or explain your main idea? Once you have chosen your main idea, you need to find information about it. There are several kinds of details:

- facts
- reasons
- examples
- sensory images
- stories or events
- experiences
- explanations

Where do you get these details? First, look back at anything you wrote when you were thinking about topics. Look at your brainstorm list, your notes, and any graphic organizers you made. To find more details to support your main idea, you might do the following:

- research
- interview
- observe
- remember
- imagine

Six Traits of Writing:

Voice the writer's own language

Identifying Your Purpose and Audience

Before you begin to write your first draft, you also need to answer two questions:

- What is my reason for writing?
- Who is my audience?

Your reason for writing may be to entertain, to inform, to persuade, or a combination of these. Your audience may be your classmates, your friends, or another group of people. Knowing your reason for writing helps you focus. Knowing your audience helps you choose the information to include.

▼ DRAFTING

Now it is time to write your first draft. In a first draft, you put all your ideas on paper. Some writers make an outline or a plan first and follow it as they write. Other writers write their ideas in no particular order and then rearrange them later. Use the method that works best for you. Check your assignment directions before you begin writing.

Try to write the whole draft at once. Do not stop to rearrange or change anything. You can do that after you finish the draft. Remember, a first draft will be rough.

Writing the Introduction

How do you begin your writing? A good introduction can be a sentence or a whole paragraph. It should tell your reader what they will be reading about. The introduction usually states the main idea. It should also catch their attention. You might begin with:

- a story
- a fact
- a question
- a quotation

Writing the Body

The body of your writing contains details that explain or support your main idea. The body may be several sentences or several paragraphs. How can you arrange your details? Here are some suggestions:

- chronological order (from earliest event to latest event)
- order of importance (most important reason or detail first)
- comparison and contrast (different ways to compare two things)
- problem and solution (steps or different ways to solve a problem)

Six Traits of Writing:
Organization order, ideas tied together

Six Traits of Writing:
Sentence Fluency smooth rhythm and flow

If your draft is to be several paragraphs long, remember that most paragraphs begin with a topic sentence. The topic sentence tells the main point of the paragraph. All other sentences in the paragraph should relate to the topic sentence.

Writing the Conclusion

A good conclusion tells readers that the writing is coming to a close. It makes a closing statement about what you have written. Your conclusion should be logical—it should make sense with the details in the body. It should also leave a strong impression with your reader. You might end with:

- a summary of what you wrote
- a suggestion or opinion
- the last event in a sequence

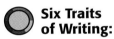

Six Traits of Writing:

Voice the writer's own language

Six Traits of Writing:

Word Choice vivid words that "show, not tell"

▼ REVISING

Now it is time to revise your draft. When you revise, you improve what you have written. You decide what you like and do not like. You decide what you want to change and how you will change it. You might add or take out words. You might rearrange sentences or paragraphs. Ask yourself these questions about your draft:

- Does my draft fit the assignment directions?
- Is my introduction interesting? Does it state the main idea?
- Is the main idea supported and explained in the body?
- Have I arranged the supporting details in a way that makes sense?
- Is there any information that I should add?
- Is there any information that I should leave out?
- Do I use transitional words and phrases?
- Do I use a variety of sentences?
- Is my conclusion logical and strong?

Here are some tips to help you revise a draft:

- Set your draft aside for a while. Then read it. This will help you see your writing in a new way.
- Read your draft aloud. This will help you hear awkward sentences and notice places where information is missing.
- Ask someone else to read your draft. Encourage this person to tell you what you have done well and what needs work.

Adding Transitions and Sentence Variety

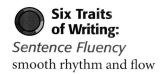

Six Traits of Writing:

Sentence Fluency smooth rhythm and flow

As you revise your writing, look for places that need a transition. A transition helps your reader move from one idea to the next. Here are some common transitional words and phrases:

also	finally	furthermore
next	in addition	therefore
first	for example	on the other hand

Also remember to use a variety of sentences in your writing. You can use declarative, imperative, interrogative, and exclamatory sentences. You can also use simple, compound, complex, and compound-complex sentences. Be sure to use a variety of sentence lengths. A mix of long and short sentences is more interesting. Do not begin every sentence the same way.

Creating a Final Draft

Six Traits of Writing:

Organization order, ideas tied together

Rewrite your first draft, making the above changes in content and organization. Use a clean piece of paper or use a computer to type your draft. With a computer, you do not have to rewrite your entire draft every time you revise it. Using a computer also makes it easier for someone else to read your draft and make suggestions.

Then read your second draft and revise it. You may have to create several drafts before you have one that you like.

▼ Editing and Proofreading

Once you have a draft you like, edit it. When you edit, you find and correct mistakes in spelling, grammar, punctuation, and capitalization. These kinds of mistakes distract your reader. You want your reader to notice your ideas, not your mistakes. During the editing step, you also look at your choice of words. Replace any vague words with more specific ones. Ask yourself these questions as you edit:

■ Did I spell each word correctly?
■ Did I write complete sentences? Are there any fragments or run-on sentences?
■ Did I use vivid and specific verbs, nouns, adjectives, and adverbs?
■ Does the verb in each sentence agree with the subject?
■ Did I use correct capitalization?
■ Did I use correct punctuation?

Here are some other suggestions to help you edit:

■ Use a computer spell checker, but remember that it cannot catch all spelling errors.
■ Edit more than once. Look for a different kind of mistake each time.
■ Read your work aloud. You may hear mistakes.
■ Ask someone else to edit your work.
■ Set your writing aside. Proofread it later. You may see mistakes more clearly.
■ Keep a thesaurus nearby. It will help you find better words. It will help you replace words that you have used too often.
■ Keep a dictionary and a grammar reference book nearby. You may have questions that they can help answer.

Proofreading Your Writing

The process of marking editing changes on paper is called proofreading. To make your proofreading faster and easier to follow, use proofreaders' marks. Draw the mark at the place where you want to make the correction. Here are some common proofreaders' marks:

Proofreaders' Marks

Delete or take out	ℒ	Insert an apostrophe	⌄
Spell out	⒮Ⓟ	Insert quotation marks	⌄⌄
Insert	∧	Change to lowercase	/
Insert space	#	Change to capital letter	≡
Insert a period	⊙	Close up; take out space	⌒
Insert a comma	∧	Begin a paragraph	¶
Insert a semicolon	⌃	Transpose letter or words	∿

▼ PUBLISHING AND PRESENTING

Think of publishing and presenting as sharing your writing with others. When you publish, you may decide to add photos, diagrams, or pictures. You may decide to add a cover. Many writers get their writing published in a newspaper or magazine or as a book. You publish a writing assignment by giving it to your teacher. However, there are other ways to publish your writing:

- Create a computer presentation such as a slide show.
- Create a poster, or post your work on the class bulletin board.
- Send your writing to a school or community newspaper or magazine.
- Give copies of your work to people who are interested in the topic. This could include family members and friends.
- Publish a class newspaper or magazine. Use it to present what you and your classmates have written.

- Get together with other writers. Take turns reading your work aloud and discussing it. Sharing aloud is one of the most common ways to publish writing.

Before you share your work you should:
- Review your paper.
- Make sure you are well prepared. Be very familiar with what you have written.
- Practice with the material.
- Practice reading your paragraph aloud.

Use this checklist to help you become a better public speaker:

✔ Speak loudly and clearly.

✔ Pause after commas and periods.

✔ Do not rush. Pace yourself.

✔ Stress certain words to add meaning to your sentences.

✔ Make eye contact with your audience.

✔ Use appropriate facial expressions and gestures.

✔ Use any visual aides that may be appropriate.

Finally, you can present your work.

Relax and take deep breaths before you present your work. During your presentation, remember to use the strategies that you practiced.

Each time you write, think about the writing process you used. Ask yourself the following questions: What would I do the same next time? What would I do differently? What parts of the process do I need to work on? Use the answers to these questions to help you the next time you write.

Appendix B: Capitalization and Punctuation Handbook

▼ CAPITALIZATION RULES

Capitalization 1 **First word in a sentence**

Begin the first word of every sentence with a capital letter.

Who won the writing contest?

Capitalization 2 **Personal pronoun I**

Write the pronoun *I* with a capital letter.

At the last minute, I changed my mind.

Capitalization 3 **Names and initials of people**

Almost always begin each part of a person's name with a capital letter.

Hernando Jones   Rosie Delancy   Sue Ellen Macmillan

Some parts of names have more than one capital letter. Other parts are not capitalized. Check the correct way to write a person's name. Look in a reference book, or ask the person.

JoAnne Baxter   Tony O'Hara   Jeanmarie McIntyre

Use a capital letter to write an initial that is part of a person's name.

B. J. Gallardo   J. Kelly Hunt   John F. Kennedy

Capitalization 4 **Titles of people**

Begin the title before a person's name with a capital letter.

Dr. Watson   Governor Maxine Stewart   Ms. Costa

Use a lowercase letter if the word is not used before a person's name.

Did you call the doctor?

Who will be the next governor?

Capitalization 5	Names of relatives

A word like *grandma* may be used as a person's name or as part of a person's name. Begin this kind of word with a capital letter.

Only Dad, Grandma, and Aunt Ellie understand it.

A word like *grandma* is usually not capitalized when a possessive pronoun comes before it.

Only my dad, my grandma, and my aunt understand it.

Capitalization 6	Names of days

Begin the name of a day with a capital letter.

She does not go to work on Saturday or Sunday.

Capitalization 7	Names of months

Begin the name of a month with a capital letter.

My favorite months are March and September.

Capitalization 8	Names of holidays

Begin each important word in the name of a holiday with a capital letter. Words like *the* and *of* do not begin with a capital letter.

They meet on the Fourth of July and on Thanksgiving.

Capitalization 9	Names of streets and highways

Begin each word in the name of a street or highway with a capital letter.

Why is Lombard Street the most crooked road in the world?

Capitalization 10	Names of cities and towns

Begin each word in the name of a city or town with a capital letter.

In 1997, they moved from Sparta to New Brighton.

Capitalization 11   **Names of states, countries, and continents**

Begin each word in the name of a state, country, or continent with a capital letter.

The movie was set in Peru, but it was filmed in Mexico.

Capitalization 12   **Names of mountains and bodies of water**

Begin each word in the name of a mountain or river with a capital letter. Also use a capital letter for lakes and oceans.

Amelia Earhart's plane was lost over the Pacific Ocean.

Capitalization 13   **Abbreviations**

If a word would begin with a capital letter, begin its abbreviation with a capital letter.

He wrote "Tues.—Dr. Lau" on a piece of paper.

Capitalization 14   **Titles of works**

Use a capital letter to begin the first word in the title of a work. Also capitalize the last word and every main word in a title. Only capitalize *the*, *a*, or *an* if it is the first word. Coordinating conjunctions and prepositions do not begin with a capital letter.

Joe and Jen are characters in the TV series *Friends for Life*.

Capitalization 15   **Other proper nouns**

Begin each major word in a proper noun with a capital letter. A proper noun is the name of a particular person, place, idea, or thing.

Matt went to Mario's Restaurant and ate Spaghetti Romano.

Capitalization 16   **Proper adjectives**

Begin a proper adjective with a capital letter. A proper adjective is an adjective that is formed from a proper noun. If the proper adjective is made with two or more nouns, capitalize each of them.

That American author writes about English detectives.

She loves Alfred Hitchcock movies.

▼ Punctuation Rules

Punctuation 1

Punctuation at the end of a sentence

Use a period, question mark, or exclamation point at the end of every sentence. Do not use more than one of these marks at the end of a sentence. For example, do not use both a question mark and an exclamation point. Do not use two exclamation points.

Use a period at the end of a sentence that makes a statement.

> A hockey player can skate backward at top speed.

Use a period at the end of a sentence that gives a command.

> Keep your eye on the puck.

Use a question mark at the end of a sentence that asks a question.

> Who is the goalie for their team?

Use an exclamation point at the end of a sentence that expresses excitement.

> That was a terrific block!

Punctuation 2

Periods with abbreviations

Use a period at the end of each part of an abbreviation.

Most titles used before people's names are abbreviations. These abbreviations may be used in formal writing. (*Miss* is not an abbreviation and does not end with a period.)

> Dr. Ramas   Mr. Bill Tilden   Ms. Mia Connolly

Most other abbreviations may be used in addresses, notes, and informal writing. They should not be used in formal writing.

> Lake View Blvd.   Thurs.   Fifth Ave.   Dec. 24

Do not use periods in the abbreviations of names of government agencies and certain other organizations.

Station MLT will broadcast a special program about the FBI.

Do not use periods after two-letter state abbreviations in addresses. This kind of abbreviation has two capital letters and no period. Use these abbreviations in addresses.

His address is 187 Third Street, Los Angeles, CA 90048.

Punctuation 3 **Periods after initials**

Use a period after an initial that is part of a person's name.

Chester A. Arthur   C. C. Pyle   Susan B. Anthony

Punctuation 4 **Commas in dates**

Use a comma between the number of the day and the year in a date.

Hank Aaron hit a record-breaking home run on April 8, 1974.

Use a comma after the year if it comes in the middle of the sentence.

April 8, 1974, was an exciting day for Hank Aaron's fans.

Do not use a comma with only the name of the month and the year.

Aaron hit his final home run in July 1976.

Do not use a comma with only the month and the number of a day.

April 8 is the anniversary of his record-breaking home run.

Punctuation 5 **Commas in place names**

Use a comma between a city or town and the state or country.

The chocolate factory is in Hershey, Pennsylvania.

Sometimes the two names do not come at the end of a sentence. Use another comma after the state or country if this is the case.

Hershey, Pennsylvania, is the home of a chocolate factory.

| Punctuation 6 | **Commas in compound sentences** |
| | Use a comma before the conjunction *and*, *but*, or *or* in a compound sentence. |

> Many people tried, but no one succeeded.

| Punctuation 7 | **Commas in series** |
| | Three or more words or groups of words used in a sentence form a series. Use commas to separate the words or groups of words in a series. |

> Jamie, Mitch, Kim, Lou, and Pablo entered the contest.

> They swam one mile, biked two miles, and ran five miles.

| Punctuation 8 | **Commas after introductory phrases and clauses** |
| | Use a comma after a phrase placed before the subject of the sentence. The phrase should give additional information about the main thought of a sentence. |

> In the old dresser, Juan found the diamonds.

Do not use a comma if the predicate comes before the subject of the sentence.

> In the old dresser lay the diamonds.

Use a comma after an adverb clause at the beginning of a sentence.

> When he was named MVP, Wayne Gretzky was 18 years old.

| Punctuation 9 | **Commas with nouns of address** |
| | Use a comma after a noun of direct address at the beginning of a sentence. |

> Fernando, that was a terrific pitch!

Use a comma before a noun of direct address at the end of a sentence.

> That was a terrific pitch, Fernando!

Use a comma before and after a noun of direct address in the middle of the sentence.

> That, Fernando, was a terrific pitch!

Punctuation 10   Commas with appositives

Use a comma before an appositive at the end of a sentence.

> The speech was given by Shelley, our class president.

Use a comma before and after an appositive in the middle of the sentence.

> Shelley, our class president, gave the speech.

Punctuation 11   Commas or exclamation points with interjections

Almost always use a comma after an interjection.

> Well, we should probably think about it.

Use an exclamation point after an interjection that expresses excitement.

> Wow! That is a terrific idea!

Punctuation 12   Commas after greetings in friendly letters

Use a comma after the greeting in a friendly letter. Begin the first word in the greeting of a letter with a capital letter.

> Dear Karla,   Dear Uncle Theodore,

Punctuation 13   Commas after closings in friendly letters and business letters.

Use a comma after the closing in a letter. Begin the first word in the closing of a letter with a capital letter.

> Love,   Yours sincerely,

Punctuation 14   Quotation marks with direct quotations

A direct quotation is the exact words a person said. Use quotation marks at the beginning and end of a direct quotation. Begin the first word in a direct quotation with a capital letter.

> "Look!" cried Tina. "That cat is smiling!"

> "Of course," Tom joked, "it's a Cheshire cat."

Punctuation 15 Commas with direct quotations

Usually, use a comma to separate the words of a direct quotation from the speaker.

> Jay asked, "Who won the game last night?"

> "The Tigers won it," said Linda, "in 14 innings."

Punctuation 16 Quotation marks with titles of works

Use quotation marks around the title of a story, poem, song, essay, or chapter.

> "Have a Happy Day" is a fun song to sing.

Sometimes a period or a comma comes after the title. Put the period or comma inside the closing quotation mark.

> A fun song to sing is "Have a Happy Day."

Punctuation 17 Underlines with titles of works

Underline the title of a book or play when you write it by hand. Also underline the title of a magazine, movie, TV series, or newspaper.

> One of the best movies about baseball is <u>The Champion</u>.

Put the title of a book or play in italic type in a word-processing program. Also put the title of a magazine, movie, TV series, or newspaper in italic type.

> One of the best movies about baseball is *The Champion*.

Punctuation 18 Apostrophes in contractions

Use an apostrophe in place of the missing letter or letters in a contraction.

> is not—isn't   Mel is—Mel's   I will—I'll

Punctuation 19 **Apostrophes in possessive nouns**

Use an apostrophe and -*s* to write the possessive form of a singular noun.

> This cage belongs to one bird. It is the bird's cage.

Use an apostrophe for the possessive form of a plural noun that ends in -*s*.

> This is a club for boys. It is a boys' club.

Use an apostrophe and -*s* for a plural noun that does not end in -*s*.

> This is a club for men. It is a men's club.

Punctuation 20 **Colons after greetings in business letters**

Use a colon after the greeting in a business letter. Capitalize the first word in a greeting.

> Dear Ms. Huan: Dear Sir or Madam:
>
> Dear Senator Rayburn: To Whom It May Concern:

Punctuation 21 **Colons in expressions of time**

When you write time in numerals, use a colon between the hour and the minutes.

> 5:45 PM   9:00 AM   12:17 PM

Punctuation 22 **Hyphens in numbers and fractions**

Use a hyphen in a compound number from twenty-one to ninety-nine.

> thirty-seven   fifty-eight   seventy-three

Use a hyphen in a fraction.

> one-quarter   two-thirds   seven-eighths

Appendix C: Speaking Checklist

Speaking in front of an audience is one way to communicate. Common types of public speaking include speeches, presentations, debates, group discussions, interviews, storytelling, and role-playing. Use this checklist to help you plan a speech or presentation.

Define Your Purpose and Audience

✔ If the speech is an assignment, read the instructions carefully. What will you be graded on? Will the speech be formal or informal? Will you stand in front of a podium? Can you interact with the audience?

✔ Decide on your purpose. Do you want to inform, entertain, persuade, explain, or describe something? Do you want to get the audience to act on an issue? Do you want to involve them in a discussion or debate?

✔ Identify your audience. Who are they?

✔ Think about what your audience already knows about the topic. Predict their questions, concerns, and opinions. What words are familiar to your audience? What may need explanation?

✔ Think about how your audience prefers to get information. Do they like visuals, audience participation, or lecture?

Decide on Your Topic

✔ Choose a topic that is right for the purpose and assignment. Choose one that you know and enjoy, or choose one that you want to learn more about.

✔ Make sure the topic is important or interesting to the audience.

✔ Determine how long your speech should be. Is your topic narrow enough? Do you have enough time to share the details?

✔ Think about the kinds of details that will help you get across the main idea.

Draft Your Speech

✔ Include an introduction, a body, and a conclusion.

✔ In the introduction, state your topic and purpose. Give your position.

✔ Establish yourself as an expert. Tell why you are the right person to give the speech based on your experiences.

✔ Get the attention of your audience so they want to listen. You might start your speech by asking a question, telling a story, describing something, giving a surprising fact, sharing a meaningful quotation, or making a memorable entrance.

- ✔ In the body of your speech, tell more about your main idea.

- ✔ Try to prevent listener confusion.

- ✔ Include supporting details such as facts, explanations, reasons, examples, stories or experiences, and quotes from experts.

- ✔ Check the order of your supporting details. Do they build on each other? Is the order logical?

- ✔ If you are describing something, use figurative devices, specific words, and words that appeal to the senses.

- ✔ If you are telling a story, make sure it has a beginning, middle, and end.

- ✔ Repeat key phrases or words to help people remember your point. If something is important, say it twice.

- ✔ Use transitions such as, "This is so important it is worth repeating," or "As I said before, we must act now."

- ✔ In the conclusion, tie your speech together.

- ✔ If you asked a question in your introduction, answer it in the conclusion.

- ✔ If you outlined a problem in your introduction, offer a solution.

- ✔ If you told a story in your introduction, refer to that story again.

- ✔ You may want to ask your audience to get involved, to take action, or to find out more about your topic.

- ✔ Revise your speech. Add missing details. Make sure the details support the main idea. Make sure the body is organized in a logical way.

- ✔ Edit and proofread your script. Choose more specific words. Check your grammar.

Select Audio/Visual Aids

- ✔ Decide if a visual aid would help your audience understand the main idea. Visual aids include posters, displays, objects, models, pictures or words on a screen or blackboard, and slide shows.

- ✔ Decide if handing out printed material, such as a list or diagram, would help the audience follow along.

- ✔ Decide if an audio recording or video clip would be helpful or interesting.

- ✔ Think about how the room is set up. Can the room be darkened for a slide show or video presentation? If the room is large, do you need a microphone or projector?

- ✔ Make sure the right technology and props are available. Do you need a projector, video or tape player, computer, overhead screen, display table, or easel? Do you need someone to hold or adjust something?

- ✔ Make sure the audience will be able to clearly hear or see your audio and visual aids.

Know Your Speech

Every speaker is afraid of forgetting his or her speech. Choose one of the following ways to remember your speech.

✔ Hold a copy of the script. Highlight key phrases to keep you on track.

✔ Write a sentence outline of your main points and supporting details. Write down anything that you want to say in a certain way.

✔ Write an outline of key words. Choose words that will remind you what to say.

✔ Write key words, an outline, or your entire speech on note cards. They are less obvious than paper. Number the cards to keep them in order.

✔ Memorize your speech.

Practice Your Speech

✔ Practice your speech several times so you are familiar with the words.

✔ If you plan to use a script, practice with it. Do not just read your script. Practice looking out at the audience.

✔ If you plan to use note cards or an outline, practice with them. Revise them as you practice.

✔ If you plan to use visual aids, practice with them. Decide when in the speech you will introduce them.

✔ If you plan to use technology, be familiar with how it works.

✔ Practice sounding natural and confident. Giving a speech is more than talking. Your voice and appearance are powerful parts of your speech.

✔ Decide what you will wear when you give your speech.

✔ Practice how you will move. Will you stand in one place or move around? What gestures will reinforce your message?

Give Your Speech

✔ Body language: Stand tall. Keep your feet shoulder-width apart. Do not cross your arms or bury your hands in your pockets. Use gestures to make a point. Try to relax; that way, you will be in better control of your body.

✔ Eye contact: Look at your audience. Spend a minute or two looking at each side of the audience. The audience will feel as if you are talking to them. Do not just look at your teacher, the front row, or one side.

✔ Voice strategies: Clearly pronounce your words. Speak at a comfortable rate that is not too fast. Speak loud enough for everyone to hear you. Vary your volume, rate, and pitch. For example, you could say, "I have a secret. . . ." Then, you could lean toward the audience and speak in a loud, clear whisper as if you are telling them a secret. This adds dramatic effect and gets attention.

Appendix D: Listening Checklist

Listening is an important skill. You hear messages all the time—from other people and from the media. You are a listener at school, at home, at social events, at work, even in the car. You are a listener whenever you are part of a conversation or a discussion. It is important to understand and analyze the messages you hear. Use this checklist to become a better listener.

Listen Actively

✔ Be prepared to listen. Complete any reading assignments that are due before a speech or presentation.

✔ Sit near the person speaking and face the speaker directly.

✔ Sit up straight to show you are alert.

✔ Look at the speaker and nod to show you are listening.

✔ Focus on what the speaker is saying. Do not be distracted by other people.

✔ Take short notes during the speech or presentation.

✔ After the speech, ask the speaker to explain unfamiliar words or confusing ideas.

Be Appreciative and Thoughtful

✔ Relax and enjoy the listening experience.

✔ Think of the listening experience as an opportunity to learn.

✔ Respect the speaker and his or her opinions and ideas.

✔ Do not talk or make distracting gestures.

✔ Do not cross your arms. Open your arms to show you are open to receiving information.

✔ Try to understand the speaker's background, experiences, and feelings.

Analyze the Message

✔ Predict what the speaker is going to say based on what you already know.

✔ Identify the main idea of the message.

✔ Determine the purpose of the message.

✔ Note details such as facts, examples, and personal experiences. Does each detail support the main idea?

✔ Determine if a supporting detail is a fact or an opinion. Watch for opinions that are not supported. Watch for unfair attacks on a person's character, lifestyle, or beliefs.

✔ Identify any details intended to trick or persuade. Watch for exaggerations of truth. Watch for cause-effect relationships that do not make sense.

✔ If there are audio/visual aids, do they contribute to the message? What effect do they have?

✔ After the speech, ask about any words or ideas you did not understand.

✔ Form your own conclusions about the message.

Analyze the Speaker

✔ Analyze the speaker's experience and knowledge. Is he or she qualified to speak on the topic?

✔ Does the speaker seem prepared? Does the speaker appear confident?

✔ Analyze the speaker's body language. Is it appropriate?

✔ Consider the speaker's tone, volume, and word choices. What do they show?

Take Notes

✔ Write down key ideas and phrases, not everything that is said. Abbreviate words.

✔ Summarize the main points of the message in your own words.

✔ Copy important visual aids, such as graphs, charts, and diagrams. Do not copy every detail.

✔ Use stars or underlining to highlight important information or main points.

✔ Use arrows to connect related information.

✔ Use lists, charts, bullets, or dividing lines to organize information.

✔ Circle anything that is confusing or needs to be explained. Ask about these items later.

✔ Use the note-taking guidelines described on page xiii of this textbook.

Appendix E: Viewing Checklist

Visual messages are messages that you see. They may or may not contain words. Visual messages include artwork, posters, diagrams, videos, photos, slide shows, and ads. Use this checklist to help you analyze a visual message.

Analyzing Photos and Videos
✔ Identify the parts and features of the photo or video. What does it show?

✔ For videos, think about how movement is used to create the message. Is it fast or slow?

✔ Are written or spoken words part of the message? If so, how do the words affect what you see?

✔ Think about how the photo or video makes you feel. What mood is created? What are you reminded of?

Analyzing Artwork
✔ Notice how colors, shapes, lines, and textures are used. Do certain features seem important?

✔ Think about the artist's purpose. What message does the art express? Does it represent something? Does it show an opinion or a mood?

Analyzing Graphs, Charts, and Diagrams
✔ Graphs and charts are used to organize information. What information is shown? Is it clear?

✔ Graphs and charts often compare facts or numbers. What is being compared?

✔ Diagrams use shapes, lines, and arrows to show a main idea. What does the diagram show?

Analyzing the Overall Message
✔ Think about the main idea. What is the author/artist trying to say? Is he or she successful?

✔ Think about the purpose of the message. Is the author/artist trying to inform, persuade, or entertain?

✔ Look for facts and opinions. Is information presented fairly? Does the message express an opinion? Is exaggeration used?

✔ Think about how the parts of the message work together. Does each part support the main idea? Do any parts take away from the main idea?

✔ Sometimes a visual message is part of a presentation, display, or speech. How does the visual message tie into the whole presentation? Does it help the presenter make a point?

✔ What conclusion can you make after viewing this message?

✔ What will you remember most about this message?

Appendix F: Reading Checklist

Good readers do not just read with their eyes. They read with their brains turned on. In other words, they are active readers. Good readers use strategies as they read to keep them on their toes. The following strategies will help you to check your understanding of what you read.

✔ **Summarizing** To summarize a text, stop often as you read. Notice these things: the topic, the main thing being said about the topic, and important details that support the main idea. Try to sum up the author's message using your own words.

✔ **Questioning** Ask yourself questions about the text and read to answer them. Here are some useful questions to ask: Why did the author include this information? Is this like anything I have experienced? Am I learning what I thought I would learn?

✔ **Predicting** As you read, think about what might come next. Add what you already know about the topic. Predict what the text will say. Then, as you read, notice whether your prediction is right. If not, change your prediction.

✔ **Text Structure** Pay attention to how a text is organized. Find parts that stand out. They are probably the most important ideas or facts. Think about why the author organized the ideas this way. Is the author showing a sequence of events? Is the author explaining a solution to a problem? Is the author showing cause and effect?

✔ **Visualizing** Picture what is happening in a text or what is being described. Make a movie out of it in your mind. If you can picture it clearly, then you know you understand it. Visualizing what you read will help you remember it later.

✔ **Inferencing** The meaning of a text may not be stated. Instead, the author may give clues and hints. It is up to you to put them together with what you already know about the topic. Then you make an inference—you conclude what the author means.

✔ **Metacognition** Think about your thinking patterns as you read. Before reading a text, preview it. Think about what you can do to get the most out of it. Think about what you already know about the topic. Write down any questions you have. After you read, ask yourself: Did that make sense? If the answer is no, read it again.

Glossary

A

Abbreviation (ə brē vē ā´ shən) A short form of a word (page 8)

Abstract noun (ab´ strakt noun) A word that names an idea that you cannot see, touch, hear, smell, or taste (page 12)

Action verb (ak´ shən vėrb) A word that tells what someone or something (subject) does, did, or will do (page 97)

Active verb (ak´ tiv vėrb) A verb form used when the subject is doing the action (page 127)

Adjective (aj´ ik tiv) A word that describes a noun or pronoun (page 67)

Adjective clause (aj´ ik tiv klȯz) A dependent clause that describes a noun or pronoun (page 327)

Adjective phrase (aj´ ik tiv frāz) A prepositional phrase that answers the question *which one, what kind,* or *how many* about the noun or pronoun in a sentence (page 194)

Adverb (ad´ vėrb) A word that answers questions about a verb, an adjective, or another adverb (page 159)

Adverb clause (ad´ vėrb klȯz´) A dependent clause that works like an adverb in a sentence (page 316)

Adverb of degree (ad´vėrb ov di grē) An adverb that answers questions about adjectives and other adverbs (page 163)

Adverb of negation (ad´ vėrb ov ni gā´ shən) The adverbs *never* and *not,* which tell that an action will not happen or that a state of being is not present (page 166)

Adverb phrase (ad´ vėrb frāz) A prepositional phrase that answers the question *how, when, where, how much,* or *how long* about the verb in a sentence (page 197)

Antecedent (an tə sēd´ nt) The noun that a pronoun replaces (page 35)

Apostrophe (') (ə pos´ trə fē) A punctuation mark that shows that a noun is possessive (page 24)

Appositive (ə poz´ ə tiv) A noun, noun phrase, or noun clause that renames or explains another noun (page 324)

C

Capital letter (kap´ ə təl let´ ər) The uppercase form of a letter such as *A, B, C* (page 235)

Clause (klȯz) A group of words with a subject and a verb (page 213)

Collective noun (kə lek´ tiv noun) The name of a group of people, places, or things (page 4)

Common noun (kom´ ən noun) The name of a general type of person, place, thing, or idea (page 7)

Comparative form (kəm par´ ə tiv fôrm) The form of an adjective used to compare two people or things (page 86); the form of an adverb used to compare two people or things (page 169)

a	hat	e	let	ī	ice	ȯ	order	ů	put	sh	she	ə	a	in about
ā	age	ē	equal	o	hot	oi	oil	ü	rule	th	thin		e	in taken
ä	far	ėr	term	ō	open	ou	out	ch	child	ŦH	then		i	in pencil
â	care	i	it	ȯ	saw	u	cup	ng	long	zh	measure		o	in lemon
													u	in circus

Complement (kom´ plə mənt) A word that completes the meaning of the verb (page 284)

Complete predicate (kəm plēt´ pred´ ə kit) The simple predicate and all of the words that describe it (page 243)

Complete subject (kəm plēt´ sub´ jikt) The simple subject and all of the words that describe it (page 238)

Complex sentence (kəm pleks´ sen´ təns) A sentence with one independent clause and one or more dependent clauses (page 330)

Compound-complex sentence (kom´ pound kəm pleks´ sen´ təns) A sentence that has two or more independent clauses and one or more dependent clause (page 334)

Compound noun (kom´ pound noun) Two words joined together to form one new noun (page 4)

Compound object (kom´ pound ob´ jikt) Two or more objects in a sentence connected by a conjunction (page 186)

Compound personal pronoun (kom´ pound pėr´ sə nəl prō´ noun) A pronoun formed by combining a singular personal pronoun and -*self* or a plural personal pronoun and -*selves*. (page 40)

Compound predicate (kom´ pound pred´ ə kit) Two or more simple predicates connected by a conjunction (page 245)

Compound preposition (kom´ pound prep ə zish´ ən) A preposition made up of more than one word (page 187)

Compound relative pronoun (kom´ pound rel´ ə tiv prō´ noun) A pronoun formed by combining a relative pronoun with -*ever*; *whoever, whomever, whatever,* and *whichever* (page 43)

Compound sentence (kom´ pound sen´ təns) Two independent clauses joined by a coordinating conjunction (page 250)

Compound subject (kom´ pound sub´ jikt) Two or more simple subjects connected by a conjunction (page 241)

Concrete noun (kon´ krēt noun) A word that names something you can see, touch, hear, smell, or taste (page 12)

Conditional verb (kən dish´ ə nəl vėrb) A helping verb that puts a condition or requirement on an action (page 123)

Conjunction (kən jungk´ shən) A word that connects parts of a sentence (page 213)

Contraction (kən trak´ shən) A word made from two words by replacing one or more letters with an apostrophe (page 57)

Coordinating conjunction (kō ôrd´ n āt ing kən jungk´ shən) A word that connects two or more equal parts of a sentence (page 213)

Correlative conjunctions (kə rel´ ə tiv kən jungk´ shən) A pair of conjunctions that connects words or groups of words (page 218)

D

Declarative sentence (di kler´ ə tiv sen´ təns) A sentence that makes a statement (page 247)

Definite article (def´ ə nit är´ tə kəl) The word *the*, which is used to talk about a particular person or thing (page 70)

Demonstrative adjective (di mon´ strə tiv aj´ ik tiv) The word *this, that, these,* or *those* used as an adjective (page 83)

Demonstrative pronoun (di mon´ strə tiv prō´ noun) A pronoun that points out a particular person or thing: *this, these, that,* or *those* (page 50)

Dependent clause (di pen´ dənt klöz) A clause that does not express a complete thought (page 221)

Direct object (də rekt´ ob´ jikt) The noun or pronoun that receives the action from a transitive verb (page 268)

E

End punctuation (end pungk chü ā′ shən) A mark at the end of a sentence that tells the reader where a sentence ends:) a period (.), a question mark (?), an exclamation point (!) (page 235)

Exclamatory sentence (iks kla′ mə tòr ē sen′ təns) A sentence that shows strong feeling (page 247)

F

First-person pronoun (fėrst pėr sən prō′ noun) A pronoun that refers to the person who is speaking (page 38)

Future perfect (fyü′ chər pėr′ fikt) Shows an action that will be completed before a certain time in the future (page 102)

G

Gerund (jer′ ənd) A verb form that ends in -ing and acts as a noun (page 351)

Gerund phrase (jer′ ənd frāz′) A gerund and any adjective, adverb, prepositional phrase, or complement the gerund may have (page 351)

H

Helping verb (hel′ ping vėrb) A verb that combines with a main verb to form a verb phrase (page 99)

Hyphen (-) (hī′ fən) A short dash between parts of a word (page 5)

I

Imperative sentence (im per′ ə tiv sen′ təns) A sentence that gives a command (page 247)

Indefinite article (in def′ ə nit är′ tə kəl) The words a or an, which is used to talk about a general group of people or things (page 70)

Indefinite pronoun (in def′ ə nit prō′ noun) A pronoun that does not refer to a specific person or thing (page 53)

Independent clause (in di pen′ dənt klòz) A clause that expresses a complete thought (page 221)

Indirect object (in də rekt′ ob′ jikt) A noun or pronoun that tells who receives the direct object of the verb (page 276)

Infinitive (in fin′ ə tiv) To plus the present tense of a verb (page 101)

Infinitive phrase (in fin′ ə tiv frāz′) An infinitive, its complements, and any adjectives or adverbs that describe it (page 348)

Interjection (in′ tər jek′ shən) A word or phrase that shows strong feeling (page 225)

Interrogative pronoun (in′ tə rog′ ə tiv prō′ noun) A pronoun that asks a question: who, whom, which, what, and whose (page 46)

Interrogative sentence (in tə rog′ ə tiv sen′ təns) A sentence that asks a question (page 247)

Intransitive verb (in tran′ sə tiv vėrb) A verb that does not pass an action from the subject to another person or thing (page 261)

Irregular verb (i reg′ yə lər vėrb) A verb that does not form its past tense and past participle by adding -ed or -d (page 106)

L

Linking verb (lingk′ ing vėrb) A verb that joins the subject with a noun, pronoun, or adjective in the predicate; it is always a state-of-being verb (page 290)

a	hat	e	let	ī	ice	ò	order	ù	put	sh	she	ə	a	in about
ā	age	ē	equal	o	hot	oi	oil	ü	rule	th	thin		e	in taken
ä	far	èr	term	ō	open	ou	out	ch	child	ŦH	then		i	in pencil
â	care	i	it	ò	saw	u	cup	ng	long	zh	measure		o	in lemon
													u	in circus

M

Main verb (mān vėrb) The last verb in a verb phrase (page 99)

N

Noun (noun) A word that names a person, place, thing, or idea (page 3)

Noun clause (noun klòz´) A dependent clause that works like a noun in a sentence (page 319)

Noun of direct address (noun ov də rekt´ ə dres´) The name of a person addressed or spoken to in a sentence (page 325)

O

Object complement (ob´ jikt kom´ plə mənt) A noun or an adjective that follows the verb and refers to a direct object (page 284)

Object of the preposition (ob´ jikt ov ᴛʜə prep ə zish´ ən) The noun or pronoun that follows the preposition in a prepositional phrase (page 185)

P

Participle (pär´ tə sip əl) A verb form that is used as an adjective (page 355)

Participle phrase (pär´ tə sip əl frāz) A participle and an adverb or adverb phrase (page 356)

Passive verb (pas´ iv vėrb) A verb form used when the action happens to the subject (page 127)

Past participle (past pär´ tə sip əl) The verb form used to form the perfect tenses (page 106)

Past perfect (past pėr´ fikt) Shows one action completed before another action began (page 102)

Personal pronoun (pėr´ sə nəl prō´ noun) A pronoun that refers to a person or a thing (page 38)

Phrase (frāz) A group of words without both a subject and a predicate (page 313)

Plural noun (plùr´ əl noun) The name of more than one person, place, thing, or idea (page 15)

Positive form (poz´ ə tiv fôrm) The form of an adjective used to describe one person or thing (page 86); the form of an adverb used to describe one person or thing (page 169)

Possessive (pə zes´ iv) Showing ownership or a relationship between two things (page 24)

Predicate adjective (pred´ ə kit aj´ ik tiv) An adjective that follows a linking verb and tells about the subject (page 298)

Predicate noun (pred´ ə kit noun) A noun or pronoun that follows a linking verb and renames the subject (page 290)

Preposition (prep ə zish´ ən) A word that shows a relationship between a noun or pronoun and other words in a sentence (page 185)

Prepositional phrase (prep ə zish´ ən nəl frāz) A group of words made up of a preposition and an object (page 185)

Present participle (prez´ nt pär´ tə sip əl) A verb form that shows continuing action (page 111)

Present perfect (prez´ nt pėr´ fikt) Shows an action started in the past and continuing to the present (page 102)

Progressive form (prə gres´ iv fôrm) The form of a verb that ends in -ing and shows continuing action (page 111)

Pronoun (prō´ noun) A word that replaces a noun in a sentence (page 35)

Proper adjective (prop´ ər aj´ ik tiv) A proper noun used as an adjective, or the adjective form of a proper noun (page 73)

Proper noun (prop´ ər noun) The name of a particular person, place, thing, or idea (page 7)

R

Regular verb (reg´ yə lər vėrb) A verb that forms its past tense and past participle by adding -ed or -d (page 106)

Relative pronoun (rel´ ə tiv prō´ noun) A pronoun that relates or connects words to an antecedent; *who, whom, which, what,* or *whose* (page 42)

S

Second-person pronoun (sek´ ənd pėr´ sən prō´ noun) A pronoun that refers to the person who is being spoken to (page 38)

Sentence (sen´ təns) A group of words that expresses a complete thought (page 235)

Series (sir´ ēz) A group of three or more words, phrases, or clauses (page 214)

Simple predicate (sim´ pəl pred´ ə kit) The main verb or verb phrase in the sentence (page 243)

Simple sentence (sim´ pəl sen´ təns) A sentence with one subject and one predicate; an independent clause (page 250)

Simple subject (sim´ pəl sub´ jikt) The main noun or pronoun that the sentence is about (page 238)

Simple tenses (sim´ pəl tens´ ez) Present, past, and future (page 101)

Singular noun (sing´ gyə lər noun) The name of one person, place, thing, or idea (page 15)

State-of-being verb (page stāt ov bē´ ing vėrb) A verb that tells something about the condition of the subject of a sentence (page 137)

Subject (sub´ jikt) The part of a sentence that tells who or what the sentence is about (page 97)

Subordinating conjunction (sə bôrd´ n āt ing kən jungk´ shən) A word that connects a dependent clause to an independent clause in a sentence (page 221)

Superlative form (sə pėr´ lə tiv fôrm) The form of an adjective used to compare more than two people or things (page 86); the form of an adverb used to compare more than two people or things (page 169)

T

Tense (tens) The time when an action takes place (page 101)

Third-person pronoun (thėrd pėr´ sən prō´ noun) A pronoun that refers to the person or thing that is being talked about (page 38)

Transitive verb (tran´ sə tiv vėrb) A verb that shows action passed from the subject of the sentence toward another person or thing (page 268)

V

Verb (vėrb) A word that expresses action or state of being (page 97)

Verb agreement (vėrb ə grā´ mənt) When a verb agrees in number (singular or plural) with its subject (page 116)

Verb phrase (vėrb frāz) A main verb and one or more helping verbs (page 99)

a	hat	e	let	ī	ice	ô	order	ù	put	sh	she		a	in about
ā	age	ē	equal	o	hot	oi	oil	ü	rule	th	thin	ə	e	in taken
ä	far	ėr	term	ō	open	ou	out	ch	child	ͭͪ	then		i	in pencil
â	care	i	it	ȯ	saw	u	cup	ng	long	zh	measure		o	in lemon
													u	in circus

Verbal (vėr´ bǝl) A verb that is used as another
part of speech (page 345)

Verbal phrase (vėr´ bǝl frāz) A verbal, its
complements, and any adjective, adverbs, or
prepositional phrases that describe it
(page 345)

W

Word (wǝrd) A set of letters that has meaning
(page 313)

Index

Acknowledgments

Photo Credits

Cover, © Fotolia; page 10, © Thinkstock/ Punchstock; page 18, © Ron Chapple/Jupiter Images; page 27, © Jack Hollingsworth/Jupiter Images; page 44, ©Ron Chapple/Jupiter Images; page 58, © Thinkstock/Jupiter Images; page 60, © Photodisc/Punchstock; page 74, © Rubberball/ Jupiter Images; page 84, © Simone van den Berg/Shutterstock; page 90, © Lorelyn Medina/ Shutterstock; page 114, © Larry St. Pierre/ Shutterstock; page 125, © Hemera Technologies/ Jupiter Images; page 130, © BananaStock/Alamy; page 143, © Hemera Technologies/Jupiter Images; page 150, © Geoff Delderfield/Shutterstock; page 152, © Michael Newman/PhotoEdit; page 164, © Blend Images/Super Stock; page 175, © Luisa Fernanda Gonzalez/Shutterstock; page 178, © Hemera Technologies/Jupiter Images; page 188, © Digital Vision Ltd./Super Stock; page 191, © Corbis/Jupiter Images; page 206, © Rob Melnychuk/Jupiter Images; page 219, © Avner Richard/Shutterstock; page 222, © BananaStock/Jupiter Images; page 228, © Creatas Images/Jupiter Images; page 236, © Creatas Images/Punchstock; page 248, © Glow Images/Punchstock; page 254, © Image Source/ Jupiter Images; page 280, © Michael Newman/ PhotoEdit; page 301, © Age Fotostock/Super Stock; page 306, © Hemera Technologies/Jupiter Images; page 322, © Kris Timken/Jupiter Images; page 332, © David Young-Wolff/Jupiter Images; page 338, © Stockdisc/Punchstock; page 349, © Norberto A. Guaschi/Shutterstock; page 353, © Stockbyte/ Punchstock; page 358, © Jose Luis Pelaez, Inc./ Jupiter Images.

Staff Credits

Melania Benzinger, Karen Blonigen, Nancy Condon, Barbara Drewlo, Daren Hastings, Brian Holl, Jan Jessup, Mariann Johanneck, Bev Johnson, Mary Kaye Kuzma, Julie Maas, Daniel Milowski, Carrie O'Connor, Deb Rogstad, Morgan Russell-Dempsey, Julie Theisen, Peggy Vlahos, Charmaine Whitman, Sue Will, Jen Willman